The Blue Chameleon

Det. Daril Cinquanta
with Dennis Bloomquist

Published by Waldorf Publishing
2140 Hall Johnson Road
#102-345
Grapevine, Texas 76051
www.WaldorfPublishing.com

The Blue Chameleon

ISBN: 978-1-944783-93-8
Library of Congress Control Number: 2016957023

Copyright © 2017

Dedication

I dedicate this book to my father, Frank Cinquanta, who was my best friend, mentor, and confidant. Dad always supported me — right or wrong — and he was always there for me.

To The Men In The Arena

"It's not the critic who counts, not the man who points out how the strong man stumbled, or where the doer of deeds could have done them better. The credit belongs to the man who is actually in the arena, whose face is marred by dust and sweat and blood, who strives valiantly, who errs and who comes short again and again, who knows the great enthusiasms, the great devotions and spends himself in a worthy cause, who at the best knows the triumphs of high achievement, and who at the worst, if he fails, at least fails while daring greatly, so that his place shall never be among those cold and timid souls who know neither victory nor defeat." **President Theodore Roosevelt**

Table of Contents

Foreword

BLUE CHAMELEON: CHAPTER 1................................ 1

CHAPTER 2: THE POLICE ACADEMEY, THEN A
HEADLONG DIVE INTO POLICE WORK................ 18

CHAPTER 3: DISTRICT TWO 22

CHAPTER 4: TRAFFIC BUREAU 26

CHAPTER 5: DISTRICT ONE 35

CHAPTER 6: COMMUNITY RELATIONS.................. 46

CHAPTER 7: DISTRICT ONE 49

CHAPTER 8: DISTRICT THREE 62

CHAPTER 9: VICE & NARCOTICS 67

CHAPTER 10: DISTRICT THREE 82

CHAPTER 11: INFORMATION DESK 113

CHAPTER 12: DISTRICT THREE 118

PHOTO CHAPTER.. 128

CHAPTER 13: SPECIAL CRIME
ATTACK TEAM (SCAT) 145

CHAPTER 14: DISTRICT FOUR.................................... 207

CHAPTER 15: SPECIAL WEAPONS
AND TACTICS (SWAT) 249

CHAPTER 16: CRIMINAL INVESTIGATIONS
DIVISION 262

CHAPTER 17: CAREER CRIMINAL UNIT 280

CHAPTER 18: THERE IS LIFE
AFTER THE DEPARTMENT 326

Acknowledgments... 380

Author Bios 381

Foreword (1956 – 1970)
By Retired Capt. Larry Britton,
Denver Police Dept. badge 56-25

The 1950s and 1960s were a time of turmoil and transition for the Denver Police Department, and Law Enforcement nationwide. There was a woeful lack of training and supervision within the law enforcement community. Most supervision was "laissez faire" at best.

While most good self-initiated police work was and is done by 10-12 percent of police personnel, another 10 percent, during the '50s and '60s, were using their positions to commit illegal and/or unethical acts against the public they were sworn to serve and protect. Drunks, racial minorities, and persons of ill repute became victims of the 10 percent of bad officers, who decided to "serve" themselves by lining their pockets and "protecting" each other in a code of silence.

It was commonplace for some officers to drink while on duty, to sleep on duty, to place bets with known book-makers, to accept gratuities in the form of free food, drinks, and money as well as other gifts, not only for themselves but also for supervisors or commanders.

Nothing exemplified the code of silence more than the scandal that rocked the Denver Police Department. The burglary scandal of the late '50s and early '60s pitted officer against officer, led to grand jury investigations, officers being imprisoned, and left a community, already suspicious of police, completely lacking confidence in city and police leadership.

The truth be known, the involvement of officers in burglaries and thefts probably had been going on for years prior to the grand jury investigations of 1960. Officers notified of a possible burglary by silent alarm, or coming upon an unlocked business would pilfer the business of safes, money, and merchandise prior to other officers arriving on scene. Other officers would target businesses for burglary, then notify precinct officers of their intention, and tell them to stay out of the area.

Remember, young officers on the job like myself were seeing veteran officers sleeping, drinking, looking the other way, as the norm. Very little self-initiated, proactive police work was tolerated. Officers who tried to be proactive were ostracized or seen as "snitches." Things had to get worse before they could get better.

Two big incidents in 1960 initiated the beginning of the end. Officer Art Winstanley was arrested for burglary. While on bond for that burglary, he was arrested again for a safe-job burglary in Aurora. When his fellow crooked officers abandoned him, he rolled over on them. This led to a major grand jury investigation.

Prior to this, a young officer by the name of Ford, working patrol at night in North Denver, saw a speeding car on West 38th Avenue. Upon stopping the vehicle, he found fellow police officers in plain clothes with the vehicle loaded with fresh cut meats. Officer Ford let them go but later finding out that a burglary had occurred at Frazzini's Meat Market, reported it to supervisors. Those officers were arrested, but a search of their homes was negative, and they were never charged. A couple days later, the meat was found rotting in an open field.

Another burglary of note had two officers breaking into a supermarket, doing a safe job and netting $50,000 to $60,000. Again, these officers had told other officers to stay out of the area. These and many more were investigated by the grand jury with officers turning on officers. 1961 saw "Black Saturday" in which a large number of officers who had been indicted, were arrested. Suspect officers were put on a bus and taken to the capital.

The majority of the officers were charged as accessories and used as witnesses. Others eventually were convicted of burglary and went to prison. Some officers refused to cooperate with the grand jury investigation. Interestingly, some of these officers, while charged as accessories were subsequently acquitted at trial. The other officers who refused to cooperate were never charged due to a lack of evidence.

As the bad apples were weeded from the department, supervision changed. Supervisors like Red Borden and Paul Montoya promoted a more pro-active attitude within the department. Officers like Jerry Kennedy, Steve Metros, Dick Scherwitz, Maurice Mullins and George Esterbrook were encouraged to take the initiative and make felony arrests.

At the same time, with laws and attitudes changing, being pro-active was not always accomplished without some sort of questions or controversy. The Intelligence Bureau personnel were seen as the elite of the department. I always wondered how they developed the information and informants they had that led to some outstanding arrests.

Having made a lot of felony arrests myself, I was promoted to detective and eventually got to the Intelligence Bureau. It wasn't long before I learned how they stayed on top of crime in Denver. I located a spiral notebook in the Intelligence Bureau that listed all the latest major crimes in Denver and possible suspects.

A unique relationship between Intelligence Bureau personnel and the head of security for Mountain Bell (the local telephone company provider) had developed. An officer was assigned each day to go to the phone company and listen to phone conversations by potential suspects. Intelligence information was gathered and eventually led to a number of arrests.

The whole covert operation was code-named "Miami." Information concerning gambling, organized crime, narcotics, murder, and dirty politicians was gathered and closely guarded. In about 1962, several organized crime figures were released from prison after serving their sentences.

The Smaldone Crime Family opened a bar called the Glass Hat and brought Bobby Shanks from Kansas City in to run it. A police raid of the joint after disturbance and assault complaints netted the arrests of Gene Smaldone, Checkers Smaldone, Mike Tomeo, Babe Tate, Jess Birdwell and most the employees of the Glass Hat. The media ate it up.

At about the same time, a Jefferson County grand jury was investigating the murder of Rob Roberts, street name "Walkie-Talkie." Sam Shanks, a relative of Bobby Shanks, had been arrested. Roberts was killed after a high-ranking Denver Police officer, on order of the Court, testified that Roberts was an informant for an Intelligence Bureau commander.

Not all high-profile felony arrests were made because of operation "Miami." For example, I learned that several known ex-cons had recently been released from prison on parole. David Foster, Ronnie Milano and Gabarino, who were known stick-ups, were running the streets together. I was in daily contact with robbery detectives and found several recent unsolved robbery cases that were perpetrated by three unknown males wearing black hats, black coats, and masks.

I developed information that the ex-cons were planning an armed burglary. A surveillance team was put together, and the suspects were surveilled and stopped during an attempted burglary with a sawed-off shotgun, wearing the clothing described in the prior unsolved robberies. While court hearings later suppressed some statements and evidence, they were eventually convicted of weapons and conspiracy charges and sent back to prison.

It wasn't until 1967 that operation "Miami" came to an end. A crook named Bob Wertz was overheard planning a burglary. Again, a surveillance team was put together. Wertz was surveilled and arrested during a burglary. The first thing out of his mouth was "you wiretapped me." While later convicted of the charges against him, Mountain Bell security personnel feared lawsuits for civil rights violations. This eventually ended Mountain Bell's cooperation with the Intelligence Bureau.

In another covert operation dubbed "Penthouse" arrests were made, evidence was seized, and valuable intelligence information was garnered. The name "Penthouse" was used due to the location the operation was centered from. The old Denver Police Headquarters was located on the corner of 13th Avenue and Champa Street in downtown Denver. The Denver City Jail was housed in this same building and operated by the Denver Sheriff's Department.

On top of the building, right above the City Jail, was a room where Intelligence Bureau personnel would listen to conversations between jail inmates and their visitors. For example, a stripper, who was the girlfriend of Bobby Shanks, was told by a homicide suspect in custody, Sam Shanks, to get rid of evidence.

Also, arrests were made after officers learned that two notorious career criminal stick-ups were planning an armed robbery. The info was gleaned during an inmate visit between two other career criminals who were husband and wife. The wife told her husband that the stick-ups were staying with her and what they were planning.

In about 1968, a new police regime was appointed, and the Intelligence Bureau was disbanded bringing an end to many covert operations. Training and supervision were changed, and so was police work. Good felony arrests and investigations became competitive between officers who were self-motivated and sometimes self-taught.

They had to be because during those years the laws were changing. Supreme Court cases were directly affecting how police work was being done and restricting police powers. Two major cases decided by the U.S. Supreme Court were Mapp v. Ohio and Miranda v. Arizona. Mapp v. Ohio addressed the future requirements of law enforcement to obtain search warrants, based on probable cause, to obtain evidence of criminal conduct. It also clarified what is referred to as the "exclusionary rule".

The Fourth Amendment prohibition against unreasonable search and seizures, as applied to the states through the Fourteenth Amendment, excludes unconstitutionally obtained evidence from use in criminal prosecutions. The case Miranda v. Arizona required police to fully inform anyone taken into custody of their right to *silence and not to make any statements upon contact/arrest or in any subsequent interrogation. Formal "Miranda Warning" rights were established June 13, 1966.*

Those who were doing good police work all along became supervisors, commanders, and mentors for the new recruits who were coming on the job in large numbers between 1969 and 1975. Officers quickly learned that good police contacts, interview and interrogation techniques, developing informants and information, support and guidance of supervisors and commanders were all key to being a top rate police officer.

I hope in some small way, I helped provide an avenue for some of those officers to be successful. I had the privilege to work with many outstanding officers and detectives. I thank them for their friendship and brotherhood. It's no small feat to become an outstanding police officer. It takes guts, determination, and commitment. The citizens of Denver and every community deserve nothing less.

To give one's life or be wounded in the line of duty is the ultimate in dedication. Daril Cinquanta was such an officer. Having been shot and seriously wounded, he thankfully recovered from his wounds. He went on to have an outstanding career earning him the nickname "Super Cop" by the Denver media.

BLUE CHAMELEON—
CHAPTER 1—
OCTOBER 3, 1971

I am working the graveyard shift at District One-North
Denver. It's a cloudy, chilly morning, about 7:55 a.m., near
the end of my shift. I stop at Winchell's Donuts on Speer
Boulevard for two twists and a chocolate milk. I am in
route to the Sunnyside Drug at 44th Avenue and Mariposa
Street to get the Sunday *Rocky Mountain News*. As I travel
down Mariposa Way, I observe a black Chevy II at the
curb.

Inside are a female driver, a female sitting in the
middle of the bench seat and a guy sitting on the passenger
side who is wearing a Fidel Castro-style green cap bearing
some buttons and pins. He is wearing shades and looking
straight forward in a very intentional manner. There's no
doubt in my mind he has seen me in my patrol car, but has
no desire to look at me. He looks like a bad ass so I back up
and get out of the police cruiser to approach him at the
passenger side window.

I ask him for ID, and he starts talking with a Mexican
accent and acting like he doesn't understand me. He finally
gives me his wallet, which contains some pictures of
children and a Social Security card bearing the name Luis
Archuleta. I remove the coat from his lap, in case it is
hiding a weapon. I squeeze the coat and place it on the top
of the roof, and ask him to get out of the vehicle. My
intention is to get him to the rear of the Chevy II to pat him
down for weapons. As he exits the car, the driver leans over
with a panicked look, as though she's about to say
something. But she remains silent.

I get the man to the back of the Chevy II, and I tell him to put his hands on the trunk. Suddenly, with his back to the trunk, he sidesteps to free his right arm, and raises his right elbow to pull a pistol from under his shirt. I am right next to him, so I smack him with my fist in the temple as hard as I can, knocking off his hat and sunglasses. I reach across his body with my left hand and grab his wrist as he levels the gun at me. I can't restrain him and hear a shot go off.

The next thing I know I'm on the ground, my service revolver, a Smith & Wesson .357 Combat Magnum, is in my hand. I feel like the wind is knocked out of me and everything has gone silent. The women remain in the Chevy II, kids are gathering around the area, and my assailant is running through the projects. I want to give chase, but I can't get my legs to work. Am I shot through the spine? There is no pain as I crawl to the patrol car, the only place we had a police radio in 1971. I also am not wearing a bulletproof vest because there are no bulletproof vests in 1971.

I awkwardly drop into my squad car and call for help, telling the dispatcher I've been shot at 44th and Mariposa Way. As I lie there, I hear the sirens approaching, so I know the troops are coming to my aid. Officers Mike O'Neill, Willie Haynes, and Jim Laxson come to my aid. The EMTs roll me onto a gurney, hoist me into the ambulance and begin feverishly working on me as the siren squeals on the trip to Denver General Hospital, seven to eight minutes away at emergency vehicle speed.

Racing back through time
As I lie on the gurney in the ambulance with emergency medical technicians speeding to save my life,

my mind races into my past, and I am standing on wooden crates, washing dishes in a three-bay stainless steel sink. I'm in Riverside, California, at our first family restaurant, the Alpinian. I'm 7 years old, and I can see my grandmother cooking, with my Uncle Joe standing next to her learning the nuances of the Italian family recipes. My Dad sweeps through on the way to the front of the restaurant, where he alternately seats and entertains our guests—and accepts payments for their meals. Everybody in our family works.

We live in a brown all-brick Tudor house on Beatty Drive in Riverside. The tail of an airplane sticks out of the one-car garage. In fact, every house we ever have has an airplane protruding from the garage. Uncle Joe is always working on airplanes. I take my first flight in the Aeronca Champ that Joe and my Dad keep at Flay Bob Airport. Life is happy and full. When I have to go to the dentist, Dad takes me to Maypes' cafeteria, then to the Mission Inn, which has a candy shop that sells suckers bearing pictures of windmills and such. We had landed in Riverside, replanting the family roots from Pennsylvania.

My Grandmother is a big-hearted lady who makes me cry, then hugs me and tells me she loves me. She spends all week before every holiday preparing dinner. If her children don't show up, she sits in a chair with her arms hanging between her legs and weeps. Eventually, my aunts and uncles call on the telephone, and she stops crying. Grandmother is Old Italian. She doesn't speak English, and everything revolves around her family and food. She wears long dresses, and her hair is always up in a bun. She wears moccasins, and her stockings come half way up her legs.

On the stove at all times were three short Hills Bros. coffee cans—one filled with lard, one with olive oil, and one with bacon grease.

Grandma disciplines me with a wooden spoon, which is always in her apron pocket. She makes wine and root beer, cans every fruit and vegetable under the sun, and is an accomplished baker. When she makes a big batch of pies, I steal one and eat the entire thing. I pluck figs off her tree and filch pretty much anything else I can get my hands on. After numerous run-ins with her wooden spoon, I realize she counts everything. One day I find some chocolates and eat the whole box. Ex-Lax.

* * * *

I was born in St. Mary's, Pennsylvania, which is near Ridgway, my family's American starting place. My Dad worked at the electric company climbing poles and reading meters. He also boxed when he was a kid. He eked out a few nickels by tucking his tie into his shirt and betting that the suckers couldn't knock it out.

While the family lived in Ridgway, the Ku Klux Klan approached my grandfather, Joseph Cinquanta, who worked in a tannery. They wanted him and his sons to join. He refused, wanting no part of it. Shortly after that, my grandfather went missing, and his boys set out to find him. They rode the rails to nearby towns such as Pittsburgh, Hershey, and Scranton, but they could never find any sign of their father. They have always believed that the Ku Klux Klan killed him. The Klan sometimes burned a cross on a hill above the family house.

* * * *

My Dad married a gal from Italy. After she bore me, she immediately returned to her homeland. I joke that she

4

saw my nose, realized I was a life-support system for that nose, and ran. Anyway, I never knew her. My grandmother, Uncle Joe, and Dad raised me.

Dad is a wonderful man—very kind and gentle. At various stages, he is a pilot, realtor, inventor and a scratch golfer. His brothers Joe, Tony and Tom, are also pilots. Gino is the hunter of the family, and routinely returns with deer, then dresses the venison on a hook on the lower porch of the house. My Dad has a trap line on Moan Run below Boot Jack Hill, and snares mink and muskrat, and then sells the pelts. Everyone contributes to feeding the family.

Joe works at Piper Aircraft and builds many planes over his life. He pilfers an entire Piper Cub from the factory floor, piece by piece by piece, then assembles it at Hunchy's airstrip on the outskirts of town. Hunchy's is pretty much a pasture, with hangars, a windsock, and a gas pump. Not long after he finishes building that Piper Cub, he flies it into the trees. Joe had always been too proud to get flying lessons, but after he had fixed the pilfered Piper, he got lessons.

* * * *

All of the brothers went to war to fight for the United States. Joe and Dad were in the Army Air Corps. Joe flew P-40 Warhawk fighters. Dad was promised a seat in a fighter but ended up training in B-29 Super-Fortress bombers. Gino went to the U.S Navy and was on a destroyer and Tony went to the Army Air Corps to fly B-17 Flying Fortress bombers. Tony was shot down over Germany but made it back from behind enemy lines only to be plopped back into a pilot's seat.

Every Cinquanta brother survived the war. After World War II, Joe flies home to see his mother in a

5

"borrowed" Warhawk. He descends from Boot Jack Hill, dives, pulls up and buzzes the town, narrowly missing a statue of a bronze hero from an earlier war, complete with upheld sword, atop the courthouse. Turns out the statue had been erected when Joe was overseas, and Joe suddenly is performing his aerobatics with new obstacles. When he lands back at Hunchy's Airstrip, a crowd has assembled.

* * * *

Largely because of my grandmother's health issues, the family uproots again, moving from Riverside to Colorado in 1959. We are in search of a site to build a new restaurant. We first stay in Colorado Springs with my Uncle Tony and Aunt Gert and their two daughters, Karen and Toni. Karen and I develop a lifelong friendship.

I attend Cur D'Ars Catholic School in Denver in third grade. My best friend is Ron Malpiede, who grows up to become a chiropractor and is a friend to this day. We get into trouble when we are caught eating the communion host wafers from a box and drinking holy wine. Being an altar boy suddenly is completely out of the question. My third-grade teacher gives me a "D" even though she is dating my Dad. I have a crush on a little blonde named Bonnie, who also is still a friend.

* * * *

When we arrive in Boulder, my Dad and Uncle Joe find a plateau south of town on Colorado Highway 93. They buy the property from Ed Hogan, who is a fine guy. During the time of building our first Matterhorn restaurant, I attend Sacred Heart Catholic School. In fourth grade, I am pretty wild, and the nuns are constantly disciplining me by twisting my ears, hitting my hands with a yardstick, or banging my head on the desk. When we go to Mass in the morning, the nuns patrol the aisles with a rubber tip pointer that they poke into the backs of children who lean back against the pew.

When I'm not in school, I help haul rock from the plateau in a wheelbarrow. We build the first Matterhorn Restaurant out of rock, including flagstone, glass, and wood. It has a spectacular view of the majestic Flatirons that loom 1,000 feet over Boulder. The restaurant has two stories, and we live upstairs. Boulder is known for severe winds that sometimes gust into the neighborhood of 100 miles an hour.

* * * *

We build a hangar in the southwest corner of our property, where Joe and Frank keep airplanes. The diagonal runway has 300 usable feet between two barbed wire fences. A second, long runway runs directly west of the restaurant. We have a fuel tank and a wind sock, and although no one has an active pilot's license, Frank and Joe fly and are instructors.

Over the decades, the family owns and flies a wide range of small tail-dragger planes, including a Swift, Steerman, Cub, Waco, and Aeronca. Joe builds a highly-modified biplane from plans for a Smith Mini Plane. He doubles the ribs and modifies the tail and wings with aluminum and magnesium alloy. Over the years, he builds and modifies Smith models N13H, N14H, and N30H. The Smith planes are amazingly aerobatic and have beautiful lines, and he receives recognition at the Experimental Aviation Association fly in at Oshkosh, Wisconsin.

* * * *

Our first Matterhorn serves mainly Italian food, including pizza. I am the youngest member of the family,

7

and I hand peel 50-pound bags of potatoes. As the salad boy, I am proud of my beautiful creations. As with the Alpinian in Riverside, all the recipes are my grandma's and the restaurant is a hit. The first Matterhorn burns to the ground because of a faulty heater, so the family decides to rebuild the restaurant toward the north end of the property.

Matterhorn II is three stories tall, and overall much more grand. Although he has only an eighth-grade education, Joe designs the restaurant and completes the architectural drawings. Again, we haul rock from the area to build the walls and pillars. Guests are greeted by massive doors, hand-hewn by Frank and Joe. A bank of windows lines the north wall, affording a spectacular panorama of the Flatirons and Boulder.

The floors are flagstone, and we have huge timbers flat-bedded from Oregon to construct the exposed beams. The Molla furniture and lighting are imported from Italy. A large copper hood arches over the open-pit kitchen. Customers enjoy walking over to watch their food being prepared. The bar and back bar are one-piece logs with bark on both sides. The ambience is completed with a large rock fireplace in the dining room and a waterfall cascading over rocks.

Matterhorn II becomes known as one of Colorado's "Big Five" restaurants. The other restaurants are El Rancho, near Evergreen; two establishments near Morrison, The Fort, and The Old Heidelberg Inn, which is owned by two of our oldest friends, Karen and Ed Sellers; and the Red Lion, west of Boulder, which is the property of our friend Chris Mueller.

After we open the Matterhorn II, Joe's girlfriend Kathy hand-stitches a large banner with five-foot-tall letters reading, "DINE-DANCE—MATTERHORN." Joe tows it behind Frank's PA-11—the airplane I fly to this day. You talk about drag. He picks it up between two poles, circles the Colorado University football games, and then drops it at about the same place. One day he circles back to home base, and the banner won't release. Somehow he successfully lands with the banner dragging along the runway behind the PA-11.

In another close call, he takes off to the north and hooks his tailwheel on the top strand of barbed wire. Fortunately, the barbed wire snaps. The Cinquanta brothers decide that is a good time to haul in a bunch of dirt to fashion a ramp, so there will be no more mishaps with objects at the end of the runway. Joe frequently performs aerobatics in the valley below the restaurant, appearing from over the rise to surprise guests as they dine. Cars full of spectators line up along Colorado Highway 93 north of the Matterhorn, until one day the Colorado State Patrol visits Joe to inform him his aerial maneuvers must stop because they are creating a hazard.

During this time, John and Nettie Wiest frequent the restaurant with their daughters, Francis and Diane. Francis is a beauty queen and a Continental airline stewardess, and she has eyes for Dad. They end up getting married and buying a home in Martin Acres on the south end of Boulder. John and Nettie take us on Sunday drives over mountain roads that cross plenty of old railroad tracks. We end up eating at many of Colorado's off-the-beaten-track restaurants. We often spend July Fourth holidays at their cabin up on a rock in Coal Creek Canyon.

* * * *

One weekend, my parents head to Glenwood Springs for a getaway, and I am experimenting with rockets. One of my metal-body designs is propelled by gun powder. I light the fuse on that baby and move back. It immediately explodes, firing shrapnel through my lower left leg, breaking both bones. Doctors at Boulder Hospital save my leg, and I suffer neither a limp nor any other lasting issues. The explosion leaves a big hole in the cement, a lasting reminder of my dubious judgment and good fortune.

I have a rough time with Francis' discipline and propensity for stepping between my Dad and me. They have three children together, then adopt the daughter of my Dad's sister. Eventually, I move out and stay at the cabin next to the Matterhorn II. Every morning when I wake up, I check the salt lick out on the plateau to see if animals showed up in the early morning hours. I'm surrounded by wildlife such as deer and coyotes. I am happy staying there because I have peaceful solitude and am entrusted with guarding the restaurant through the night.

It is a carefree time, with life offering great rewards. Dad and Uncle Joe give flight lessons to lots of people, mostly friends, such as our pianist Don Pearson, Bert Kennedy, Troy Hubbard, Elmo Bruner, and Joe's girlfriend, Kathy Harder. I am learning the basics of flying, and we find time to pitch back toilet paper rolls from the airplane, then do a wing over to cut the paper strands to shreds. A lot of these maneuvers are achieved in a 90-horsepower clip-winged J-3 Piper Cub with a controllable-pitch prop.

Joe has installed plexiglass 360 degrees around the cockpit and on the floor. The Piper Cub becomes "Patches" one day when Joe flies through a hailstorm that punctures numerous holes in the fabric. He returns back to land and taxis down to the hangar. Madder than hell, he cuts out the 100-plus puncture wounds with a pair of pinking shears, then covers the holes with butyrate dope and canvas patches.

* * * *

For most people, a broad range of family, friends, and acquaintances from the framework of a life. As I roll through the years, my wonderful family provides support and inspiration.

One of my younger brothers is a real athlete who plays football for two colleges. He might be good enough to make a roster as a receiver in the NFL but sustains several serious concussions, so the doctors tell him it is too dangerous to continue playing. However, that setback opens the door for him to pursue his talents as an actor and director, and he works in numerous movies. He is Mr. Personality—good looking, always in shape and daring in his roles as an actor.

My other brother is a talented actor, director, and screenwriter. Nowadays he writes children's books. He is also a self-taught musician who plays piano, saxophone, and clarinet. He recently married his partner, Tom.

My sister is an art teacher and artist. Her uniquely styled paintings and illustrations have appeared in numerous exhibitions, and many of her signed and numbered prints have sold over the decades. Her daughter is a singer and performer who is on tour. She is married to a great guy. Her son is an up and coming sportscaster.

My other sister is an executive secretary who runs a law firm. Her husband is an entrepreneur and makes cigar box guitars that are unique and beautiful as a hobby. One of her sons is a computer programmer, and the other is a computer industry technical writer.

My stepmother has her own cosmetic line. Her mother, Nettie, is the most well-read woman I have ever known and could talk knowledgeably about anything. She and John are very good to me, and her sister Pee Wee is a great aunt. On occasion, when I am in my teens she watches me. Sometimes when she falls asleep, I sneak out of my bedroom window and take her car for a joy ride, returning before she wakes up. Jim is a doctor and amasses an impressive collection of German uniforms and other World War II memorabilia.

* * * *

Growing up in Boulder in the '60s can only be described as living in the movie "American Graffiti." I attend Baseline and Douglas junior high schools, and I am expelled from both. The first time was for playing mumblety-peg with a pocket knife on the lawn, and the second expulsion was for making out with a gal behind the wrestling mats.

As teenagers, our lives revolve around work, cars, 3.2-percent alcohol beer and girls. Boulder kids align with cliques called the Rah Rah's, Haystackers, Downtown Bad Asses, Hill Rats and Jocks. Our most valuable asset is a fake ID that gets us into the legendary bars and clubs on The Hill and scattered around other parts of town. Tulagi's, The Sink and the Olympic top our regular circuit. We routinely buy quart bottles of beer at the Cornucopia just north of Boulder High School that we open with a "church key." Life is good.

I enjoy playing sports, but I am never around long enough to be a starter on any team. We hang out on The

Hill, and our corner is 13th and College, where we "profile" for the babes, wearing Roughout boots or penny loafers, khakis, Gant button-down shirts, sweaters and navy blue London Fog coats. We try to hustle the college girls, which is only good practice. Our group, the Hill Rats, includes Kent MacDonald, Scott Robertson, Bill Schwen, Steve Doughty, Jake Sanchez, Dave Howell, Bob Cornelius, the Friersen brothers, Jerry Asbury and Kent Kettering.

Cornelius is a natural pool player, and we cruise to nearby towns to hustle. On occasion, we narrowly escape after taking the suckers' money in Lafayette, Denver, Longmont or Louisville. I work at The Golden Cue for a while and teach Colorado University freshman coeds how to play pool. Some jobs, you should pay the employer …

The first friend I ever lose is Don Zarina. We specialize in making and eating Italian food together. We ride motorcycles, Don on his Ducati and me on my Honda. Don gets swept up in the draft and is shipped to Vietnam. He never returns after being shot in combat.

Cruising is a way of life. Some nights it ends in drag racing. Other times we just meet friends or girls at Twin Burgers, which has a dark area surrounded by trees where we park to make out. We often hit free street dances on The Hill, or at Crossroads Mall or Basemar Shopping Center. The Astronauts and Moonrakers are Boulder bands that make a splash in the national spotlight. When we go to the Holiday Drive-In, we try to set a record as to how many friends we can hide in whatever car we are in that night, including my '66 Pontiac GTO or Kent's '56 Chevy Nomad.

Every now and then, we make a run to The Scotchman in North Denver for a "Horrible Burger" or a "Hot Cookie" which is a Cinnamon Coke, or a "Hollywood Coke" which is vanilla and crème. One night we hit on the Italian girls at the car wash near the Scotchman. They smooth on lots of red lipstick, paint their fingernails the same fire-engine red shade, wear lots of jewelry and are a lavish style of gorgeous we aren't used to seeing. Some of the North Denver fellas figure out from our license plate prefix that we are from Boulder, and we take a beating because we are outnumbered, and North-Siders know how to fight dirty.

In the summer, we cruise out to Boulder Reservoir, just north of town. It is our beach. The girls go there, and we follow. From age 14, I am never without a motorcycle. I first ride to The Rez on a Honda 150, but I upgrade over time to a Triumph Bonneville, an Indian and a Harley Heritage Softail.

One night Kent and I find a woodsy and snatch the pony keg from the frat boys and escape on my Honda. It works once, so we keep doing it. One time we also nab the steaks they are cooking. We are quite the vision, the two of us riding away with a pony keg on that puny motorcycle. Considering that almost all the Frat Rats live on The Hill, we are fortunate to be able to laugh about it for weeks, and not be jumped somewhere along the way.

I am fond of my classmates at Fairview, but get kicked out for mixing it up with a fellow classmate. I am then enrolled at Boulder High for the next year. During the summer of my senior year, I meet a surfer girl, Nancy from California. She is a dish. Blonde, petite and built. She resembles Susan Somers from "American Graffiti," and we spend much of the summer together at a small lake west of Martin Acres. Ah, summer love. We eventually go our separate ways.

When I first attend Boulder High, I become familiar with Minnie and Jake, whose images are displayed in cement on the front of the school building. As with most of my academic endeavors, it doesn't last. I am expelled from Boulder High for being wild, drag racing, drinking beer and smoking in the parking lot. Eventually, I decide to live with it, and just earn my G.E.D.

I lose my driver's license three times before age 18, and it comes back to haunt me later in life. Boulder cops are masters at writing "chicken shit" tickets. During one of my "appearances," Judge Rex Scott wisecracks that my fines have been instrumental in paving a large portion of Broadway Avenue.

I am dating a gal who gets pregnant, and we have a beautiful daughter. She is smart and turns out to be an outstanding woman. Our daughter eventually gets married and has a little boy, making me a grandfather. It's funny how things work out in life.

* * * *

At some point, Uncle Joe, who is the chef at the restaurant, packs up his handmade mobile home, his airplanes, and Kathy, and is gone. He leaves a note: "Adios, keys are on the bar." I become the chef and Dad is the maître-D and co-bartender. We felt that Joe wanted to start a life of his own, and he did. Joe and Kathy had a daughter, Leanna, who became a pilot and award-winning dressage rider.

Eventually, Dad leases the restaurant to a Boulder group, and I am off to San Francisco. I try to join the military to get into flight training, but none of the branches will accept me because of my poor eyesight. The U.S. Army says they might let me fly helicopters, but I don't like the uncertainty of "might," so I pass. In San Francisco, I get to frequently see Uncle Tony and Aunt Gert, who live on The Presidio. He is a lieutenant colonel and is still flying for the Army, which is great career advancement for someone who lied about his age to fly B-17s during World War II.

I work as a civilian for the 6th U.S. Army Adjutant General's office. I have a top-secret clearance, and we are moving everything from tongue depressors to bodies to and from Vietnam. Under the floor vents are beer and various forms of drugs. We are on the Presidio in San Francisco in 1967, and Haight Asbury is just over the hill. I leave Boulder with no love lost for the hippies who have invaded The Hill. I have always figured the hippies who overran Boulder in the '60s stayed and became government workers. Regardless, I fall in love with romantic San Francisco—the cable cars, sourdough bread, freshly caught fish, the frequent rain and The Buena Vista bar, home of Irish coffee.

* * * *

I eventually move down the coast to Southern California to attend college. I find a house near the Strand in El Porto and get a job at Bentley's Limited, a traditional men's clothing store. I enroll at Harbor Junior College and take some police science classes. I realize I have always wanted to be a cop and think it would be fun to chase "bad guys." I enjoy going to school and get great grades, probably because I am fascinated by the subject matter.

My cousin Ron is a cop in Los Angeles. Ron advises me to test at all the smaller departments. He tells me I will probably fail the tests but will be ready to test for the L.A.P.D. because all of the smaller departments pattern their exams after the Los Angeles' test. I take Ron's advice, and he proves right: I fail them all. I go to L.A. and pass the written and the oral components. Now I need to decide whether to stay in L.A. or return to Colorado.

I'm having a great time on the California beaches, learning how to surf and play volleyball. Manhattan Beach is overflowing with stewardesses and teachers. I date an R.N. who also is a stewardess and has the Hawaii flight. Airline employees can walk their companions onto flights when there is an empty seat. My only obligation is paying for food and drinks and enjoying the layovers. And that gal has the largest collection of small liquor bottles that I have ever seen.

I'm conflicted, but I decide to go back to Colorado to be with my family. I'm disappointed to leave my long surfboard behind in L.A. because I can't afford to ship it. I enroll at Colorado University and get a job at Orbach's men's clothing store. I apply to small police departments around Colorado, and as I anticipate, I bomb out on each attempt.

When I finally test for Denver, I am accepted. They make me take the lie-detector test twice because they don't believe that I have never tried marijuana or other drugs. I pass both polygraphs. I am scheduled for the first class of 1970, in March, and am assigned badge number 7014. I am living in Boulder with my girlfriend Lindsay when I am accepted into Denver Police training.

CHAPTER 2—
THE POLICE ACADEMEY, THEN A
HEADLONG DIVE INTO POLICE WORK—
3-70 to 5-70

The morning I prepared to make my first drive from Boulder to the Police Academy, I put on my academy uniform and stopped by to see my Dad for a few minutes. He hugged me and pulled a card out of his pocket and placed it in my hand. It was a holy card depicting St. Michael. My Dad hoped the archangel would watch over me and protect me from evil in my inherently perilous new career. He told me to always carry that card with me, and it remained in my wallet through every day for the next quarter century.

In 1970, the Denver Police Academy is in the basement of the District One station at 2195 Decatur Street in North Denver. It's in the shadow of Mile High Stadium, and across the street from a park with which I will become very familiar. I enjoy the daily commute from Boulder to the academy with Gene McGuire. I know he will be a fine cop because he was a serious, smart and a no-nonsense kind of guy.

Law enforcement is in a rapid evolutionary period, and there are five women in our class: Eleanor Boehm, Patty Jeung, Wilma Ptacnik, Norma Davidson and Ruth Campbell. The guys are Rich Phillips, Gerald Fitzgibbons, George Kennedy, Larry Lindsey, Gary Wagner, Rich Boroff, Rudy Sandoval, Gary Omdahl, Mike Scanlon, Brian Deasy, Dan Hendricks, Ross Monahan and Rod Huskey. Our training staff is Capt. Ruby, Technician Doug Carr, and Lt. Jerry Kennedy.

The academy is fun and challenging, but I have a hard time staying awake during class. Capt. Ruby puts me on notice that if I fall asleep again, I will be kicked out. Every night we have to type our notes from the day and place them in a three-ring binder. This is excellent practice for completing and filing our investigative reports. I type one-fingered, so Lindsay helps me by transcribing my notes every night. After our studies at the Academy, the rookies go on Friday night rides with the veteran cops through Denver's four districts.

In 1970, the districts are divided east-west by Broadway and north-south by Ellsworth Avenue. District One is North Denver where the bulk of the Mafia is located, along with primarily Hispanics and whites. District Two is the east side, which features Five Points and Curtis Park, and has predominantly black and Latino neighborhoods. District Three includes East Colfax Avenue, Broadway and Denver University, and is a melting pot of nationalities. District Four is southwest Denver, including The Westwood Projects, and is home to mostly Hispanics and whites.

All four districts are loaded with bad guys. Every Friday night I anticipate a high-speed chase or coming upon a stickup, but for me, it doesn't happen. Rookies seldom drive the patrol car and take all of the reports from citizens. We can't be too talkative. Some of the Old Heads are nice and can empathize and reminisce about when they were rookies. Others consider us a nuisance and are not at all happy to have us in their cars.

When I come on board, the Department is using the Ten Code. Some of the common codes are 10-0 Caution; 10-7 Out of service, which we use while eating; 10-26

Detaining suspect; 10-31 Crime in progress (robbery, burglary, homicide, kidnapping or shooting); 10-32 Man with a gun; 10-33 Emergency; 10-37 Suspicious vehicle; 10-38 Stopping a 10-37; 10-80 Chase; 10-89 Bomb threat; 10-99 Subject wanted; 10-96 Mental case; 10-90 Alarm (burglar—silent or ringer).

Academy training includes self-defense and pursuit driving, which are more fun than work. We learn the legal ins and outs of search and seizure, constitutional law, search warrants, courtroom testimony and accident investigation. We are told over and over that booze, broads and bills will get us into trouble quicker than anything else.

In the '70s, cops are treated with respect and are liked by citizens and feared by bad guys, for the most part. If we are strapped for cash upon entering the academy, we are advised to go to Gart Brothers to see Kibby Gart. He sells us a new rookie gun for $5 a month. Sounds like a deal to me, so I get a Smith & Wesson .357 Combat Magnum on a K frame that also shoots .38-caliber ammo. Our class of rookie cops goes to the firing range often and becomes proficient with our side arms. I earn an expert rating.

* * * *

One early April morning I am driving my maroon and white '69 Chevrolet Chevelle SS-396 from Boulder to the Academy. I am not even out of Boulder, taking the back way along Broadway southbound, heading downhill and sweeping to the right as I enter the open spaces south of Boulder. A car cuts me off, and my Chevelle skids from the pavement and leaves the road to strike a rock and a telephone pole, then rolls.

The Boulder P.D. officer who responds to the accident is Dale Stange, who wrote me countless tickets when I was a teenager and was instrumental in getting my license suspended three times. He looks at me with a shocked expression and asks for my driver's license. He says he can't believe I am becoming a cop, as blood pours from my head onto my shredded uniform. Officer Stange shocks me by not writing a ticket.

I call the Academy to tell them I'm going to be late for class. Lindsay picks me up and drives me to the Academy after I am sewn up at the hospital and change clothes. I show up mid-morning, looking terrible.

* * * *

During my first year on the job I have a week break, so I drive my Buick GS-445 to Tempe, Arizona to see a gal I had met at the Teen Fair in high school. Jan is a Cherry Creek High School girl—a tall, beautiful brunette with a great personality. I think it's love. We are both in high school, and she occasionally sneaks up to Boulder in her Chevy Impala SS to party with me in the cabin next to The Matterhorn II.

One night she is driving back home, doesn't make a sweeping turn in Marshall heading for the Boulder turnpike and rolls that sweet SS. She gets a ride back to my cabin, and I have to call her folks. Boy, are we in trouble, and I don't see her for about three years.

So now I am driving to Arizona State University to see Jan, over flooded roads and through torrential rains and mudslides. I get there to learn from her roommate that Jan has flown to California to meet some guy. I sleep for half a day and then spend a couple of days with her roommate, who is great fun. I motor my GS-455 along the scenic route back to Colorado through southern California. I remain friends with Jan and her brother Dave to this day.

CHAPTER 3—
DISTRICT TWO—
6-70 to 7-70

My class graduates from the Police Academy on June 12, 1970, and I am thrilled to put on the uniform and hit the streets. I am assigned to District Two. I report to the night shift and am standing at roll call, wide-eyed, looking over all the officers. These men look like commandos, wearing both a revolver and an automatic pistol. Most of them have nightsticks and/or saps, which are leather filled with lead buckshot.

One officer, Charlie Flos, is standing roll call with a cigar clenched in his teeth. I am waiting for the sergeant to jump him, and when it doesn't happen, I figure Charlie must really have some juice. We go to the parking lot, and officers are taking shotguns out of their personal cars. Are we going to war with the bad guys in this district?

The officer I am riding with this first night, unbeknownst to me, is part of the "Wild Bunch"—a group of cops who take no shit off blacks and do not hesitate to "thump" them. I am riding with the most brutal of "The Bunch." He is average size, about 5'10" and 175 pounds, with a crew cut. But he's muscular and mean, a military vet who never quenched his thirst for combat.

We respond to a call on a report of a guy pulling a knife on the marshal serving him civil papers. The senior officer tells me to cover the front of the house, and he walks to the rear with the marshal. I hear loud talking, so I walk around to the rear. A 25-year-old black guy with a pimply face and short-cropped hair, probably 6'2" and 250 pounds, is in the kitchen brandishing a butcher knife, so I

22

pull my gun. The senior officer says, "Put your gun away. It creates too much paperwork if you shoot him."

The guy with the knife runs into a windowless room. Without a flashlight, the senior officer follows him into the dark room, pulls out his nightstick, finds him and beats him to a pulp. In succeeding days, I witness incident after incident in which the wildest of the Wild Bunch physically abuses people, and the people being assaulted are not all blacks.

On a warm summer night, a couple of patrol cars meet up and dump a black prisoner into the trunk of one of the police cruisers. They slam down the trunk lid and drive him to "The Bottoms" in the switching yards by the Platte River, where he endures a long roller coaster ride over the railroad tracks. Another night they hold a black dude by his belt over a bridge railing, threatening to drop him to the pavement if he does not finger his accomplice in a burglary.

I haven't experienced brutality in my life, and I am not violent. I am willing to give someone his "licks" if he has it coming, but what I'm witnessing is excessive. I am less than one month into the 12-month probation and have a hard time sleeping. I fear being fired, or "rolled up" in an investigation and sent to prison if this predator they are calling my "partner" kills someone.

Sgt. Casey Simpson pulls me aside one night and says, "You do not have to be like these brutal cops, Daril." I tell Sgt. Simpson my feelings, which coincide with his, and come to believe he saved my life.

Sgt. Simpson teams me with Paul Coliano, a mellow professional cop who is not at all mean, much less brutal. I learn a lot from Paul, and we have fun chasing bad guys. A

23

couple of Italians, we eat at The Dome and Rossi's in the Denargo Market. Work is fun and life is full.

* * * *

One night when Paul is off duty, an Old Head pulls me aside and orders, "We are going for a ride. You single rookies cannot make probation unless you do Molly." The route takes us to North Denver. He pulls into an alley and lays on the horn. No one emerges from the back of the house. The Old Head says, "You lucked out tonight, rookie, but we'll be back so you can meet the 'Brown Bear'."

Molly has a soft spot, or several soft spots, for cops and firemen and services many of them at the blare of an emergency vehicle horn. The brass must have forgotten about having me "experience" Molly, but I eventually do meet her at All Star Wrestling event at the Denver Coliseum later in my career.

* * * *

District Two includes Five Points, the most notorious part of Denver. I learn about the historic Rosonian Bar; the gambling shack; Jimmy Overall's, the bootlegger who sold booze after hours; the Capris; Zona's Hot Links; and Dial-a-Dinner, which has great chicken. The Dahlia Lounge is also a fine place to eat.

Five Points is the intersection of five roads, including Broadway, with the downtown Denver skyline shooting up immediately to the west. Cops call it the "Lilly Pad" because we assemble there like so many frogs. Ironically, the blacks in the neighborhood to the East are referred to as "Frogs." The Points is full of narcotics, gambling, and fencing of stolen goods. Criminals and their clients are coming in and out of the area—prostitutes, pimps and johns, and street-corner dope dealers.

I handle the first shooting of my career at the Crystal Bar. A gal has been shot in the shoulder with a small caliber gun. I learn then that smaller slugs are prone to ricochet off of internal bones and travel through the body. The bullet ends up around her pelvis, and she leaves a bleeder trail, which kills her.

* * * *

Not long on the job, I get tired of shining my gear. It's tedious, and I have better things to do than polish leather. So, I get a patent leather Sam Brown Belt and all of the cases that attach to it, as well as patent leather shoes, and I look sharp. I carry a Colt .25 semi-automatic pistol as a backup along with a sap, and sap gloves for extra punching power. No issues with punching power with my primary gun—a Smith & Wesson nickel-plated .357 Combat Magnum.

One night on patrol an Old Head tells me he likes me and wants to buy me a steak dinner, but first, he has to drop by an old building in Lincoln Park to see an informant. We pull up to a warehouse with no signage. The Old Head introduces me to Harry Zeitz, the owner of The Buckhorn Exchange. Animal head mounts, antique guns, and memorabilia line every wall.

Harry seats us and says he will bring us our dinner. I have never before gone to the restaurant and not ordered my meal. I get worried real fast because I have five dollars on me—not enough to cover a steak dinner if my partner doesn't buy. Harry brings out two huge T-Bone steaks, and announces, "On the house!" I quickly learn that most restaurants in Denver feed cops at half price or entirely free. I leave my lone five-dollar bill as a tip, and consider it the bargain of the month.

CHAPTER 4—
TRAFFIC BUREAU—
7-70 to 8-71

One night at roll call the sergeant announces three cops are going to the Traffic Bureau. He says the brass drew names from a hat. My name is announced, and it feels like my world is tumbling down. Traffic is the last place in the Department that I want to be. I am a habitual, lifelong traffic violator. Now I am expected to write traffic tickets? That makes me an instant hypocrite.

But in July 1970 I go to the Accident Investigation Bureau, and I feel my ambitions to be a "Crime Fighter" start going cold on the back burner. Throughout my career, I am put in situations in which I need to remind myself, "Never lose your sense of humor," and I plan to be as happy as possible as I make this assignment work. I guess I did find some decent Italian restaurants while working in Traffic...

* * * *

At some point, I am paired with Mike Frazzini, the brother of Jerry the Narc. We hit it off and take off on an adventure of seeking out police work. We make so many DUI and narcotics arrests during our accident investigations that it makes working the Traffic Bureau tolerable.

Mike is a funny guy with an endless sense of humor. We are laughing all of the time. He is tough, and I never have to look over my shoulder to see if he is there to back me up. A cop's partner is his biggest asset on the job. A lousy partner makes life miserable. The ideal partner is fun, has your back and stands with you shoulder to shoulder in a fight. Mike and I are a good team and are developing informants.

After we develop informant information, I believe I need a search warrant, so I go to the Vice & Narcotics Bureau. All these dicks are standing around posing and flapping their gums. They are wearing leather jackets and zipper boots, and are smoking cigars. I later find out they are emulating their commander, Jerry Kennedy.

I am on a mission, so I ask the detectives if one of them would show me how they are writing their warrants. They all look at each other and Jerry Frazzini—the brother of my partner— comes over, looks at my badge, flicks it with his middle finger and says, "You are nuts. Get the fuck outta here." They all enjoy a snide laugh at my expense. I never forget.

I return to the Narcotics Bureau late that night and find they do not lock the door. I open their case files and examine their affidavits for search warrants and realize they are not putting a lot of effort into establishing probable cause for issuance of a search warrant. I later learn their philosophy is to not put much meat in an affidavit. The less information they offer at the front end, the less the defense has to attack at trial. They also specialize in "flyers"— search warrants that have jet fuel dripping from them because they are based on creative writing.

However, my first affidavit is the result of informant information, corroboration, and verification. I'm not taking any chances because I know my search warrant may not be well received, me being a lowly traffic officer on probation daring to trespass in the exclusive club of detectives. Mike and I get the search warrant signed by a judge and execute the warrant to seize hashish, lids of marijuana and some blotter acid, which is liquid LSD on squares of paper. We collar four people. Now this is fun! We soon are receiving commendations from Sgt. Chuck Saterberg.

* * * *

AIB assigns cars to each district for accident investigations. The officers in the accident cars also are responsible for DUI duties and writing "movers," which is what cops call traffic tickets. The unspoken quota was 10 moving violation tickets for traffic officers, and one mover for patrol cops.

One night I am teamed with Steve Tanberg, a meticulous cop who does things by the book, and enjoys police work and looking for the criminals. About 8 p.m. one night in February 1971, an armed robbery call comes out at the Gigantic Cleaners at 101 Madison Street. Steve and I are at Headquarters and hear the robbery call being aired over the police band.

We decide to cover a possible escape route and position ourselves at Broadway and Speer Boulevard. A green VW beetle matching the description of the getaway vehicle flashes in front of us, and we give pursuit. We stop the Volkswagen at West 8th Avenue and Kalamath Street and arrest both occupants, recovering the stolen money and the gun used in the heist. It's the first stickup arrest for both of us, and we are on a high.

* * * *

Success in police work results from paying attention to details, following instincts, and getting lucky. So, it's a metaphor for life. Another night Tanberg and I are in a tall, skinny white guy's house interviewing him about a traffic accident. He is in his underwear, standing in the dimly lit kitchen with his hands behind his back. He is acting

28

strangely. I think his dick is hanging out of his pants, so I move over to get a sight angle. When I see his hands, I realize he is holding a pistol. I jump the guy and grab his arm that is holding the revolver, and the fight is on. Steve and I end up pinning him onto the stove to disarm him.

* * * *

I work with one character, Dave Shigley, who is always happy. I think he might be taking "happy pills," but over time I figure out he is just a great guy who always has a good attitude. He's fun to work with and is open to chasing criminals. We patrol East Colfax and Washington Park and arrest the dopers on "Monkey Island," which is on the lake in the park. Shigley and I make a lot of good pinches. Down the road, I become friends with his brother, Maynard, and we fly planes and ride our Harleys together.

One night we are at DGH on a DUI. The guy has driven his car into a pole, and the glass lens in the streetlight comes loose and crashes through the top of his convertible, hitting him in the head. He is getting stitched up when I receive a message from the hospital staff to telephone Capt. Hindes.

I have no idea who Capt. Hindes is, but I immediately return his call. He introduces himself as the captain of District Three and says he understands his "very good friend" has been in an accident. He asks about the driver's condition, which is not good because that streetlamp lens was heavy and fell a long way to hit him.

We are in the emergency room with him. I give Capt. Hindes the update. He never asks for special treatment, but I know what his call is about. I write the driver a careless driving ticket and don't bother with the suspected DUI, and take him home. This wasn't about kissing up to rank or currying favor. It was a professional courtesy. It's an extension of the unspoken rule: Do not write a fellow police officer a ticket, no matter where he or she works. During my career, I found that a cop could fix anything outside of murder and sex crimes.

* * * *

One night, Frazzini and I arrest a black guy on an assault warrant. I ask him point blank, "Did you do this assault? He says," Hay-ellll no! I's crackin' hip with some pink toe." I arch a brow and ask him, "What the hell are you talkin' about?" He explains that he was "laid up" with a white woman during the time of the crime. I buy his alibi and never forgot "crackin' hip with a pink toe." Then we put his ass in chains.

Mike and I continue making many narcotics arrests outside our AIB assignment. We also find a restaurant called The Western Drive-In that bakes up great pizzas. Many nights we order two large pizzas and polish off both. Our bond extends beyond our police shifts on the streets of Denver.

We learn that Mike O'Neill in the Narcotics Bureau is filing on all of our street cases. The other detectives do not want to file our cases because we had a lot of collars resulting from plain view, furtive movements and seizures made after an individual granted us consent to search.

* * * *

When I come on the job, they hand me a badge and a gun and tell me I can arrest all the bad guys I want. I take them seriously. I believe coming in that a policeman on the street is the most powerful person in society because he can take an individual's property, freedom and sometimes even his or her life. I quickly learn that many of my fellow officers do not share my philosophy or my enthusiasm for doing police work.

I have a business plan and a scientific approach that involves contributing to and having immediate access to the bureau cards in Intelligence, Vice/Drug, and Juvenile Bureaus. During my career, I work all four Denver police districts and make a "Bad Guy Book" in each. On any given interaction, I note the subject(s), who they were with, vehicle info, and any unusual physical characteristics such as facial and hand features, deformities, gait, speech and clothing, and shoes. I pay attention to little things. Tattoos have always been very important in the police investigation.

When I start on the job, I can tell where a contact did time under the influence of the art of his tattoos. Whether they were from California, New Mexico or New York, there were distinguishing "artistic" styles. Then inmates from one part of the country were ending up in some other state penitentiary, and their tattoos would no longer be telltale signs of where the suspect was from.

Joint tattoos are joint tattoos. There is no mistaking them because they are all one color. It's a matter of necessity in that the prison tattoo artist generally doesn't have much to work with in terms of ink. Many criminals put their name or initials on their shoulders, then get popped because their tattoos don't match their phony IDs. I figure if the ID doesn't match the tattoos, the individual is probably wanted.

I make hundreds of contact cards and arrest letters, which I send to the Intelligence Bureau and other bureaus to be cataloged. I study the juvenile files of suspects, so I know about their parents, siblings, and patterns of childhood crimes and behaviors that often carry into a pathway of adult criminality. Prior to interviewing suspects, I always know far more about them than they realize. I can often see it coming when a suspect tells a lie. I am versed on rap sheets and the files from the Intelligence, Narcotics, and Juvenile bureaus.

While in Traffic I make frequent trips to Headquarters to collect the special bulletins put out by the Narcotics, Robbery, Theft and Burglary bureaus. I also gather the daily bulletin, which features the new wanted parties. I make lists of their mug shot numbers, then have the gals in the ID Bureau pull the mugs for me. I figure out early that the name of this game is "know your opponent."

My entire career, I pull mug shots and study them. I make a file of wanted felons, which I carry in my police car. I show the mug shots to informants and use them to leverage individuals that I corner for minor offenses, often develop those individuals into informants who lead me to cheap arrests on major crimes resulting from my mug shots. I do my homework. I'm studious and methodical, focused and professional.

* * * *

Sgt. Saterberg is the Traffic cops' guardian angel. When we draw heat from Lt. Horan, Saterberg smooths him out. Saterberg talks me into staying in traffic until I complete my probation. The best supervisors are like Saterberg, the good guy who protects the men under his command and verbally disciplines, rather than writing us up.

When we are young, we tend to not look at old people and envision them as younger men. I learned that Wally was a real cop in his day. In April of 1961, a silent alarm comes out at the Glendale Drug Store. Wally and Larry Peters, another of the best cops on the job, enter the store and Wally notices there was not a soul in sight, and it is too quiet.

Larry goes right, and Wally goes left. In a split second, all hell breaks loose. Wally is hit in the groin and thigh by "Nervous" Derrera, and Wally shoots Nervous. Then a man named Tony Brunetti jumps up, and Wally thinks he is another stickup and shoots him. Turns out Brunetti is a customer who had been on the floor.

Meanwhile, Officer Peters is in another part of the store and is surprised by the second stickup, Tony Acosta, who puts a gun to Larry's head and pulls the trigger. The pistol misfires. Larry immediately shoots Acosta. Two other customers escape with minor wounds, but it is unknown who shot them because of the volume of the gunfire. A witness described describes the sounds in the drug store as "like popping popcorn."

Wally felt terrible about shooting Brunetti, who sued the Denver Police Department over the incident. He got no money. Officer Peters had a guardian angel on his shoulder that night that must have placed his finger between the firing pin and the bullet. The *Denver Post* headline the next morning reads, "Five shot in a holdup in North Denver."

Horan and Peters were true heroes that night but were never commended or recognized. Retired Capt. Larry Britton continues to try to get the Denver Police Department to honor Larry and Wally for their heroic actions.

* * * *

In August of 1971, I draft an affidavit to kick in the door to a judge's house to make a narcotics arrest. I get it signed by another judge and off Mike, and I go. The affidavit is based on the fact that the judge's son is peddling dope with both hands. While the judge is sitting on the bench in mountain courtrooms, the son is at his home dealing drugs.

We seize weed and LSD. Even though we score a significant bust, this is the straw that breaks the lieutenant's back. Lt. Horan sneers, "So you want to do narcotics and everything but traffic work, huh? I am sending you to District One!" The lieutenant then added, "If you don't stop making all these felony arrests, you are going to get shot. Now get out of here." My initial reaction was, "Yeah? Now I am going to a REAL District!"

CHAPTER 5—
DISTRICT ONE—
9-71 to 12-71

I arrive at District One in September 1971. At the end of my first roll call on the night shift, Sgt. Torsney announces, "You new guys meet me at my car after shift." I get back to the station parking lot at the end of the night shift and Sgt. Torsney strides out of the station and pops open his car trunk. "If you don't drink with me, you don't work for me!" he shouts. He yanks out a bottle of whiskey, ice, and cups, and pours a generous slug for each of us.

The sergeant is old school. He operates by his own set of rules and tells us, "You do not turn in any resistance or any major report without me reviewing it first." He is trying to prevent us from falling into the internal department traps that often derail inexperienced cops.

* * * *

Because I am a rookie, I get bounced to morning shift, which is graveyards, which is miserable. The graveyard is responsible first and foremost for finding any kick-in burglaries committed during the night at businesses in the precinct. Thieves go out under cover of darkness, kick in a door or two, and steal the contents of the business.

If we don't find a kick-in first, it is reported by the business owner or another citizen the next day, and our butts are on the line, with the brass chewing our asses at roll call. Every morning, I am stopping anyone who looks like a criminal and clearing him or her. Along the way, I am making felony pinches and seizing weapons and small quantities of drugs.

One morning I get a call from a fellow cop to meet him

at the Forney Auto & Train Museum, west of downtown, next to the Platte River. I pull into a group of patrol cars. "Stay off the fucking radio, you little fucker, or you won't make it in this district," I am told. Further, I am informed my fellow officers won't cover me in the future if I call for backup on my stops. I suspect I am waking them up from an on-duty nap. One morning after roll call, I see one Old Head putting a pillow in the trunk of his patrol car. I realize that sleeping on the job is routine for a few officers, and it's referred to as "cooping."

* * * *

Bob Hollingshead and I develop an informant base on a drug seizure who tells me he will introduce me to some heroin dealers. We contact the Narcotics Bureau, which jumps in with both feet when they find out one of the bad guys is a cop shooter. I make three buys of heroin packaged in balloons, and we make five arrests. Two of these bad guys are armed with guns. This is my first undercover experience, and I feel the rush of being a cop, buying from the dope dealers and arresting them.

* * * *

One morning I stop a Cadillac driven by a "character." We don't exactly hit it off. He jumps me, and suddenly I'm fighting for my life. This guy is tough. He is a short, muscular, balding Hispanic dude, and I know I have to end this scuffle before he gets my gun and shoots me. I pull my Kel Light, a long, solid steel flashlight, and nail him in the head, which dazes him. I get him cuffed, and I am exhausted. His head is split open, and there is blood all over. Eventually, the cover car shows up. I search the suspect's car and cannot find any drugs or a gun, and figure I could have missed the evidence.

36

When I walk the suspect into the Detective Bureau, Sgt. Larry Britton, a legend on the department, is manning the desk. He looks up and says, "Willie 'The Hat!'" I come to learn I had duked it out with a known heroin dealer and very violent man. Then Sgt. Britton tells me I cannot put Willie on the elevator to the jail until he gets sewn up at Denver General Hospital. I go to the ID Bureau and get Willie Ortega's mug shot and rap sheet, and he's listed as a heroin dealer. Willie isn't wearing a hat when I arrest him, and I can never draw any connection between Willie and his nickname. He goes to the hospital, then to jail.

* * * *

I am dating a gal who is earning her teaching certificate, and she tells me she has a fantasy of fooling around in a police car with a policeman. She asks me to fulfill her fantasy. I know it will be tricky to pull it off, but we drive to the Bottoms and park between two buildings. It's pitch dark, and we start peeling off each other's clothes. It's a bit of a project to get off my Sam Brown belt, but we eventually have my pants down and are having sex in the back seat of the patrol car.

Suddenly, two persons are beating on our side windows and shining their flashlights into the car. They get an eyeful with a naked blonde dish straddling me, and then they disappear into the darkness. I almost pass out from shock, and I know my female companion also is in total disbelief. I always suspected it was the two on-duty sergeants, thinking they were going to catch me sleeping, and they probably were as surprised as we were. Sex was always better in uniform.

* * * *

One morning Sgts. Kenney and McNellis ask me to

meet them at Eddie Bohn's Pig & Whistle on West Colfax Avenue for breakfast, where I get to meet Eddie in person. He was an old-time boxer from the era of Jack Dempsey. Dempsey had Colorado roots and was known as the Manassa Mauler based on his childhood home of Manassa, Colorado. Bohn and Dempsey were long-time friends, but Eddie also used his celebrity to meet other celebrities. The walls of the Pig & Whistle are lined with memorabilia, and Eddie tells us some great stories.

These sergeants are "old school" and care for the officers under their command. Taking me to see Eddie was their way of welcoming me to the district, showing me "the ropes," and telling me they support my police work. They never mention the naked blonde in the patrol car episode. But if they had wanted to, they could have filed internal charges on me for that escapade.

* * * *

Arriving back in the very urgent present...

Everything around me is still hazy, yet amazingly clear, and suddenly I am lying on my back on the gurney in a speeding ambulance. I hear the siren and realize we are pulling up to DGH. I open my eyes to see my shirt is open and I have an IV stuck in my arm and I am wearing an oxygen mask. They wheel me into the emergency room filled with doctors and nurses.

The ER crew begins working on me, and I see a huge syringe filled with blood. I wonder where in the hell the blood came from. "He's bleeding out," I hear a nurse or doctor say. They put a chest tube in me, and it is excruciating, considering they are plunging a hard, clear plastic tube with a beveled tip between my ribs into a cavity that's filling with blood.

Just before they roll me into the operating room, my folks show up. They find out from the morning TV news report that I have been shot. The Denver Police Department provides an around-the-clock guard when an officer is injured in the line of duty, but no one from the department went to my parents' house to notify them and drive them to the hospital to be with me.

I get out of surgery and am in ICU, and I can taste doughnuts. An Old Head in District Two had told me to never eat when I come to work, in case I get shot, because I will be terribly sick. I am terribly sick, and it will be ten years before I can eat another doughnut. I have tubes everywhere—in my nose, throat, penis—and there is a machine helping me breathe.

I realize how severely injured I am, but I know I am alive. I remain in the hospital for several weeks. Denver General Hospital Emergency Room is known as "The Gun and Knife Club," and most of the personnel are there because they are trauma specialists. The DGH crew saves the lives of many severely injured people, including cops and robbers. They treat me so well that I have no desire to leave. The nurses are great, and I believe Dr. Preston saved my life.

One day, Denver Mayor Bill McNichols and Police Chief George Seaton came to visit me in the hospital. Another happy day, my family arrived with a pot of spaghetti and meatballs, which boosts my recovery. The press was ringing my phone off the hook and wanting interviews, which I declined.

One day, Tony Lamonica, a long-time reporter for several of the biggest radio stations in Denver, called to request an interview. I asked if he was Italian, he said yes, so I granted the interview. He showed up with a radio as a present. I gave him an interview and we two paisanos became lifelong friends.

A North Denver girl named Maria sent me a card and came to see me in the hospital, and we eventually dated. She was good looking, and an exceptional person from a great family and her mom could really cook. Maria gave me a Denver Police Department ring that l wear to this day. She became a stewardess and is still a flight attendant. Looking back, I guess Maria and I were just too young to have a serious relationship at the time.

In the days following the shooting, I received many cards and letters from citizens. I also heard from Colorado Governor John Love, State Representative Mike McKevitt, Denver Manager of Safety Dan Cronin and police officers from around the state. I was impressed that people who do not even know me supported me because I was a cop.

I learned from Lt. Don Brannan and Det. Dale Lawless that the girls in the Chevy II were Nancy Lopez and Darlene Marquez. They said they knew the shooter as Luis Archuleta. I also learned the cops had the shooter's coat, sunglasses, and "Fidel Castro" hat, and one of the buttons showed the emblem of the Crusade for Justice. Intelligence information indicated that the Crusade had driven him to Mexico after the shooting.

In 1972, the DPD was notified by the FBI that a subject in Monterey, Mexico was using the name of a deceased person, and was arrested for trafficking in drugs and being in a shootout with the Federalis. He had been advocating the use of violence and firearms to the leftist leaders in Monterey. He was closely associated with the

Chicano movement in the USA and turned out to be a full-blown militant.

Mexican authorities used fingerprints to determine he was Lawrence Pusateri, wanted out of California for escape from Soledad prison on 5-11-71, where he was doing time for burglary. Pusateri stated that the Mexican Police were beating him. The FBI intel indicated that while he was incarcerated in Mexico, he boasted that he was in a shootout with police in Denver. The U.S. Consulate and the FBI interviewed him, and he confirmed the shootout. He wanted out of the Mexican jails and eventually was extradited back to Colorado.

In February of 1971, Lt. Brannan and Det. Lawless traveled to California and met with his mother and other family members. The family identified the man in the pictures in the wallet carried by "Luis Archuleta" as Larry Pusateri, Jr. The FBI extradited Pusateri back to the United States, taking him into custody at the border. In March of 1973, Pusateri went to trial in Denver, where he was represented by Rollie Rogers. The assistant district attorney was Leonard Chesler, who proved to be a great lawyer and friend.

Investigators and prosecutors earned a conviction of 9-1/2 years to 14 years for aggravated assault on a police officer and sent Pusateri to Colorado State Penitentiary in Canon City. The jury acquitted Pusateri of assault with intent to murder, which made zero sense considering the facts we were able to prove in the trial.

In August of 1974, Lawrence Pusateri and Sidney Riley were transported to the state hospital in Pueblo for minor medical procedures. All inmates in the Colorado Department of Corrections needing medical treatment went to the state hospital. When they arrived at the hospital, they were joined by an armed accomplice and grabbed additional guns that had been stashed in the bathroom.

The trio took the guard hostage and sped away from the hospital in a waiting vehicle. They made their getaway and let the guard go unharmed. To complete the Hollywood-style slice of reality, Sidney Riley was captured within weeks, and Pusateri remained at large. Just 17 months into his sentence, the man who had shot me was on the loose.

In 1975, I developed information that he was at an address in San Jose, California. I requested that San Jose police go to that residence, and neighbors provided a positive ID on Pusateri. But we were a week too late. My ongoing investigation indicated he had gone to Mora, New Mexico; Los Angeles, and that he had even visited Denver. I figured out that Nancy Lopez's husband was Tilo Lopez, who was in Soledad Prison with Pusateri, and that Pusateri came to Denver to lay low. The women in the Chevy II on the day I was shot had lied. The FBI put out an unlawful flight to avoid prosecution warrant on Pusateri.

After my three letters of inquiry, *America's Most Wanted* agreed in 2009 to air a segment on Lawrence Pusateri. John Walsh and his film crew traveled to Denver to recreate an accurate account of the day I was shot. The actor wore my uniform, and the producers used a cop car similar to the one I was driving in 1971. Pusateri had been wanted since 1974 and at over 35 years became one of the longest-wanted fugitives on *America's Most Wanted*. However, the airing of the program did not lead to his arrest.

I was in the hospital for several weeks for treatment for liver and kidney wounds. For my actions the day I was shot, I received the Denver Police Department Medal of Honor, as well as the Police Purple Heart, Veterans of Foreign Wars award and the military order of the Purple Heart.

* * * *

After my release from the hospital, I spent time in my Boulder apartment, regaining strength for a return to work. I was living with Bob Hollingshead, who started dating a gal he eventually married. He and Anita had two great daughters. I moved to the Camelot Club Apartments in Wheat Ridge, where I lived with Greg Meyer. He was tall, good looking, and maintained perfect hair by using plenty of hair spray. I used to tell everyone he slept with a hairnet and shaved his legs. Greg was funny, with an amazing line of bullshit, and must have been a car salesman in another life.

Greg and I did a lot of police work together. He was a really good narc and invented the "black box"—a wooden box containing a tape recorder, which he would start when he placed suspects in the back seat. He recorded them after he searched their person and vehicle, then let them go back to their car. It was incredible what he would learn listening to the tape. Suspects seemed to have the compulsion to talk about hiding a gun or dope, or to blurt out that they were using a fake ID to operate under an alias. The bad guys would be shocked when he found the contraband on his second search of the vehicle.

I came home one day to Camelot Club, and Greg was in bed with a gal I was dating. When I opened the front door, I heard movement in Greg's room and caught them in the act. It wasn't a big deal because I wasn't that into the gal, but I made it one, to screw with Greg's head. It was a matter of principle. He had broken "The Code of the West."

Although cop shops are highly sexually charged, it's understood among police that you never have sex with a fellow officer's wife, ex-wife, girlfriend or ex-girlfriend. About a month later, I called Greg to meet me at the apartment. He showed up, and I was in the sack with a gal he really liked. Paybacks are a bitch. We eventually laughed about it, and each moved on to our pursuit of "the perfect woman."

Greg and I later moved to a house I bought with some of the 15 grand I received for getting shot. Attorney Marshall Fogel represented me in my Worker's Compensation case. He was Denver cops' go-to attorney for a range of legal problems, including personal injuries and divorces. He was a funny guy who dressed up in a raincoat like the Peter Falk character "Columbo" to do a hilarious "schtick" at our Narcotics Unit lunches. Fogel also has one of the premier baseball memorabilia collections in the country and has always been my supporter and friend.

Cindy and I came home one night to find drunken Greg standing on a stool in the hallway, posing naked as if he were a statue. As we passed him, we acted nonchalantly and said, "Hi, Greg." Greg eventually succumbs to peer pressure from other narcs, who constantly encouraged him to get away from me. That hurt in light of my belief that we were friends. Years later he apologized to me.

Over the years, some other cops were my roommates: Dave Michaud, Larry Britton, Bill Barrow, Vic Lovato,

Gary Rennert and Kenny Brown. I have always hated to eat alone, and they all loved my cooking.

I married Cindy in 1977. She is smart, great looking and has a sense of humor. Her family is first class, and we all shared many good times together. I introduced my friend Dan Archer to her sister Julie, and they married and had two sons. Cindy became a widely known speech pathologist, publishing innovative flip books for people with speech problems. She achieved a Master's degree and helped many children over the years. I believe our marriage suffered from several influences, and the biggest problem was my job, which disrupted our life on a daily basis. We were both sad when our marriage ended in 1984.

CHAPTER 6—
COMMUNITY RELATIONS—
1-72 to 8-72

In January of 1972, I returned to work after recovering from the shooting and was assigned to Community Relations in District One. The North Denver storefront on West 38th Avenue and Mariposa Street was surrounded by what was left of Little Italy. I became the partner of Tech. Ralph Benfante, who resembled Tony Curtis. He was one hell of a cop and ended more stickups in progress than anyone else in the department.

Ralph would sit on a 7-11, robbers would show up, and he would confront and arrest the gunmen. By the time I joined him, he had done a lot of police work. Ralph's informants fed him information, which we passed on to the respective bureaus or acted on ourselves. Ralph had a knack for persuading wanted felons to walk into the storefront and give themselves up.

One day I took a stroll to nearby Columbus Park. I saw a number of men wearing brown berets and figured I should know them. I grabbed my camera and took many rolls of photos over many weekends. One day we were talking to a kid who came into the storefront for some help. Just for the hell of it, I showed him my stack of pictures from the park and asked him if he knew any of the people.

He said they were all members of Corky's Crusade for Justice. Rodolfo "Corky" Gonzales graduated from Manual High School and became a boxer, and eventually a poet and Denver University grad. He organized and led the Colorado Chicano movement.

The kid said he did not like the Brown Berets because they went into the neighborhoods to solicit money for The Crusade. He then started identifying the men in the pictures. He knew every name. We sent copies of the labeled photos to the Intelligence Bureau. Then we matched up their cars and plate numbers. Suddenly, they were no longer anonymous shadow figures. They all had names.

Frankie Rino, a popular Denver lounge singer, started hanging with us at the storefront. He had a great voice, was a friend of Ralph and wanted to be a Denver cop. He came by frequently to show us his new guns, and we went to see him perform at Denver nightclubs. Frankie was a real talent and had quite a few Las Vegas gigs. Of course, he had a big entourage of ladies, so we hung around to catch his overflow.

Then Tony Lamonica, the radio newsman who interviewed me in the hospital after I was shot, started running with us. We were all Italians, liked to eat, and became good friends. We teased each other mercilessly and did stunts like rearranging the things on the tables at Tony's house, which was meticulously arranged. He never said anything about our rearrangement, carrying on a conversation as he subconsciously moved the pictures and vases and other table items back where they had been when we came in.

Capt. Moe Miller nicknamed Ralph "Teddy Bear Eyes." Ralph always carried his hat under his arm because it messed up his perfect hair, though he never admitted to that.

A little old Italian man often came into the storefront to talk. We called him Mr. Fallico. One day he came in with two bottles of "Dago Red" that he said he had made for us. It was a delicious wine. He brought us bottles of wine a couple of times after that, and we told him how good it was. He showed up with a woman about a month later. I asked him, "No Dago Red?" He explained that he would make another batch in a couple of weeks. His female companion commented, "You better clean that bathtub good." Ralph and I rolled our eyes and glanced at each other with that "I really hope she's joking" look.

In Community Relations, we gave talks to community groups and students. This was not my thing. Fellow Community Relations officers Bob Baltz, Al Sandoval and Dick Alligood were all good guys. However, giving community relations presentations was a distraction from my focus, which remained catching bad guys.

When I could get to Headquarters, I resumed my practice of pulling mug shots and forming friendships with the detectives in the various bureaus. Ralph and I made some quality arrests while working the storefront and gathered reams of information. Without any orders or guidance, we had turned the storefront into a satellite intelligence bureau.

CHAPTER 7—
DISTRICT ONE—
8-72 to 12-73

In August of 1972, I returned to patrol in District One, which had been my last assignment before being shot. I worked under Lt. Larry Britton—a legend with a photographic memory for criminals. He taught me how to handle and talk to career criminals. The key was establishing mutual respect. Larry and I made a number of on-site arrests. We both enjoyed "routining" bars. I quickly learned which partners were comfortable on the street. They could "routine" bars with me and roust the bad guys.

When a cop enters a bar, he needs to profile everyone in a few seconds, registering a mental record of the people and what they are doing at that instant. Bars are volatile because the patrons can turn on the cops in a split second. The environment is often dark, and someone can come out of the shadows with a knife or gun.

We always found wanted felons, dope dealers who were "holding" and gun-toting bad guys in the bars. Plus, I developed some solid informants out of bar pinches and came upon active informants who had dropped out of contact. So, I'd pull them outside and pressure them.

On Fridays, we would look for junkies with fresh needle "tracks" so we could threaten them with jail time for illegal use of narcotics. They knew that going to jail on a Friday would ensure they ended up going through withdrawal through an entire weekend, so they rolled over with information.

Larry and I were routining bars one day and entered Richie's at W. 26th Avenue and Elliot Street. We spotted

Patrick Runningbear, an escapee from the Department of
Corrections, playing pool, and took a loaded revolver off of
him. These arrests were commonplace for us. Larry and I
were on a roll and stopped all sorts of career criminals
because we immediately recognized them. Working with
Larry was advanced police training.

One day, I saw Buster Snider coming into the station at
the end of his shift. Buster was famous, or infamous, for his
tally of traffic tickets. I said, "Well, Buster... how many
chicken shit tickets did you write today?" He responded,
matter of factly, "About 80." Then he fired back, "Well,
Daril... How many people's rights did you violate today?"
I chuckled and replied, "I lost count." Although we had a
philosophical difference in reasons for wearing a badge, I
liked Buster, the undisputed champion traffic ticket writer
in the history of the Denver Police Department.

My business model was based on cataloging criminals
and informants. Buster had his assembly-line approach to
writing traffic citations. He took home a case of moving
violation tickets, and while watching TV, filled in all the
generic info. Buster had long, open boxes of tickets that
were labeled by violation. Each shift, Buster lined up the
partially filled out citations in the back seat of his car. I
think he could write a ticket in 90 seconds. But even Buster
had a code of conduct. He never wrote a ticket on another
cop, or a cop's wife or other relative, or even a cop's
"chippy."

Buster caught a lot of media flak because he operated
his cruiser as a ticket mill, but over the years I saw a good
cop who made arrests beyond traffic stops. If another cop
called on the radio for help, Buster would be there.
Department lore includes a story of cops calling for help

and Buster sliding through the doors of a large disturbance, laying down his motorcycle and coming up off the concrete swinging his nightstick. Bad guys once strung a wire across an alley and lured him into a chase. Buster hit and snapped the wire. It could have killed him, but Buster Snider was one hell of a tough cop.

* * * *

I became District One Collator in November of 1972. I was assigned Car 150, a "wild card" that traveled the entire district. I also put out a bulletin detailing the active criminals in the district who were committing armed robberies, burglaries, dealing dope and committing any other crimes. There was a shortage of undercover cars in the department, so I sometimes drove my 1973 Buick Riviera on duty. Fellow cops called it "the Batmobile."

One day I saw a pair of keys to an unmarked vehicle hanging on the hook in the sergeant's office, so I snagged them. I drove my prize to the underground parking at the Holiday Inn near Mile High Stadium. In the weeks to follow we used the car to make some quality arrests. We gassed the car in the normal manner at the police pump.

All good things come to an end, and sometimes they end ugly. I got caught driving the missing unit. The administration had made a stolen car report. Someone in the department turned in a case on me and tried to get the District Attorney's office to file auto-theft charges. The D.A.'s office ignored the complaint, considering I was using a police car to do police work, fueling it according to regulations, and had not converted the vehicle for personal use or profit. One of my sayings was "never lose your sense of humor." I had to make sure I found the humor in the disappearing vehicle episode.

That month I arrested three stickups wanted for a series of robberies. Officers Bill Martinez, Gerry Fitzgibbons and Steve Fugate and I located and arrested Nancy Woodruff, who was wanted for the homicide of Toby Maes. Every time the department issued a bulletin for a murder suspect, the cops roamed like wolves, trying to make the arrest. Cops are competitive and want bragging rights for a big pinch on the street.

* * * *

Bill Martinez, Tom Casper and I developed a new informant who gave up a "chop shop" that was hiding numerous stolen automobiles and motorcycles. Later in the month we knocked off a second chop shop containing five stolen vehicles that were being dismantled. We arrested four suspects and revealed in the pinches.

Martinez and I were stopping bad guy after bad guy, and my District One book of contacts was growing. I was pulling mug shots and trying to learn who the main players were. Bill and I contacted a career criminal, Sammy Blan, and recovered a stolen gun from his vehicle. Blan cleared up seven burglaries before we were done with him. We also tracked down Bruce Cooley, who was wanted for murder out of Boulder. Shortly after that, we caught DOC escapee Lloyd Phelps, who was doing time for burglary.

* * * *

I was learning how to run my police car as a business. I didn't waste my time writing tickets and dealing with misdemeanor arrests. In terms of keeping the turbulence to a minimum, I learned it's not what you do to people, but how you do it to them. If you articulated the reasons for the stop, it usually defused their reactions.

Every stop presented a potential confidential informant waiting to be developed. I used traffic offenses as probable cause to make stops and ID the drivers, then clear and search their cars. If the pieces of the stop did not fall into place for a good arrest, I used the seizure as leverage to turn the occupants into CIs. I am still amazed how many fugitives I arrested from information gathered during traffic stops. I usually showed them my mug shot file.

Over many year's work, I compiled a small army of informants who gave me info and educated me about the M.O. (*modus operandi*) of individual criminals and their families, friends, "fall partners," vehicles, girlfriends, and companions. I always tried to spend time talking to the people I arrested or stopped, and I strived to learn something from each of them.

I learned that women were crucial as informants and in locating wanted parties. *"Cherchez la femme"* (seek the woman) and you shall find the man. I followed countless females who led me to dope houses and wanted parties who were hiding out.

* * * *

Hollingshead and I were assigned to car 116, which patrolled Lincoln Park, including the Lincoln Park Jets (projects) and Santa Fe Drive. The boundaries were West Colfax Avenue to Ellsworth and eastward from Broadway. Bob was a tough Vietnam Vet, and he sometimes thumped people, for which I got blamed on more than one occasion. He was a streetwise cop and a great partner and even was my roommate for a time.

One day we arrested five individuals with loaded guns. In one month, we had rolled up over 100 felons and had a lot of fun doing it. Those arrests were for serious crimes, including armed robbery, burglary, escape, drug possession and trafficking, parole violation, and possession of stolen property. We were so prolific, the disbelieving command pulled all our daily logs and verified the arrests with the jail sheets. They determined we had done the work and told the truth about it, establishing some kind of performance record.

Bob had taken the day off, and I was working car 116 solo in the Lincoln Park Jets. I was talking to Don Danhour and Larry Blumer, a couple of really good cops who made a lot of pinches and were working the Las Casitas projects. A stickup call, including ID on the getaway vehicle, came out at Wineberg Jewelers on Santa Fe Boulevard.

I covered the Eighth Avenue escape route, and they took West 13th Avenue. Soon, a car matching the description rolled by, rear plate flapping in the wind. I gave pursuit and stopped the vehicle west of Federal Boulevard. I was holding them at gunpoint and trying to coax the driver from the car.

He opened the door, extended his left arm and leg from the vehicle and shouted he could not hear me. The driver was trying to lure me toward the car so he could get a clear shot at me with the revolver he was holding in his right hand. The troops arrived, and we arrested Richard Meno Espinosa, Lila Duran, Gilbert Duran and Larry Larson without a gun battle.

We recovered the stolen money and jewelry from the vehicle. I always believed each day was a gift, and I had a strong desire to go home each night at anyone else's expense. The same jewelry store had been hit a month earlier and Lt. Paul O'Hara arrested the stickups single-handedly, recovering the loot.

* * * *

Lt. Britton, Hollingshead and I executed a search warrant at Dial-a-Dinner on Larimer Street. We had received information that the Cocas, who owned the place, had machine guns, and were fences in possession of a treasure trove of stolen property. The informant was spot on. We seized automatic weapons and stolen merchandise from numerous burglaries.

The Coca family had dug a cavern under the restaurant in which they built a firing range, complete with a steel can swinging from a wire that they used as a target. They refused to open the antique safe, so we had to call Old Man Dire of Dire Lock and Key. He cracked the safe, which contained a cache of silver, gold, cash and jewelry. It was a shame because that joint served great chicken, and the District Two officers were ticked off we shut down one of their favorite restaurants.

* * * *

One day, Bob and I were driving around The Bottoms near West 4th Avenue and Bryant Street. Like much of the lowland along the Platte River, it has always been an industrial area, filled with warehouses and manufacturing. We jumped a large group of thieves breaking into and pilfering the contents of semi-tractor trailers.

We made 17 arrests with the help of our district cars dedicated to burglary investigation. Apparently, after the band of thieves had broken in and taken the choice merchandise, they called their friends and families, who then helped themselves to the remainders.

* * * *

Bob and I were knocking off a high number of escapees from various institutions. We were locating them by routining bars and developing informant information. We had developed a rapport with DOC officials, and they sent us intelligence sheets when inmates escaped. These data sheets showed mug shots of the escapees and detailed who they were talking to on the phone and who was visiting them when they were in the can. This detailed information gave us a substantial edge.

We had linked up with a score of parole officers, including Fred Lane, Tom Maddock, John Parmenter, Nicole Archuleta, Paul Upah, Trixie Miller and Max Winkler. The level of trust was so great that the PO's allowed us to put holds on their parolees without calling them, ensuring the inmates would not get out of jail until the hold was released.

Sometimes we had information that a parolee was in violation, but we lacked probable cause to secure a search warrant for his or her home, so we would encourage the parole officer to make a home visit in accordance with the parole agreement. The parole officer would often "toss" the house, finding contraband such as guns or drugs that spun the offender back to prison.

Bob and I were connected, and we had all sorts of ways to defeat the crooks. We developed a relationship with Al Bennet, director of Camp George West in Golden. Camp George was a kind of halfway house for cons pending parole. There were lots of runners, and Al loved chasing them with us. He was a good old boy and called them "varmints." He was a real fugitive hunter and enjoyed riding along with us as we tracked down the escapees. Camp George West, the state hospital in Pueblo or any correctional institution labeled anyone who broke out or walked away as an escapee because each one remains an inmate until "killing his number" of conviction days, regardless of the level of incarceration.

Escapees are a real challenge and are potentially dangerous because they are desperate to not return to a cell. Over the remainder of my career, I never forgot that I was shot by a prison escapee, and I tracked down and captured over 100 fugitives.

* * * *

One fall afternoon I went for lunch at Patsy's in Little Italy, Denver's oldest Italian restaurant. I grabbed a handful of Stark's wafer candies and started to walk into the dining room. I glanced over a high booth and saw Chubby, the owner, counting money and inspecting betting slips for off-track betting. Chubby was a bookie for the Mob.

I said, "Chubby, Chubby, Chubby! What are you doing?" He looked over his shoulder, moaning as he scooped up the slips and money. I asked him, "What are you going to do, eat them?" I laugh at the grimace on his face, and his obviously startled condition.

He did not know what to do. Chubby had gotten sloppy in his old age, and I had caught him red-handed. I did not arrest Chubby. Instead, I ate pasta and meatballs. He quickly exited with his gambling slips and cash, thinking I might change my mind. The next time I came in, he thanked me for giving him a break. I never paid for another meal in Patsy's. Chubby would always tell me someone picked up my tab.

* * * *

I loved North Denver restaurants, including Little Devils at Carbone's, which is now Lechuga's, the home of the Mini Hots and Tooty Toots. People coming from all over town to pick up those delicacies. Gaetano's was the mafia hangout on 38th Avenue owned by the Smaldone family. Pagliacci's kitchen crew would leave a large pot of their great soup on a table for the cops in the winter.

Mancinelli's had the best sandwiches, and the Subway had the top pizza and sausage cannolis. When customers got out of hand at Subway, Danny and Ray Longo enacted their brand of justice, using martial arts skills to knock them down and often out. Then they dragged the bad actors to the sidewalk, unconscious, and called the Denver Police Department. Dispatchers would then send officers to 38th and Lipan on a "man down." Other Denver Italian eateries we frequented were Little Pepino's, The Marigold, Carl's Pizzeria and Cugino's.

I extended my affection for Italian restaurants outside Denver, to places such as Arvada Villa, Little Nick's, Café Jordano, Mama Sanino's and Sano's. I know all the owners and go to those restaurants because the food is great. The Three Sons was owned by the Sanino family, who became my friends.

* * * *

One day, Bob and I were working car 116 when an informant called and said he was at the Burnham Tavern. He said a guy was mouthing off that he was going to set me up and shoot me. The informant said he had never seen the man in the neighborhood before, but that the guy had a gun in his trench coat. Hollingshead and I decided we had to arrest the talkative guy to find out who he was.

He walked out of the bar, northbound on Mariposa Street. We confronted him mid-block, patted him down to seize the weapon, and arrested him. We IDed the guy, who wasn't wanted, then jailed him to get his mug shot and prints. Bob and I figured we were making an impression on

58

the criminal element if someone was going to put out a contract on me, or even spout off that he was.

* * * *

Bob and I were getting progressively better at making quality pinches, including many cases in which we obtained and executed search warrants for dope and stolen goods. At night, I worked on my "projects" outside the district that involved suspects such as stickups, burglars, and dope peddlers. Throughout my career, I chipped away at ongoing investigations based on personal interest and informant information.

Routining bars solo was a really bad idea, but I was trying to establish a reputation as a fearless and potentially crazy cop. I figured I would live longer if violent criminals thought I was a threat and a little crazy. When I showed up alone, they knew right away I had "heart." I was getting into physical altercations and had put my gun in more than one bad guy's mouth to bring him closer to Jesus.

When you are in a fight, you never quit fighting until you win or you die. Eventually, I got less resistance from the characters who frequented the bars. They were getting to know and fear me. When officers went toe to toe with a criminal, they never complained to the City of Denver or the Denver Police Department.

* * * *

"Crazy Joe" Lovato came up wanted for murder, escape and child molestation out of Utah. I developed information that he was hiding out in Boulder. I took mug shots and information on Lovato to Boulder Police Department, and the next day he was spotted walking in town. He was arrested and ended up back in Denver.

I spent time with him at the Denver City Jail and obtained a written confession to the aggravated robbery and murder of an 87-year-old cashier in a Utah movie theater. Salt Lake City Police verified that the details outlined in Lovato's confession were accurate. I traveled to Salt Lake during the trial and testified as to how the confession was gained. The Lovatos were a huge Denver crime family of bank robbers, stickups, burglars and drug users, and I ended up arresting just about all of them over my two decades on the force.

District One was a target-rich environment. The Casa Del Barrio housed militants who had no use for cops. The Phillips 66 station at West 8th Avenue and Kalamath Street was owned by Juan Haro, the vice chairman of The Crusade for Justice. The Crusade stood for Chicano Power and openly preached hatred of police. They claimed they were oppressed by the government and police and demanded equal rights for Chicanos.

I was in District One for more than 18 months and generated a lot of heat within the Chicano community. I always felt that if the bad guys were not complaining, I was not doing my job and needed to make it even hotter for them. The honest citizens and business owners loved Hollingshead and me for cleaning up the precinct, especially Santa Fe Boulevard. The not-so-upstanding residents looked at us as a threat because we could arrest them as long as we were in the district.

The Chicano activists were putting a lot of pressure on Denver Police Chief Art Dill and Division Chief Paul Montoya, both of whom were always in my corner. Paul was more of a friend than a supervisor, and he was worried about my safety. He had received calls from his friends regarding threats toward me. In December of 1973, the Chicano movement won, and I was transferred to District Three. The charge to shove me out was led by Helen Lucero, a Chicano activist. Oh well, I knew it was only temporary. My philosophy was that they could contain me for eight hours a day, and then I would be free to work on my projects.

CHAPTER 8—
DISTRICT THREE—
1-74 to 6-74

In January of 1974, I transferred to District Three and was assigned to the day shift. After one shift, I drove to District Four to verify some information on drug activity that an informant had given me. I spotted the wife of a wanted fugitive, Ruben Nolasco, driving south on Federal Boulevard, so I followed her to a house and watched her go inside.

Her husband had so many warrants that the printout stretched as long as my arm. He had been arrested in the commission of a burglary in which he was shot, and immediately escaped from Denver General Hospital. He had been wanted for six months, and the warrants were for multiple counts of burglary, escape, and parole violation. I called for backup, and the District Four Officers showed up along with Lt. Torsney, who was toting a shotgun.

I knew the Nolasco couple, so I knocked on the door. She answered, and I stuck my foot in the open door as she tried to slam it closed. I heard Lt. Torsney jack a shell into the shotgun and I called out, "My foot is stuck in the door! Do not shoot!" When I told Nolasco's wife that the house was surrounded, she quit pushing on the door. Six officers went in and hauled Nolasco off in chains.

District Three command was so unimpressed by my great arrest that they put me on guard duty at the Mayor's house. Mayor Bill McNichols had a putting green on the lawn, so I practiced my stroke when the weather permitted. But the brass soon relented, and I was only on the greens crew for a couple of weeks.

Then I was assigned desk duty. I soon realized that the "well to do" also complain about the police, usually for discourtesy. My practice was to handle the complaints with a personal and creative touch, rather than referring them to Internal Affairs. I then called back the complainants as "Captain Klaback" to inform them the officer had been disciplined for his discourtesy and a written reprimand would be placed in his file. End of complaint. I not only amused myself but saved the officers from a time-wasting official inquiry that could have resulted in several days suspension.

* * * *

One night, I was off duty, and I dropped by The Turn of the Century nightclub on Hampden Avenue. As I got in my car to leave, I spotted Pat Sheehan waiting for the valet to bring his car. I knew Sheehan was wanted for assault, parole violation, investigation of bank robbery and bond jumping. I ran up to arrest him, and the fight was on. As I was trying to handcuff Sheehan, the valet drove up with his car and opened the door, so of course Pat was trying to get in and drive away. I told the clueless valet to summon the officers inside the club to help me.

In the meantime, Sheehan's girlfriend, Tana Byers sneaked up and blindsided me and then took off. The off-duty cops came out and helped me arrest Sheehan and get his car towed to the impound lot. I arrested Byers at her parole officer's office days later.

* * * *

I was working the Hampden car and had recently received the list of all parolees for Denver. I tried to keep busy as I waited for my informants to produce. I learned that several parolees lived in a complex where Hampden

63

Avenue turns north and becomes Havana Street, leading into Aurora. I found a few of them were parole violators and got a couple of them at the addresses they provided to the Parole Department. I also acquired tenant lists from the apartment managers for the complexes along Hampden Avenue. I cleared some individuals I thought might be wanted, and also scored arrests of a few felons who were new to me.

* * * *

Colfax Avenue runs all the way through metropolitan Denver, from Golden to Aurora, and much of it is a hotbed of criminal activity. So, I continuously requested a Colfax car. The brass wouldn't let me work any of those precincts, but I made small narcotics arrests and executed search warrants whenever I could.

One night I was on East Colfax looking for a car and a black suspect in a robbery. I was on a side street in an old apartment building that was on my list of places to check. I was in plain clothes dressed grubby as to not look out of place. A few white guys were on a second-floor balcony as I entered the lobby to check the names on the mailboxes.

Several people came down the stairs and bumped into me as they left the building. My right leg started hurting, and when I looked down, I realized I had been stabbed. I went outside, and no one was in sight. The bleeding wound was not deep. There is no way they knew I was a cop, so why had they sliced me? I never figured out who or why.

* * * *

Larry Britton and I made a stop of an interracial couple in a suspicious car on East Colfax Avenue. We questioned them while they were in their vehicle and requested ID. The woman opened the door, striking my head. Their attitudes were not good before the assault, and they were upset that we had stopped them.

We ended up arresting them, and they later alleged that we harassed them and that the man was beaten and the woman was subjected to lewd and obscene remarks. There were no signs of abuse on his body because all of their claims were fabrications. I questioned the woman, so I know her claims were false. We found out that both of their fathers were cops in another state, and I figured they resented growing up in an authoritarian home environment. They sued for some "free money," but they got nothing.

* * * *

One day, I was driving down Broadway, and I saw a uniformed cop receiving resistance from a bad guy. I cut across to help him, and as I pulled up to the curb, the cop had the guy on the ground, wailing on him with his nightstick. It was impressive to watch him work.

The bad guy had gotten in his licks but was now paying for his poor decision to attack a police officer. This cop was Mike Staskin, and I immediately struck up a friendship with him. He would become one of the best "who done it" detectives I ever worked with. He was very smart, and his detailed investigations were bulletproof in court.

* * * *

One night Larry Britton and I were out cruising East Colfax for bad guys. We dropped by a bar frequented by pimps before they went out to corral their "stables" of girls and collect their money. About eight "pimp mobiles" were parked on a triangular parking lot. I took out my tire tool, and we deflated all of their tires by loosening the valve stems.

We then sat back and waited for the excitement. They all came out at the same time dressed in their finest pimp costumes and promptly lost it. They jumped all over the place and filled the late-night air with "Motherfuckers!" and "Ain't this a bitch!" Another job well done.

CHAPTER 9—
VICE & NARCOTICS—
7-74 to 6-75

In July of 1974, Capt. Kennedy took me up to the Vice & Narcotics Bureau with the intention of making me a detective. He was the D.P.D champion at singling out promising patrolmen and promoting them to detective. I immediately learn "GITB" means "Get It in The Book." There is a large book filled with date-stamped forms officers fill out when they make a pinch. Capt. Kennedy had earned the reputation as "The Man" because he believed in police work and expected everyone to produce.

He would enter a room and say, "What about it? What have you done today for the good of the order?" He also often said, "Do something, something happens. Do nothing, nothing happens." He fostered a healthy, productive level of competitiveness, and the narcs were trying to make the largest seizure for bragging rights.

The detectives in the unit were George Esterbrook, Alan Dalrymple, Robert Hollingshead, Darrell Wisdom, Mario Luchetta, Tom Sanchez, Tom Laska, Gary Wagner, Bill Baldi, John Gray, Steve Barnhill, Joe Garcia, Mike Martinez, Jim Lux, Dick Thompson, Ray Libinoti, Mike Christopher, Gerry Frazzini, Stan Baker, George Fortunato, Tom Cooper, Dale Leonard, Tom O'Neil, Johnny Humphries and Danny Schreiner.

It was about how much "dust" we seized, contrasted to today's emphasis on the seizure of money and assets. I learned to protect the identities of my informants because there were cops willing to steal them if we got sloppy. The detectives in the bureau were quality, pro-active narcs who worked their informants and were always ready to "run" on someone, meaning we were prepared to execute a warrant or make an arrest.

* * * *

Vice/Drug Control Luncheons were at The Wellshire Golf Club, and Art Hutchison was master of ceremonies. He was a natural comedian, and our routine luncheons rose to the level of recognition events filled with praise and even "celebrity" roasts of everybody in attendance. No one was safe from his wit, and he relentlessly picked on personality traits and idiosyncrasies. Any recent missteps would be announced to the entire crew. It was a great fun release, for those of us who were not thin skinned.

* * * *

I had to work General Vice and teamed with Tom O'Neil, Dale Leonard, Danny Schreiner, and Jim Lux. I was out with O'Neil and Leonard on East Colfax, which was lined with street-corner prostitutes. Upon arresting a prostitute—male or female--I often wrote a HOI, Health Order In, requiring him or her to go to DGH for a health exam. Nobody in the process enjoyed it, but it was a measure truly designed to protect public health by keeping prostitutes infected with STDs including HIV off of the streets until they could be treated.

My fellow officers spotted a gal who looked like a bag lady and said, "There's Colfax Annie, get out and make a whore deal with her!" I said I didn't think she looked like a whore. A deal consists of the offer of sex for something of value. So I caught up with her and tried to get a deal down. She went wild, swinging her purse and swearing at me.

When I got back to the car, they were rolling with laughter. They had set me up. I learned that they mixed it up, writing bars for liquor violations, making whore deals, doing the porn theaters like The Hayloft for public lewdness, also hitting the parks for gays. "Whores stroll. Gays troll."

Routining the gay and lesbian bars resulted in busts for sexual activity in the restrooms, cars and the parking lots. This was a perverted assignment. Because I was new on the detail, my considerate co-workers used me as "whore and gay bait." I managed to put down deals, and my partners would cover me until I gave them the "bust signal"—such as putting my arm out the window or hitting the brake pedal a few times in a row. Schreiner would sometimes disappear, and I would have to drive to Headquarters and arrest them in front of the building.

* * * *

Some hotels provided a free room with an adjacent room for whore and narcotics deals. During the National Western Stock Show, really good-looking prostitutes come into Denver from other states to work the hotels. We would take them up to the room for a whore deal, making sure we got them naked before we gave the bust signal so the detectives next door would get to check them out.

If we gave the high sign before they were naked, we got all sorts of shit. Sometimes after the shift was over, we would come back to the room and have card games, small parties or bring a girlfriend.

The men's rooms at Denver city parks have adjacent storage rooms with platforms that we stood on to peer through the vents. The first gay guy would come in and whip out his stuff over the urinal. Then here came the second guy, and they would stand there looking at the other's dicks, like a couple of peacocks. Then one would drop to his knees and take the other's stuff into his mouth. When we ran around to arrest them, the fight was on. I soon learned that many of these guys were "closet queens," and this was their double life.

Their public personas included pastors, businessmen, firemen and family men with wives and kids. Every once in a while, we'd pop a cop. Most of these guys using public restrooms as a playground had a lot to lose, and I always thought it was odd they would risk being "exposed" by having sex in public places.

* * * *

Working the porn theaters was really sick. I would go in and take a seat, and the theater would go dark, and the movie would start. I could never figure out how there was no light to see with a movie going on. All of a sudden there were the sounds of people moving around, playing musical chairs. Then I would hear the zippers and slurping sounds.

The first time I did this detail, there suddenly was someone next to me, and he is squeezing my dick and resisting arrest. It took our entire team to get him under control, and we found out he was a husband and businessman with lots to lose.

* * * *

When we did the bars, I was rousting the patrons to see if I could get a cheap pinch while my partners were writing liquor code violations. There also was kinky stuff going on in the bathrooms, and making those busts was never my thing.

Over time we came up with a compromise, with everyone working vice in our team making the kinds of busts they preferred, and me working the bars in the parts of town where I knew the criminals. This also enabled me to execute some drug warrants and kick some doors in.

One night I filled in for a fellow officer at The Broadway, a gay bar. I had never worked off duty there. I was sitting on a stool at the end of a short hallway just inside where the bouncer was stationed. A guy sat down on the stool next to me. We made small talk, and out of nowhere, he grabbed my crotch. I grabbed him, and we tumbled to the floor. His arm was broken, and he was on his way to the hospital and jail. I charged him with everything I could apply to the case.

About a month later I got a subpoena to go to court on the case. When his case was called, the defendant approached the podium without a lawyer. He told the judge that he was going to change his plea to guilty, but he wanted an opportunity to apologize to Officer Cinquanta.

The defendant stated he found me "irresistible" and that's why he grabbed me. I could not believe what he had just said and turned around to make sure there were not any other cops in the court room. There is one, and I know what is coming. Days after the hearing, cops were going out of their way to call me "Precious" and "Irresistible."

* * * *

Greg Meyer and I developed an informant who had information on a heroin ring out of the San Luis Valley in southern Colorado. The kingpins were Ybarra and Marquez who were moving kilos of heroin in the Denver area. I executed a search warrant at a house in Arvada when all of the occupants were leaving in four cars. Cops stopped all four cars, but they contained no drugs. Then, no one was in the house.

The exterior looked like an ordinary home, but the interior was set up for a standoff. There were guns and binoculars at every window. The downstairs contained long tables bearing electronic scales, drug packaging materials, and partial 50-pound bags of lactose, which is used to cut heroin for street sales. I had missed. Just bad timing.

I executed a second warrant on the San Luis Valley cartel at a "staging area." We arrested two dealers in the otherwise empty apartment. Meyer and I seized 1.5 pounds of high-grade heroin in a small briefcase under the kitchen sink. This seizure set a record, but we missed the kingpins. Word hit the streets that the drug ring was offering a $10,000 bribe for us to get off their backs.

* * * *

We had to deliver one of my informants to county jail who had been in the city Jail for two weeks, from which he then would end up in the state penitentiary in Canon City on a drug conviction. I liked him, and he was a good informant, so I checked him out and let him call his wife. She came to the police building, and I had a policewoman search her. Then I let the informant and his wife have sex in the interview room. I knew he would remember my gesture and would call me when he got out.

Informants nickel and dime cops for money to buy diapers, milk, car repairs, food or whatever. We were always doing favors or fixing cases for them, but they were essential to my success as a detective.

Meyer and I took down some high-volume speed dealers, including negotiating an undercover buy of 10 pounds of "white crosses." We showed up at a suspected drug house, and the occupants were armed with a rifle.

They were standing behind an open suitcase containing two large bags of methamphetamine.

We knew this could turn to shit real quick. We were at the point where we had to show the money, so I opened the briefcase and pulled out my sawed off shotgun at the same time Greg pulled his gun. They gave up immediately rather than starting a toe-to-toe shootout. Now, this was my idea of General Vice.

* * * *

Meyer, Britton, Hollingshead and I had so much intel on drugs from our combined informants we started regularly going out at night and kicking in one or two doors. Greg named our covert group "ODNU" (Off-Duty Narcotics Unit). We reveled in it but knew if word got out, the brass would not receive it well. Our quartet executed several search warrants, all of which nabbed heroin, guns and stolen property.

Greg and I went undercover with Doug "Duke" Martin of the Drug Enforcement Agency. He thought he was related to his idol John Wayne. We introduced him to a dope peddler and meth "cook." Duke was able to make numerous buys, and the combined investigation led to a cocaine supplier from South America.

One of my informants introduced us to a drug dealer in Indian Hills, a small town west of Morrison, Colorado. We had no idea that we'd come across a vein of dealers of weed, LSD, speed and coke. Martin and I made about 10 buys from individuals in separate trailers and cabins.

* * * *

Greg and I went after a dangerous career criminal, Sammy Abeyta. We had information that he possessed stolen property from his burglaries. We hit the house with

Det. Tom Laska and Alan Dalrymple. At the finish line of the horse race to the bedroom, Abeyta grabbed a pillowcase and attempted to remove one of many loaded handguns. I was fully prepared to shoot him. We seized a lot of stolen goods, guns, rifles and narcotics. We put him in chains, narrowly averting a shootout.

Years later Sammy was shot in front of the 5th Avenue bar on Santa Fe Boulevard. He told the cops that I had shot him and left him lying there to die. It was not true, but many bad guys would say that I busted them when I was nowhere near the scene at the time.

* * * *

In one case, the bad guy robbed a neighborhood bar, and the patrons overpowered him and took him to the floor. They broke empty beer bottles on his head and face, leaving horrible glass cuts. He went to the joint, where he told the other cons I had done that to him. I guess it was fashionable for criminals to say that I had done these things to them when they were talking to other criminals.

* * * *

Det. Stan Baker was one of my favorite narcs. He was a born undercover agent. Some cops did not believe he could buy from the Hispanics because he was white, but he did. He shaved his head, had Denver General nurses give his arm needle marks. Stan completely bought into the role, getting a driver's license under a phony name and crafting an undercover wallet full of documents consistent with his alter ego. Dr. Jack Smuthers had just been born.

Dr. Jack's CI was a dealer whom I had busted months earlier. We hit the informant's house but couldn't find his ounces, so I started cutting open the furniture and called for a bulldozer. They fell for my bluff, and his wife went crazy and told him to give me the dope because she did not want her house leveled. He took me into the back yard and pulled the drugs from under the grass. He then showed me how to flip a shovel blade over the dope to create a pocket that will not collapse, even when it is stepped on. The informant ended up being killed committing an armed robbery in San Jose, California.

Together with the CI, Dr. Jack made over 100 buys from the Hispanic dealers. Dr. Jack made The Chariot Lounge in North Denver his base of operations, meeting many of the dealers there to buy dope. One suspect showed up with a carload of Dilaudid and other narcotics stolen in a pharmacy burglary. Dr. Jack bought the whole load for $2,500.

Eventually "Operation Roundup" was put in motion and the bad guys who sold Dr. Jack the dope were rounded up in one day and put in jail. Stan was a hell of a boxer who fought in the Police Department Smokers. He quit the job early and became very successful in business. He contributed to The Denver Police Museum and is a big supporter of Police in general.

* * * *

One of our black detectives was a lady's man. His come-on line was always, "Hello, pretty lady!" His motto was "Ugly and Fat Chicks Need Love, Too." We never left him alone with our girlfriends at the Parlour or Copperfield's. Officer Romeo was a true predator, with a veneer of class. We stumbled upon the motel where he was taking his white chicks. One day while he was splitting the sheets, a stream of detectives put their business cards under his undercover vehicle's windshield wiper blade.

* * * *

Teaming with Dets. Tyus and Schaffer, I did an in-progress investigation based on informant information. We followed a career criminal 60 miles north to Greeley and watched him break into a farmhouse. As soon as he left with the loot, we arrested him.

Det. Tyus, Mike Rosales and I acted on informant information that led us to career criminal Anthony Martinez. He was wanted for bank and grocery store robberies committed over the past four years. My informants paved the way to a string of these types of arrests. I teamed with other detectives while I was off duty to make these busts, but not draw heat from the higher ups.

Det. Gary "The Sal" Salazar was an outstanding narc. He had his share of CIs and was always kicking in doors. He did a Title 7 wiretap on the Nunez heroin ring that resulted in the indictment of 22 people and a significant seizure of heroin. Wiretaps are long-term, labor-intensive investigations. But the months of labor can yield big returns.

Sal and his partner Ron Hannah got into a harrowing shooting at The Inner City Parrish. They were a block away when a shooting occurred, and calls were coming in for police assistance. They pulled up to see a large crowd beginning to scatter. They saw the guy shoot someone and ordered him to drop his gun. He turned and missed two shots at Sal. Sal returned fire, hitting the shooter in the stomach and head, while Hannah fired one bullet. A suspect named Aragon was DOA at the scene.

Sal and I did many investigations over the years, and he proved to be a true friend. Sal and Ron deserved the Medal of Honor for stopping a madman surrounded by unarmed citizens, but they received no commendation.

* * * *

One time we were executing a search warrant on a house, checking each room for suspects. I found a bowl of heroin, lactose and another ounce of brown heroin on the bed. When I came back to that bedroom, I saw that the ounce was mixed with the heroin and lactose in the bowl. Our seizure of 1.5 ounces had grown to about four ounces. I never did find out who cut the dope.

Another time we were searching a dope house for tar heroin. I took several items from the refrigerator to see what was really in the containers. I pulled out a nearly empty quart container of orange juice. When I came back to put all of the items back into the refrigerator, I noticed that the orange juice had tripled in volume. For all I know, someone peed in the container.

We were on a search warrant on an apartment, and a dog ran up to Ray Libonati who was about 6'5", and peed on his leg. Mike Martinez said, "The dog thought you were a tree, Ray." From then on, Ray would be known as "Tree."

* * * *

I executed a search warrant in Curtis Park for heroin in probably the dirtiest house I had ever been in. Clothes were a foot deep throughout the house. Dishes caked in food residue were all over the kitchen, and the bathrooms were filthy. We were having a difficult time finding the dope, but I was confident that it was there because the occupants were outside when we rolled up, and they had no opportunity to destroy it. I looked in the oven with a flashlight and saw a pan that appeared to be moving. Cockroaches were having a party on the entire inside of the pan, among about 20 balloons of heroin.

Testifying in court separates the men from the boys. In this arena, I had better be prepared and be on the top of my game. The defense is going to do everything in their power to make you look like shit and win their case. If they are attacking me, rather than the evidence, I know I have a great case. Going after the police did not really work back in my day. I learned to be very effective with juries by almost always making a connection with them by directing my answers to them, making eye contact and talking plain English.

When officers are stiff in their testimony and rely on police descriptions and lingo, they bore the jury. I tried to be down to Earth and explain what I did in terms that humanized myself. Sometimes I even interjected some humor. As a policeman, you always ride out of battle on the same horse you rode into battle on. In other words, you never change your testimony from your written reports … never.

One day I was about to walk into the courtroom when the defense attorney said,"Are you here today to test a lie, detective?" This lawyer had some nerve because when the court was under session, he immediately presented a fabricated defense that I knew was so far from the truth that I questioned whether he was talking about the same case. I love it when a defense attorney sticks to the facts of the case and doesn't try to present smoke and mirrors.

* * * *

I was nearing one year in General Vice and Capt. Kennedy was preparing to put me in for detective. Out of the woodwork, Chief Tom Rowe bounced in to see Capt. Kennedy. Rowe was carrying a stack of folders and stated, "We got Cinquanta!" Capt. Kennedy looked up and said,

"Better men than you have tried and failed." Rowe's case stated I had gone to court and received money for dates on which I had not appeared.

I took their investigation "evidence" to the D.A.'s office, where I pulled all the jackets of the listed cases. In my time on the force, I noticed that when I went to court, the Assistant D.A. always wrote on the jacket that I had appeared to testify. All but one jacket bore the notation that I had appeared in court. Perhaps I screwed up the date on that one case. I reduced their big pile of horseshit case against me to a single dog turd, but it didn't stop Rowe from transferring me to District Three.

I heard that Mayor McNichols and Capt. Kennedy even disagreed with Division Chief Rowe's final decision. That event brought me to the realization that it was "me against them." I was developing my detractors, largely fellow cops who did not share my enthusiasm for doing police work and probably resented the "ink" I was receiving in the papers. I had frayed their egos and sparked a degree of envy. The irony was that any of them could have done the police work I was doing if they applied themselves and developed some knowledge and informants.

* * * *

In July of 1975, Skip LaGuardia took a shotgun blast to the face as he exited his vehicle and was walking to his front door. It was a gangland-style shooting. Skip had a 9MM automatic handgun in his hand but did not have an opportunity to fire. Skip was the owner of The Alpine Inn at West 36th Avenue and Tejon Street. LaGuardia was a bookie and may have gotten the nod to move up in the crime family. I went there for spaghetti and meatball day.

Skip was a good cook, and I ate with him. Skip tipped me off that Ralph Pizzalato had picked up a contract for my murder. He didn't have to tell me. Pizzalato was a thug enforcer with the Smaldones. Pizzalato was found stuffed in the back seat of a car at the rear of The Alpine Inn, shot to death. They had played tic-tac-toe on the sole of one of his shoes.

Skip's shooter came out of the shadows, then dropped the sawed-off shotgun after the killing. Days prior, Pauline Smaldone was shot in the abdomen and leg as she exited her home. Pauline is the wife of crime boss Chauncey Smaldone and operated his crime family out of Gaetano's Italian Restaurant at West 38th Avenue and Tejon Street. Speculation was that the killing of Skip and Ralph Pizzalato was in retaliation for Pauline's shooting.

Gaetano's was one of the "joints" cops were barred from eating in. But that didn't stop us from stopping in to roust them. Didn't much matter when we paid an uninvited and unwelcomed visit to the banned restaurants, there seemed to be a who's who of organized crime at the booths and tables.

* * * *

Elvis Presley was a huge proponent of the Denver Police Department, particularly when Jerry Kennedy and Ron Pietrafeso were involved in his visits to Denver. When the legendary singer was in town, Kennedy led a security detail that usually featured officers Pietrafeso, Bob Cantwell, Jerry Frazzini, Gary Wagner and Bobby Simmons.

On a January 1976 ski trip to Vail with his wife Priscilla, Elvis decided he liked his Lincoln Mark IV so much that he was going to buy one for Capt. Kennedy.

Elvis told Kennedy to call a dealership, and they were on their way back down Interstate 70 to Denver. He ended up buying four vehicles for Denver cops that day.

When Jerry Kennedy's brother died, Elvis flew in to sing at the funeral. For some reason the organizers thought the people at the funeral wouldn't recognize Elvis Presley. He was an extremely generous man and purchased a handful of solid gold thunderbolt necklaces emblazoned with the letters "TCB," for "taking care of business." He gave the necklaces to his protection team.

Elvis collected badges and guns. On one trip to Denver he was proclaimed an honorary Denver police captain, and was awarded a badge and a Denver Police ID card by Chief Art Dill. Elvis also financed construction of a gym in the basement of the District Two substation.

The security team would take Elvis to the Colorado Mine Company, which was owned by Cindy and Buck Scott. Chef Nick Andurlakis would prepare his invention, the "Fool's Gold" sandwich, which consisted of a sourdough loaf stuffed with peanut butter, blueberry jam and a pound of bacon.

A year or two later, Andurlakis would deliver sandwiches to Elvis at his private jet at Stapleton Airport. Presley reportedly had his pilot detour the plane to Denver expressly for a batch of Fool's Gold sandwiches prepared by Nick Andurlakis.

CHAPTER 10—
DISTRICT THREE—
6-75 to 7-76

In June of 1975, I was shipped to District Three. Lt. Steve Metros was there to give me regular guidance and counseling. As a patrolman and detective, Metros was a "super cop." He had walked Five Points with great cops like Mike Dowd and made countless big busts. Even the blacks called him "Mr. Metro." The old-time career criminals would address a police officer as "Mister"—out of respect.

Patrol officers soon notice the criminals looking at their badge numbers to see whether they are working around rookies or experienced cops. My badge number is 70-14. I came into the force in 1970, as the 14th officer hired.

On November 28, 1969, Metros and Dowd had just left the court after testifying in a narcotics case. They were traveling down West Colfax when they spotted a T-Bird containing four male occupants. They identified Louie Fernando Gomez, "The Mexican Godfather," but did not recognize the driver or other occupants.

The driver stepped on it, and the chase was on. The two vehicles weaved through the alleys and streets ending up near 15th Avenue and California Street by the longtime Denver Post building.

The driver bailed out of the car, and Dowd was on his heels. As Dowd followed him around the corner, the bad guy pulled a revolver from a shoulder holster and began firing from point blank range. When the gun smoke cleared, Dowd was riddled with six slugs, and the shooter took five. Dowd survived the shootout, but the bad guy died on the sidewalk.

The dead man was identified as "Mad Dog" Sherbondy, a notorious criminal wanted for escape from a life sentence at Colorado State Penitentiary for killing an Eagle County Deputy Sheriff in 1937 when he was just eighteen years old.

As the shooting was going down, Metros took the trio of occupants at gunpoint. All three were armed career criminals. Sherbondy possessed two dynamite bombs, maps, and plans when he was taken out. The four men were planning a string of armed robberies. The gun seized from Sherbondy had been used in the execution-style murder of a security guard 20 days earlier. The security guard died on his first night on the job.

Lt. Metros repeated various sayings, and they echoed in my mind throughout my career. "There is no such thing as a free lunch." "No Shortcuts." "Nothing is forever." "No one will remember that pinch in a week." "Hit the books and make rank." As great a mentor as he was, I didn't listen. I just wanted to catch criminals.

I thank God he mentored other cops who were better listeners and followers. He really cared for everyone in the department and wanted to see them succeed. Over the years, Steve Metros wrote me many commendations. When I anticipated he was going to chew me out, I brought him a bag of popcorn—one of his few weaknesses.

* * * *

I was working with Bob Smith in an East Colfax car. Bob was a good cop who liked to arrest criminals. He was fun to work with and cool, building hot rods. We both loved cars. I had a '57 T-Bird and a '57 Chevy Bel-Air. We made drug-related arrests and decided we hated patchouli oil, a preferred fragrance of the hippies. Because of where we went to make busts, we often reeked of its smell by the end of the shift.

Some nights we cruised East Colfax, talking to the working girls. Strawberry was a good-looking redhead who showed us her tattoos, especially the flower on her chest. She was not shy about showing off her perfect breasts at the same time. Many of the girls liked the cops and gave us information.

America was in a culture war, the "Love it or Leave It" contingent against the "Stop the War/Flower Power" group. Dets. John Gray and Jimmy Laurita were legends as a team, and they focused on the hippie element. They executed a lot of warrants and arrested a bunch of speed freaks.

* * * *

In May of 1975, Smith and I were cruising near Denver East High School, just north of the gold-domed state capitol on the edge of City Park. A car with two bandits may have seen us and thought we were going to stop them. The driver got over-excited, and they ended up nose first in the East High School fountain, water cascading over their car.

The doors flew open, and they bolted, leaving a rifle in the car. I chased my guy across Colfax Avenue into a residential area. I was dying because I smoked cigarettes and I had no idea how long I would be able to chase this asshole.

During the pursuit, I collapsed onto my knees. Both legs were stinging and aching. My guy was on his knees in the middle of the street. I managed to get to him and cuff him. I think he smoked, too. I took him back to the fountain and saw that Smith also caught his guy. We found out our desperate alley runners had been involved in an aggravated assault with the rifle they had stolen in a burglary. We also seized a shotgun and knife from the vehicle. Both suspects had extensive records.

My knees were killing me, so I went to the doctor the next day. He said there was nothing structurally wrong with my knees and referred me to a Dr. Rosenberg. Based on blood and urine tests, he determined I had lupus. I knew just about nothing about the disease but had heard of people dying from it. It was like I had been punched in the stomach. I went into panic mode.

I was referred to a lupus specialist, Dr. Donald McIntyre, who confirmed that I had this horrible, incurable disease. I was put on a high dose of prednisone, an anti-inflammatory steroid. I started looking like the Pillsbury Dough Boy. I researched the disease and learned it could attack any part of the body. In fact, they call it the "body against itself" disease. In my case, it was going after my kidneys.

I immediately decided that I would not tell the Denver Police Department, fearing they would dump me into a desk job or medically retire me. I accepted that this was a lifetime disease and I had to learn to live with it and despite it. I made sneak trips to the hospital to get biopsies that confirmed the degree the disease was attacking my kidneys. Lupus was swelling my ankles, which caused me to take diuretics. I had to mask my constant fatigue. I also had rheumatoid arthritis in my joints.

I quit smoking two-plus packs a day, cold turkey. I rarely drank so I did not have to deal with quitting that vice. Some years into dealing with this disease, I became very ill because it had escalated and was running hard through my body, attacking my kidneys with a vengeance. Dr. McIntyre started me on chemotherapy with Cytoxan, which eventually caused my lupus to go into remission.

People with lupus are never free of the disease, but the chemo minimized its destruction of my kidneys. I have learned to live with it, and life has gone on. Dr. McIntyre retired, and Dr. Rick Halterman has kept me alive. After being shot, I felt that God had spared me because he had something big that He wanted me to do for Him. Now this. Was He testing me? I have always felt that I had a personal relationship with God, so I just had to put my trust in Him.

* * * *

In the months following my diagnosis and initial treatments, I put together information on two fences, which I passed on to the Fencing Unit. They ran with the information and arrested both fences. I believe Jimmy Reed was involved as an undercover officer. He was a phenomenal detective and looked nothing like a cop.

Jimmy was heavyset, and mostly disheveled, especially his hair. He wore a coat with all sorts of pockets that generally contained everything you could think of and a lot of things you'd never expect to find in a coat pocket. If he'd gotten into a fix, I seriously doubt he could have located his gun.

But Jimmy Reed was convincing, and he could buy dope and sell items that he made the fences believe were stolen. He was funny, and I know the Fencing Unit liked him. Jimmy passed way too early.

* * * *

Steve Barnhill and I developed two informants who related that two Indians from Pine Ridge, South Dakota were in Denver with a quantity of stolen firearms that they wanted to sell. We met with Federal Bureau of Alcohol, Tobacco and Firearms agents Larry Tomlinson, Stew Kenney, Diane Paccione and Carl Newton. Also at this meeting was Capt. Shaughnessy.

We explained that the informant had traveled to Pine Ridge to purchase automatic weapons and returned with one carbine. The informants had been burned for $225. It was decided that I would go undercover with the informant to purchase the stolen handguns. ATF supplied $400 in buy money.

When we knocked on the door of a west Denver apartment, we were met by a gun-wielding Indian male. I observed a second Indian male on the couch with a handgun. After a few minutes of conversations, they both put their guns on the coffee table. They displayed four handguns that they claimed were stolen from Edgemont, South Dakota and asked if it would be OK to unload them in Colorado. I got them to reduce the price since they had previously burned us in South Dakota.

I purchased the guns and ammunition for $300, then turned the conversation to what else could they get a hold of. They said they planned to burglarize an armory for automatic weapons. I said I would pay $125 per weapon. They approved. When asked about explosives, they stated they could get dynamite. When they asked if I could get them some heroin, I replied, "No."

The two Indians said they hoped to be back in Colorado next weekend with the automatic weapons. I told them I would buy up to $2,500 worth of guns and explosives every two weeks if they could produce the goods. Before I left, I asked to buy their personal guns. I did this in case ATF wanted to arrest the suspects then, and if they no longer had guns, they couldn't shoot it out. I didn't figure the situation was made less dangerous by the fact they had been drinking and smoking weed.

They accepted my offer of $100 for their personal guns, adding they could always score more guns when they got back to the reservation. We gave the weapons to the ATF agents, who said they would wait a week and arrest and charge the two Indians. One of the suspects was found to be an escapee from a correctional institution. The weapons were found to have been taken in a burglary in Edgemont. The ATF ended up arresting them after they failed to come up with automatic weapons and dynamite.

* * * *

I began working with Mike Klawonn, a big, tough cop. He loved to do police work and was a good partner with a sense of humor. Mike and I caught three men who had robbed the Crossroads Liquor store and recovered the car, shotgun and the proceeds of the robbery.

Klawonn and I also tracked down an escapee from the Colorado State Reformatory, Blas Ben Leroux. I arrested Leroux three more times over the years, including one arrest for aggravated robbery that landed him in the penitentiary, then twice more for escape.

* * * *

In March of 1973, Patrolman Steve Snyder and Carol Hogue were parked near the Crusade for Justice Headquarters at 1567 Downing Street. Suspect Louis Martinez had jumped from their police car, and Snyder chased him on foot. Officer Hogue found Officer Snyder a short distance away, shot in the face and abdomen and carrying the assailant's gun and his own. Snyder told

Hogue that he had shot the suspect, but Martinez had run from the scene. Martinez was later found outside a medical clinic, dead.

During this time, Officer Hogue reported being fired upon from the Crusade apartment building. A score of officers responded and were met by gunfire. Officers Dave Dawkins, Daniel O'Hayre and Eugene Gold suffered gunshot wounds but survived. Officer John Singleton's leg was broken by shrapnel. Officer Robert Weyand suffered a hand injury, Det. Joe Erhart sustained a side injury, Det. Randy Sayles suffered an arm injury, Det. Pete Diaz incurred a nose injury, Klawonn suffered a hand injury, Officer Tim Gimeno sustained an elbow injury, and Officer Woodrow Schell suffered a hand injury. During the shootout, one was killed, and 19 were injured.

The exchange of gunfire set off an explosion suspected to be stored dynamite, which nearly destroyed the building. A search of the building produced semi-automatic weapons, handguns, and dummy hand grenades.

Corky Gonzales was the leader of The Crusade for Justice and accused the Denver Police Department of civil rights violations, conspiracy, brutality, and murder of Louis Martinez. The Crusade's activist attorney Ken Padilla alleged DPD was guilty of "committing mass violations of civil rights." Ernesto Vigil, Gonzales' right-hand man, claimed,"The real cause of the problem is that police are an armed force that carries out the policies of a society that oppresses Chicanos."

The shootout was emblematic of The Crusade for Justice's true motives and intentions, which were rooted in violence and antisocial beliefs. Four subsequent bombings occurred in rapid succession, including fire bombings, but they could not be tied to the Crusade.

* * * *

Little did I know in 1974 as I was skulking outside an apartment door in the Sun Valley Projects, listening to the conversation of several men inside, that I was about to meet one of the greatest informants I would ever develop. I was off duty in plain clothes, looking for a suspect in The Wuthering Heights armed robbery. I hoped he was one of the men inside the apartment.

At about 10:30 p.m., a character came out of the door, startling me. I put my gun to his head and whispered, "Police. Shut the fuck up," as I led him to my personal car. I cuffed and searched him, finding a bag of weed in his blue jean coat. As I took him to Headquarters, he told me that the guy I was looking for was not in the apartment. At the ID Bureau, I pulled Joey Cordova's rap sheet and mug shot and learned he was not wanted. He had prior convictions for burglary, robbery, and narcotics.

Cordova told me he was on probation and the marijuana would violate him, sending him back to the penitentiary. An informant was born. Cordova agreed to work for me in exchange for me not filing the marijuana charge or notifying his probation officer. He stated he had never been a "snitch" for any cop, which contradicted what a detective had told me. Apparently, the ex-con was more reliable than the detective, because Joey said he had never heard of the cop, nor did he work for him.

In the following weeks, Joey gave me information that turned up a wanted murderer, several escapees, and some dope dealers and users. His information generated search warrants for drugs. I was skeptical when he told me about an armed robbery in progress, but the robbers showed up as he had anticipated. The duo got out of the car, holding guns and approaching their target, then pulling down their masks when we rolled them up.

Joey also informed me of a bad guy who was going to burglarize the Wishbone restaurant in Thornton. The burglar had hidden in the ceiling during business hours. After the patrons and staff had left, he received a coded signal of rings on the phone in the restaurant that the coast was clear and dropped from the ceiling. He hit the cash box and broke a window to get out. We waited for him to get into the getaway vehicle, which would complete the conspiracy.

One officer in our surveillance team exited his undercover vehicle and unloaded on them with a shotgun. The chase was on at speeds exceeding 100 miles per hour. Several police cars were involved in accidents and gunshots were exchanged during the chase. Officers from District One helped us nab the suspects after they bailed out of their vehicle in North Denver. Guns, checks, and money were recovered. I always loved chases.

One of the suspects from the Wishbone burglary was out on bond, and we instructed Joey to stay close to him. We followed the guy to Greeley and arrested him after he burglarized a farm house. We put a wire on Joey and listened in on their conversations. The suspect had been spouting off about kidnapping Denver Mayor Bill McNichols, then demanding a ransom of $50,000 and the release of three associates from the penitentiary. Joey was asked by the bad guys to go along on the crimes, and we permitted it because he gave us a man on the inside.

Joey knew an amazing number of career criminals. He offered me deals whenever he learned about criminal activity. We had turned a corner in our relationship. He knew he could trust me and was sharing information on criminals and their whereabouts, as well as their M.O.'s, associates and girlfriends. He filled me in on past crimes and tipped me off on upcoming crimes. Cops learn to expect informants to double deal.

Det. Greg Meyer received independent information that Cordova had committed an armed burglary. Cordova was charged but was granted immunity for his testimony against his "fall partner," Russell Billings. He was also involved in shooting Lloyd Dalrymple in the face for refusing to store stolen goods. Dalrymple refused to cooperate in the prosecution. I explained to Joey that he had been "eyes and ears" to two of the in-progress crimes, making him a witness who might have to testify.

* * * *

The Bomb Plot Case

During the late '60s and early '70s, Denver and Colorado had experienced a rash of bombings. One militant, Kiko Martinez, allegedly was sending letter bombs. One bomb went to the home of Denver policewoman Carol Hogue. None of the bombs detonated and the accused bomber was somehow acquitted, yet was convicted of lying to federal agents.

Members of the Chicano movement were blowing themselves up while building explosive devices. A militant put a bomb in a *Rocky Mountain News* vending machine and summoned cops to the location, hoping to blow them up. Instead, he blew himself to pieces. They found his sphincter on a rooftop.

I suspected Corky Gonzales' Crusade for Justice was at the core of the bombing frenzy. In 1975, Denver was the bombing capital of the United States. I mentioned the bombings to Joey, and he told me he might know something about it and would get back to me.

Joey and I got together one day in 1975. He told me he was not in agreement with rumored plans to kill a lot of cops and citizens. He told me that Juan Haro—a leader in the Crusade for Justice and one-time candidate for Denver mayor—was building bombs at his Phillips 66 station at West 8th Avenue and Kalamath Street. There was a report that the Crusade planned a series of bombings to coincide with Mexican Independence Day on September 16, 1975.

I went to Capt. Bob Shaughnessy, head of the bomb squad, to tell him what I had learned. He was typing away in his tiny office in the old Police Building. I began telling him about my intelligence regarding a bombing conspiracy. Not even looking up at me, he told me to call him if I got my hands on some of the bombs. He obviously thought I was full of shit.

I asked Joey to go to Juan to ask for some bombs to blow up the Arab grocery stores, claiming they were ripping off the Chicano community. Joey called me several evenings later to tell me he had some bombs and wanted to know what he should do with them. I told him to meet me at West 6th Avenue and Kipling Street in Lakewood, where he gave me a bag containing four hand grenades. Haro had filled empty U.S. Army surplus grenades with gun powder, nuts, bolts, and nails, then replaced the missing firing pin with a fuse. I took possession of the deadly devices and sent Joey home.

I could have delivered them to Headquarters, but I wanted to show them to Shaughnessy. I waited until about 3:00 a.m. to call dispatch, going "two-way"—meaning only the dispatcher could hear my transmission. I told him to please wake up Bob and ask him to respond to my location to take these bombs off my hands. I sat in the dark, quiet night, picking up the sound of the far-off sirens getting closer.

They showed up with the bomb-disposal canister, and I handed a bag of bombs to the captain. He immediately asked to debrief the informant, which I told him was not going to happen. Shaughnessy became very upset, shaking and stuttering. He called Capt. Hindes and awakened him, then spoke to him out of my earshot. Capt. Shaughnessy handed me the phone and Capt. Hindes said, "Now Daril… you have really upset Bob, and I want you in my office tomorrow at 9:00 a.m."

I was not about to give up my informant. I knew I would lose control of Cordova, and I could sense the magnitude of the investigation to follow. The next day, Hindes and I reached a compromise. My partner Mike Klawonn and I would be put on special assignment to work the investigation.

To give my informant credibility, a phony bombing of an Arab grocery store was arranged and covered by the newspapers. In a second Arab grocery store, a look-alike undetonated device was "discovered and turned over to police." This cemented my informant, Joey Cordova, with The Crusade.

J.C. Tyus and Steve Tanberg were assigned by Capt. Shaughnessy to work with Mike and me. Conversations with the informant and Juan Haro were recorded in succeeding days. The informant learned that they were planning a series of bombings around Mexican Independence Day. The plot targeted Denver Police Headquarters and all four substations, as well as The International Chiefs of Police Convention. Stolen cars containing the bombs would be parked close to the target buildings.

A Bureau of Alcohol, Tobacco and Firearms squad from Oklahoma was deployed, and our combined investigation had a lot of cohesion. We set up a command post at The Ramada Inn at Simms Street and West 6th Avenue. I had previously told Joey that I would not be able to protect him from being required to testify. He said he understood. However, I told him when the time came we would move him and his family out of harm's way.

ATF agent Robert Valdez went undercover with Joey to the Phillips 66 station and received four explosive devices from Haro. At that moment, we had locked up our case against Juan Haro, and also verified that The Crusade for Justice was an early terrorist organization in the U.S.A. and Colorado, and probably was responsible for the many recent bombings in the state.

Mexican Independence Day 1975 came and went without incident. On September 17, Anthony Quintana and Joey hot-wired two cars, then stole them. They drove them to Juan Haro's Phillips 66 station, where they installed reworked ignitions and "cool" license plates. While the cars were being worked on, Corky Gonzales and Louie Gomez, the "Mexican Godfather," drove up. Corky took a handkerchief from his pocket, opened one of the car doors and wiped the handle. They walked around the cars looking them over. I later learned Gonzales was giving thumbs up on the vehicles while being careful to not leave thumbprints on them.

The cars were dropped at the Children's Hospital parking lot and the Alameda Square Shopping Center, near Juan's house. As Investigators, we were now greatly concerned that other conspirators were stealing cars and building bombs. Regardless, we had to protect six target buildings from the car-bombing plot.

Later that night, Joey told us Juan would build an explosive device and that night would drive the stolen car containing the bomb to the District Four substation. Their plan was to park the vehicle as close as possible to the wall of the substation, ensuring everyone inside would be killed. He also indicated Juan could be armed with a gun or his body would be rigged with an explosive device when he delivers the bomb-rigged vehicle.

At about 8:30 p.m., the stolen car was moved closer to Juan's house. Joey Cordova and Anthony Quintana, carrying a garbage bag from the trunk of his '57 Chevy Bel Air, entered Haro's house. After about an hour, Haro carried a garbage bag from his house to the back seat of his car. Quintana transported a box to the trunk of his vehicle.

Haro attempted to drive off, but police cruisers immediately blocked him into the driveway. Tyus pulled Haro through the open window of the vehicle. I opened the garbage bag to find a ticking bomb, complete with a stopwatch, blasting cap, wires and 27 sticks of dynamite wrapped with tape. Being that close to a bomb ticking toward detonation in 15 minutes was an adrenaline rush.

Capt. Shaughnessy and the bomb squad moved in and disarmed the device in a narrow window of time. They had guts and did a fabulous job. Mike and I moved Haro to a safer location. I told Haro if the bomb detonated and killed anyone, he would be charged with murder. He stated, "I built it. Let me disarm it. You just have to cut a wire."

A search of Quintana's car yielded bomb-making paraphernalia and dynamite. I executed a search warrant on Haro's home and seized numerous guns, a grenade launcher, scanner and equipment used in the construction of the bomb. A search warrant at Haro's Phillips 66 Station produced no other bombs, but 21 blasting caps were seized.

The second car was not picked up by the conspirators, but Corky and a companion, Ernesto Vigil, were observed driving by it. We suspect something spooked them. While we were making the arrests, all the substations were on alert as was Headquarters and The IACP convention.

In the evening, District Four was to be bombed; a Cooperative Endeavor meeting was in progress at the station. According to the Bomb Squad's analysis of the strength of the device, about 50 citizens and police officers likely would have been killed.

The next day, a woman's car was observed where 121 sticks of dynamite had been dumped in the Adams County Landfill. A search of her home yielded instructions on how to make bombs. The explosives matched the dynamite sticks used by Haro. The woman was not charged because authorities could not prove she had discarded the dynamite in the landfill.

A stolen Ford Mustang containing a bomb was left in the Regency Hotel parking lot at W. 39th Avenue and Fox Street during the convention of the International

Association of Chiefs of Police. It exploded during the night, launching half of the Mustang onto Interstate 25. Nobody was hurt. The Crusade for Justice was suspected of planting the bomb. If that suspicion is correct, it was the only bomb they successfully detonated.

The bombing plot investigation was the biggest in Denver Police Department history. ATF officials told me this was the first time in U.S. history that a terrorist bomber was caught with a ticking 27-stick dynamite bomb, en route to a target in a stolen vehicle. I have never felt more pride. We had saved many lives and stopped the bombings in Colorado.

The investigation likely would not have happened if Joey Cordova had not had the conscience to decide it was wrong for the Crusade for Justice to kill police officers— and innocent citizens. Yes, he was a dangerous career criminal. However, Joey Cordova was a hero in my eyes. All of my informants were "dealing or stealing" to support their drug habits. But you can't catch a terrorist by talking with a priest.

An article in *Rocky Mountain News* stated additional informants were giving information to a detective about planned bombings. I never saw or heard anything about any additional informants because there were none. The cases filed were based on one source: Joey Cordova. Over the years, one detective persistently claimed he had cracked the case, which also was untrue. This duplicity and desire to steal credit for other people's work have not set well with me over the years.

The defense team in The Bomb Plot Case was Stan Marks, Ken Padilla, David Manter and Jonathon Olom. The state prosecution featured chief deputies Peter Bornstein and Dick Spriggs, both great attorneys. I got sideways with them on one big issue—the "confession." They felt that putting me on the stand would invite scrutiny on about 15 deals Joey had done for me before the bomb plot investigation.

In the state case, the defense tried to discredit everything, including the confession, which Judge Leonard Plank allowed into evidence. They unsuccessfully attacked my search warrant on the conspirators' house and tried to create doubts about my informant. They claimed the investigation was a police conspiracy, that Haro was entrapped and that we wanted him dead. Juan Haro's defense followed a time-tested strategy in the federal and state cases regarding the hand grenades and the bomb plot: "Deny. Deny. Deny."

In the federal case, the judge was Sherman Finesilver, and the assistant U.S. attorney was John Kobayashi. Haro was convicted of possessing the hand grenades and received a six-year sentence. He testified he had never seen hand grenades or dynamite. Haro also denied building any bombs. He had the backing of Corky Gonzales, The Crusade, and many activists.

If the state case had been filed and prosecuted in federal court, Juan Haro would have sat in prison for decades. Federal court judges don't put up with any nonsense. The defense would not have gotten away with the tactics they pulled in the state case. Haro was acquitted in the bomb plot case.

Arresting several of the ringleaders and exposing The Crusade for Justice as a terrorist organization stopped the bombings in Colorado. Up to that point, 24 explosions occurred in Denver in the mid-1970s, and about 10 went off in metro Denver and Boulder. About 15 bombs were disarmed before they detonated.

The Bomb Squad was dispatched 339 times, picking up 73 explosive devices. About 15 suspected bombs were disarmed before they could be detonated. The targets included banks, restaurants, school administration buildings and buses, hotels, bridges, parks, electrical transmission centers, a radio station and the home of the regional CIA chief.

After the trials, The Crusade distributed a flyer nationally that read, "This Man's Life is in Danger." It showed Joey Cordova in the crosshairs of a gun sight. The Crusade listed his alleged "crimes" against their movement. It listed his "partners in crime" as Denver District Attorney Dale Tooley, Denver Policemen Daril Cinquanta, J.C. Tyus and Robert Shaughnessy, the FBI and ATF, and other federal officers. At the bottom, it read, "There is no love. There is no peace. There is no place. There is no home... for an enemy of the people." They evidently wanted Joey and us dead.

In 1998, Juan Haro wrote a book called "The Ultimate Betrayal." He claimed that in August of 1975, Corky Gonzales stated he wanted to blow up all five Denver Police stations and the International Association of Chiefs of Police convention at Currigan Hall on September 17, 1975. Haro said Gonzales outlined his plan, and Haro stated he would do his part.

Juan claims that Corky introduced him to Joey Cordova, but I doubt it. Haro also said a box of 24 hand grenades was brought to him at the gas station around September 16, and that the people delivering the grenades stated that Corky told him to deliver them.

Haro claimed that in September Gonzales carried 16 red sticks of dynamite to him so he could proceed with the plot. On September 17, Corky brought Juan additional ten sticks of dynamite which he told Juan were to be used for the job that night. Haro wrote that Gonzales had ordered him to steal five cars, but only two were taken.

Haro's book indicates they proceeded to make the bombs. In the book, he claimed Cordova assembled the bomb that was in the car, but that contradicts his confession to me when we arrested Haro in the parking lot. He stated, "I built the bomb, let me disarm it. You just have to cut a wire." I believe all three of them constructed the bomb.

When Haro claims in his book that he was not going to deliver the bomb to the substation, but to a field, I say bullshit. Haro deviated from Gonzales' original plan in that he was going to deliver the bomb. He then told Joey that he was going to plant the stolen vehicle containing the bomb at the District Four substation. His statement in the book contradicts their plan. Remember, Juan states in his book that he is an obedient soldier who follows the chain of command.

Starting in 1966, Juan had his nose so far up Corky's ass that killing a station full of policemen and citizens meant nothing to him. I believe that if Corky—his "El Hefe"—wanted him to plant all the bombs, he would have done it. Corky Gonzales was "The Boss," and the mastermind behind The Crusade for Justice, and I don't believe anyone moved on anything without his orders or approval.

The conspirators possessed more than enough dynamite and blasting caps to build all six bombs. Why they did not attempt Corky's goal of bombing all the targets will probably never be known. Juan's book also confirms that he committed perjury when he testified in his case about his knowledge of the hand grenades and dynamite.

Here's something else to think about: a lawyer cannot put his client on the stand if he knows he is going to lie. I cannot help wondering if the attorney allowed Haro to testify despite knowing Haro would not tell the truth.

Winning this high-profile case that was trying to fly under the "civil rights" banner would have established the reputations of the defense attorneys, boosting future business. The court case resulting from Denver's biggest investigation generated boundless publicity.

Legal experts can eternally debate whether the Bomb Plot Case was about winning or justice. For me, it was about saving lives and ending the bombings in Colorado. I accomplished that.

All the negative things Juan wrote in his book and the nonsense about me that Ernesto Vigil put down in another book, "The Crusade for Justice" mean no more to me today than that I was just doing my job. They alleged I had entrapped Haro and allowed my informant to commit crimes, that I was brutal and various other unsubstantiated garbage.

Besides the fact that their allegations are untrue, nothing will change the fact that Juan Haro was a terrorist bomber and the Crusade for Justice, led by Corky Gonzales, was a militant terrorist organization hell bent on killing policemen.

Sometime after the Haro trial, somebody threw a Molotov cocktail at my parent's house. Someone called the school office to try to get my brother and sister released from class. We never found out who did either act, and we could not tie it to any group or person. But I moved my family members and set up everything in fake names.

* * * *

Developing and utilizing informants is an art. Ideally, informants fear me and respect me at the same time. The first thing I do is define their motives for working with me. Is he trying to avoid jail time on a case I put on him or is he seeking vengeance, money, elimination of competition in the drug trade or insurance against future cases brought against him?

Anyone working off a case has to turn three deals. If he or she catches another case while we are working off a case, the deal is null and void.

I caution informants to not entrap anyone; doing a crime needs to be the target's idea, not the informants. I explain that if he is eyes and ears to a transaction or crime, he instantly becomes a witness and risks getting burned or forced to testify. Any case that is dismissed does not diminish an obligation to me.

If he is working for money, the CI needs to know the department has a meager informant fund. I often suggest that a potential informant calls Crime Stoppers so we can work their tip. It's embarrassing to dole out a C note for say... information leading to arrest in an armed robbery.

One day, a group of wealthy businessmen approached me to let me know that if I needed informant money for a big deal, I should ask them. This resource made my big picture view much bigger. Informants are constantly breaking the law.

Most of my informants were using dope the entire time I was working them. If they had a "burner"—a heroin habit—going, they were dealing or stealing or worse to support their habits. If I caught them doing a major felony while I was working them, they were gone.

I kept detailed records on every informant, including the date I developed him or her, and the nature of the business relationship, such as working off a case. Then I recorded each deal we made, including the arrestee's name, what was seized and the date.

Each informant had a file cataloging everything he had ever done for me and the compensation he received. I was covering my ass with this detailed information, bracing for any allegations the department or legal system leveled at me regarding an informant, or just in case an informant tried to make false accusations against me.

One key to my success working informants was telling them my mission was to solve a wide spectrum of crimes. My informants knew I wanted information on all felonies, including stickups, burglaries, theft, narcotics, speed labs, counterfeiting, auto theft, unsolved crimes and wanted fugitives. Because they were part of the undercurrent of criminal enterprise, and that stream was so deep, they always produced.

The process eventually got so ridiculously productive that I was issuing "Get Out of Jail Free" cards, which we called "insurance." Informants and non-informants would call to say, "I will give you this deal, and you will owe me one, okay?" It became difficult to keep up with the flow of information, so I cherry-picked the best deals and always recorded them in the informant files.

Female informants are in a world all their own. Once they liked and trusted me, I had them forever. Once in a while, one would get infatuated with me and would want to bed down with me. Obviously, I had to keep them at arm's length. Most of them were very effective because the bad guys freely talked in front of them.

The females would turn all sorts of big deals. While they were working for me, they frequently caught cases from other cops such as "boosting" (shoplifting), possession and use of narcotics, and prostitution.

I developed a woman informant in 1972 who turned me deals until the mid-1980s, when she was killed. She was my first high-level CI, based on the quality of her information. One woman CI was turning all sorts of deals for me, then turning around and catching cases filed by other detectives. They were not protecting her as I did, and she was murdered wearing a "snitch jacket." I would never put my informants on "Front Street" where they would get burned and possibly killed.

I always gave some time and watched for other people to come through the doors of the crime house before initiating the bust. In most cases my informant was not near the arrest site, and was not eyes and ears to the crime, thus protecting his or her identity. The bad guys used the females to drive getaway vehicles on their crimes, carry their guns and dope, deal their drugs.

After the Haro trial, I realized I needed to tape record my informants and my instructions to my informants. Anytime I had a deal in which the information indicated that the bad guys were going to commit an armed robbery or a burglary, I taped the informant's statement and my instructions. I wanted to cover my ass in case my informant actually committed the crime, and it included gun play, and somebody got hurt. The "deal" tape went into each informers' files.

In almost all violent crime and search warrant cases, the informants disappeared, so I had no problem protecting their anonymity. Cops kept informers' identities secret even from our partners, sharing only what was needed in the context of the case. It limited confusion in court when only one officer testified on the identity and role of an informant. However, having dual informers in one investigation kept both informers honest, because we compared their information for similarities and discrepancies.

* * * *

One male informant was giving me info that resulted in execution of a series of search warrants. We scored on all of them and then one day I start getting calls from the people we had hit. They wanted their stereos and televisions back. Funny thing was we did not take any. We took only the items registered as stolen.

I figured my CI was going in after we left the residences targeted in the search warrants in order to steal the belongings. The next deal he gave me, we did counter-surveillance. As soon as we left, he broke in and stole the TV. Our team swooped in, arrested him and got him sent to prison.

* * * *

Another male informant double-dealed me. He was a career criminal and was turning some quality deals. I received information that he was doing burglaries while packing a gun. In another town, a lone suspect had forced his way into a home, tied up the family members at gunpoint, and robbed them. The teenage daughter came home during the robbery, and the burglar raped her and tied her up.

The description of the rapist matched my informant, and the victims positively IDed his photo. I got him to meet me under the pretense of verifying information, and officers from the other jurisdiction and I arrested him in possession of the gun used in the robbery and rape. He confessed and went to prison.

* * * *

I have always been focused on the victims. My goal was to catch the bad guy and hold him accountable for the damage he inflicted on the victims. I wanted to be the victims' champion. I took care in making sure I sent the bad guys to prison for the crimes that they committed. If cops caught a criminal "right," we didn't have to look over our shoulders in years to come, worrying about him coming after us. That's why I verified and corroborated every scrap of information I got from informants.

As a rule, informants were not giving up their knowledge of criminal activities out of altruism. Rather, they tended to be self-serving. When informants refused or forgot to call me and kept me hanging, I often roughed them up when they resurfaced. If they really pissed me off, they went to jail.

Det. Larry Subia accused me of being too nice to them and kissing their ass, but he was wrong. When they were taking care of business, I was civil and treated them right. I always kept my word. But I was a handful when they crossed me, and they knew it. Because they feared and respected me, they didn't give me bad information and were clear in pointing out when information was iffy.

* * * *

When I compiled information in my affidavits for search warrants, I took great care in verifying and corroborating everything. My affidavits were long and detailed, including all aspects of my investigation, whether it centered on drugs, stolen property, evidence in an ongoing criminal enterprise or any items that I wanted to seize in a prior criminal offense. I had a reputation for writing affidavits that could not be defeated.

I am proud of the numerous commendation letters I received from D.A.s from Denver and other counties acknowledging the quality of my affidavits. They appreciated my hard work on the front end because it saved them from scrambling in the prosecution phase or losing a case needlessly. Defense attorneys tried in vain to suppress my evidence, picking at each element only to find out everything alleged in my cases was true.

Cops constantly have to deal with defense attorneys calling them liars, accusing them of entrapping or setting up their clients, falsifying affidavits, and planting dope. I always figured if defense attorneys were attacking me, it meant they didn't have anything to argue against in my case. The defense tended to tell enough lies for both sides of the aisle, so why would I lie?

Throughout two decades of police work, I was not without sin. I pushed the envelope as far as I could to catch the bad guys. I sometimes rearranged pieces of the puzzle, but presenting the developments out of sequence didn't alter the truth or the outcomes. Cops have a saying, "You ride the same horse out of battle that you rode into battle on." In other words, officers never deviate from their written accounts or prior testimony. Does the end justify the means? Sometimes. Every cop has to find his or her level of conscience.

I did not fabricate "once upon a time" affidavits, or "salt" someone by planting evidence, and I never witnessed any other cop doing it. I never intentionally entrapped anyone or allowed an innocent defendant to go to prison. When we found out an informant set up someone for a fall, we dropped the charges.

Cops know when an informant has entrapped someone because the accused individual will have an immediate outcry. I repeatedly coached informants that we wouldn't prosecute any bad guy who didn't dream up the crime himself and that the informant could not participate.

* * * *

The "chase" was everything to me and was the foundation of my existence as a policeman. I wanted to solve "who done its" and outthink the bad guys. Suspects I arrested went to prison for the crimes they committed, and they knew it, contrary to any "jailhouse" bullshit they might spew.

Catching fugitives was fun. On a certain level, I took it personally, and my goal was to show them I could outsmart them. While it all played out as a game or at least competition, I never forgot that every criminal was potentially very dangerous. Very few people want to be caught, or sent or returned to prison. So many criminals were packing when we arrested them that I lost count of how many guns I seized over the years. I'm certain it was in the hundreds.

* * * *

While in District Three, an informant put Mike and me onto a check ring that was netting about $10,000 in merchandise every time they went active. We managed to catch them with stolen checks, IDs and proceeds from their crime spree.

* * * *

Steve Barnhill was one thorough, meticulous cop. We nicknamed him "Barney Beagle," because when we executed search warrants, he would find dope hidden in strange places where nobody else had looked, or ever thought to look. Barnhill, Klawonn, Bob Ortiz, Gene Shaw, Gary Leutheuser, Bill Baldi and I devised a scheme of dual rolling and stationary surveillance on two criminals who had traveled to Colorado Springs and "copped" drugs and returned.

We executed two search warrants, scoring 1-1/2 ounces of heroin, stolen checks, and credit cards. We arrested eight suspects in the credit card ring investigation. This was not a huge criminal enterprise, but it was my policy to pursued most of the felony tips that came my way.

Barnhill, Vince DiManna and I developed another informant who introduced me to a speed dealer. We made a quick-hit bust on the dealer when I purchased 200 white crosses.

Barnhill and I sat on a car containing a fully automatic Japanese Nambu rifle for 24 hours until a guy came and drove off in the vehicle. It was only one weapon, but he went to jail, and we went home to sleep. Barnhill and I did many search warrant cases for drugs and ran on all sorts of fugitive information. He was fun to work with and was an expert bow hunter and fisherman.

* * * *

During this period, I was getting a stream of tips on "Who done its." I supplied information to Wheat Ridge P.D. that resulted in the arrest of two men for armed robbery. I gave Boulder P.D. info on the culprit in an armed robbery, which they turned into a positive ID and an arrest.

* * * *

Officer George Palaze, a fellow Italian, arrested a bad ass named Tommy Abeyta for burglary and put him in the rear of his police vehicle. Abeyta slipped his cuffs, rolled into the front seat of the running car, and drove away. I was embarrassed for George, who put out a department-wide offer of a steak dinner to whoever arrested Abeyta. I immediately began drumming up information. After all, what's better than a free steak dinner?

After a number of dead-end leads, I learned Abeyta had worked at a sugar factory near Lafayette, a small town between Denver and Boulder. The company indicated he no longer worked there but provided a Lafayette address. We teamed with Lafayette P.D. for surveillance on the house.

We never saw Abeyta but decided to hit the place, having seen a female enter it through an open door. Our burglar and auto thief was hiding inside, and we nabbed him as well as a gal wanted by the FBI for escape. Lafayette P.D. let us process Abeyta in their building before we transported him back to Denver. It was a great present for George, and one of the most delicious steak dinners I've ever eaten.

* * * *

Numerous informants passed me scraps of information regarding active fences, which I handed off to the Fencing Unit. I had worked on various cases with three great undercover detectives named Jimmy Reed, Bobby Tabares and Yolonda Cunningham. They flipped the tips into cases against three fences.

Jimmy could walk through a crowded mall and be one of the last people anyone would suspect to be a cop. He was disheveled, his heavyset body surrounded by a coat of pockets that contained a completely imaginative and unimaginable array of miscellaneous things. No one would dare stick their hands into Jimmy's pockets, for fear that they would get bit by something living in there.

In response to a rash of armed robberies, Reed once went undercover as a pizza delivery guy. He got stuck up, was instantly in a shootout, and put a slug in the bad guy.

Tobares was a big Hispanic dude who had the gift of the gab and could convince anyone to deal with him on stolen merchandise or dope. Bobby had classic Elvis hair, and he was a very talented undercover detective. Yoli was a natural undercover and was able to lay out a line of words that led straight to an arrest. She lulled criminals into a false sense of possibility.

CHAPTER 11—
INFORMATION DESK—
8-76 to 1-77

Out of the blue in August of 1976, I was transferred to the Information Desk at Denver Police Headquarters. I had no idea what the underlying reason might have been, but I figured there was one. My job was to man the desk, screening people as they entered the building. The arraignment court was upstairs, below the Denver City Jail.

Al Walker was stationed with me at the Information Desk, and he kept me laughing every day, but he wasn't enough distraction to keep me from having to figure out how I was going to cope with this gawdawful, tedious, boring assignment. So, I started clearing people coming into the building and finding some of them were wanted on felonies and misdemeanors. We initially caught some flak, but after we got our first arrest of a guy packing a gun, nobody questioned what we were doing.

As a police officer, I realized again and again that what mattered was not what we did to an individual, but how we articulated our reasons for doing it. It was the same on the street: Explain why. Some cops were threatened by this concept because their egos prevented them from ever explaining or apologizing for anything.

Al and I also were making dope arrests. Perhaps they were high, but what else could be going through these people's minds to inspire them to enter a police building holding drugs?

Al focused on the Open Items List of traffic warrants of wanted persons and scored more busts than me. We were having a good time and somehow managed to turn this wasteland of a job into genuine police work.

* * * *

It's brilliant when all of the divisions of a police department work as a cooperative team. It's rare, but it does happen. I passed on information I developed during the day to the Special Crime Attack Team, and they made the pinches. The first deal I turned SCAT on to was a wanted stickup. They captured him and a companion who was wanted for escape from the DOC.

I kept feeding information to the SCAT, and they kept scoring arrests. It seemed like an ideal fit, so I tried to get into SCAT—to no avail. I also was trying to go back to narcotics. I apparently had my detractors, but most of them remained anonymous. Somebody in the department—or several somebodies—was blackballing me on jobs I had already proven I had the aptitude and passion for excelling at.

So, as I sat at that information desk, my mind flashed on to people who might be blocking my attempts to get accepted into either position. I had no desire to be a case detective because it would take too much of my time, and would restrict me to the cases the brass thinks are important at any time.

I needed freedom to pursue as many cases as I could solve. My only ambition on the job was to make detective and chase bad guys. I had no desire to make rank, for either the title or the chance to supervise. For me, it was all about making good arrests.

* * * *

I developed informant information on James "Sonny" Compos, who had been on the run for two years after

escaping from Soledad Prison in California while serving
2-15 years for possession of narcotics with intent to sell.
My ears always perked up when I heard the words
"Soledad Prison," because that's where the guy who shot
me had escaped from. When he was arrested in California,
Compos possessed two kilos of heroin and one pound of
cocaine.

Information indicated that he was dealing heroin in
Denver. A delivery of heroin by the girlfriend of Compos
was scheduled for a North Denver address. The plan was to
use the helicopter and follow her to Compos' "cool pad" to
arrest him. The surveillance team consisted of Dets. Steve
Barnhill, Tom Laska, Mario Luchetta, and Dick Thompson.

Her vehicle was there when the team arrived, so the
helicopter was summoned. Surveillance followed the car
northeast to an Adams County address. At that time,
Adams County Sheriff's Office was contacted for
assistance. Officers Carl Southard, Ron Blasko, and SCAT
Det. Henry Stang also responded.

Vehicles filled with cops surrounded the building, and
the apartment manager confirmed Compos was in unit 304.
Henry Stang observed Compos looking out a rear window
of the apartment. Officers entered the apartment to arrest
Compos. He and his two female companions possessed a
sawed-off shotgun and a revolver.

Compos had rented the apartment under a phony name,
Pete Pacheco, and had a forged ID for that alias. The
females were arrested for harboring a fugitive.

* * * *

I developed a first-time informant who said two guys
in Boulder had illegal machine guns and explosives they
were willing to sell. The source gave me the address and

115

the name of at least one of the occupants. I took the CI to be interviewed by the FBI, and they accompanied us to Boulder. Then my partner and I went to Boulder P.D. to brief them on the intelligence.

An undercover officer accompanied the informant on more than one occasion to the home in attempts to purchase a weapon or explosives. The occupants blew off the woman, shaking their heads and saying they did not know what she was talking about. Boulder P.D. followed through on the initial informant claims, obtaining a search warrant for hand grenades, M-16 rifles, and a sawed-off shotgun that she claimed she saw in the residence.

When Boulder P.D. executed the search warrant, they found nothing resembling weapons or explosives. Small quantities of drugs were discovered, but the two men denied owning it and had no known history of illicit drug use. They acknowledged knowing the informant who claimed they possessed illegal firearms and explosives but added they had shunned her. The men agreed that their disinterest in her romantically must have spurred her to make the false claim to police, and also figured she planted the supposed narcotics.

Sometimes cops end up chasing their own tails, or the tails of people falsely accused. And when that happens, my partners and I always moved on to the next caper.

Unfortunately, the men were awarded $90,000 in a civil lawsuit, and I was fined $10,000, which was reduced to $2,500. I feel that in the interest of due diligence any law-enforcement agency would have needed to execute a search warrant to prove or disprove the informant's claims.

Police don't have the luxury of taking a wait-and-see approach when the safety of the community hangs in the balance. I strongly disagreed with the decision to penalize Boulder monetarily when they were only following through on a threat that had gone through the Denver Police Department and the FBI.

Of course, I took the heat and this boondoggle would be brought up in future attacks on my credibility. My detractors never mentioned that the CI was a drug addict and alcoholic who had lied.

CHAPTER 12—
DISTRICT THREE—
1-77 to 8-77

In January of 1977, I transferred back to District Three. I guess the brass figured I had done my penance at the Information Desk. During this time, Lt. Britton put Mike Klawonn and me in for the Distinguished Service Cross for cracking the Bomb Plot case. It was as big as any case in the history of the DPD, and we didn't get even a whisper of recognition in the year after it was successfully prosecuted.

Lt. Britton told me they were going to award me the more meritorious Medal of Valor, but that never happened. While I didn't care about rank or prestige within the hierarchy of the Denver Police Department, I did care about being honored for outstanding police work.

I teamed up with the U.S. Postal Service to arrest five individuals who were stealing checks out of mailboxes. The crime ring also was convicted of forgery for passing at least $18,000 in falsified checks.

* * * *

I received a tip on a paraplegic known as "Eskimo" whom I had arrested in 1976 for counterfeiting Colorado Driver's licenses. Now, I learned he was at it again, doing business from his hospital bed at Denver General Hospital. I executed a search warrant with a D.A. Investigator buddy of mine, Ken Hawkins.

In searching Eskimo's hospital room, we seized counterfeiting paraphernalia, balloons of suspected heroin, marijuana, pill capsules, needles, and syringes. As we were finishing up, in walked career criminal Angelo Macias, and the fight was on. Macias was scrambling to make his exit,

118

and we were trying to tackle him. Hawkins and I put his head through the plasterboard, and balloons of suspected heroin went bouncing all over the room.

A nurse walked in and asked us what's going on. I told her we were there to eliminate the drug dealers who were trying to compete with the DGH pharmacy in the sale of narcotics. She was displeased. We put a hold on Eskimo and took Mr. Macias to jail with the evidence that we seized.

Eskimo was the first counterfeiter I had done. He had an interesting system. Using an 8"x10" format, he cut clear plastic sheets and used rub-on letters to place all of the boilerplate information that goes on a Colorado driver's license. He then used the rub-on letters to create the person's description, including name, date of birth, address, and physical characteristics.

The Colorado State Seal was placed between the sheets along with a photo of the check passer, and a red or blue background sheet to match the style used by the Department of Motor Vehicles at the time. The next step was taking a photo with a Polaroid SX70 camera. Eskimo laminated and trimmed the final product.

Criminals at the next level down the chain had a vital tool to go on a check-cashing spree, netting thousands of dollars in property and money. Eskimo also made driver's licenses for wanted parties who needed a new identity, and he turned out a high-quality product.

I became DPD's resident expert on ID counterfeiting. I was able to separately nab "The Paper Lady," Joyce Shiloh; and Bill Rezab. Both were known counterfeiters who used the same method as Eskimo. Rezab was the most sophisticated counterfeit artist I ever encountered and was equipped with a 35mm camera and a darkroom. While it seemed the crimes of Eskimo, Shiloh and Rezab were low levels, there is no way to estimate how much damage they enabled other criminals to inflict on businesses and individuals. One violent criminal equipped with a false ID to evade capture was capable of harming dozens of citizens.

* * * *

During this period, I was teamed up with Don Rask—once named "National Policeman of the Year." He deserved to be the poster boy for the department. He was tall and looked like a fashion model in his uniform. Rask could gain someone's respect in a short conversation. He was a born leader and turned out to be a great partner. Everyone liked and respected Don.

I had suspected they put me with him to slow me down, and I was able to confirm my suspicion with Don. The problem with the brass' strategy was Don liked to do real police work, and he was really good at it. We hit a rhythm of making stops and arresting bad guys—and enjoying ourselves and the process of doing it.

Rask and I routined the lowlife bars where the bad guys hung out and pulled out a string of known wanted criminals. Don had style and substance, and I reveled in working with him and learning from him.

* * * *

Barnhill, Ed Roy and I were drafting an affidavit for a search warrant for Sammy Abeyta, who was dealing heroin. We already had an arrest warrant for him for a stabbing. One day we learn that he had just shot a man over money owed on a drug transaction. We decided to run on his address to get him off the streets. Abeyta's drug habit seemed to be spinning him out of control, and we decided we didn't want him to hurt anyone else.

We got backup help from Sgt. Angerman and District Four officers Alverson, Newell, O'Hayre, Burkhalter and Britten. One of the surveillance team members overheard a female inside say, "The pigs are already here." The team tried to talk them out because we knew they were armed, but they would not comply.

We kicked in the side door and entered the house. The toilet was flushing as we came through the door, so … there goes the heroin. We seized a gun which we found was purchased at Sportline sporting goods in Arvada with a forged check. Arvada Det. Jeff Waller immediately put a hold on Abeyta for forgery.

Abeyta had needle marks on both arms extending from his elbow to his hands, which told us he was trying to feed an enormous habit. Slashes on his right wrist were consistent with him being assaulted with a knife. We had Baker-4—the crime lab—photograph his wrist, then finished the process of getting another dangerous man off the streets and keeping him there.

My informants were giving me substantial information on escapees from various institutions, so I knocked off three of them who had been incarcerated for armed robbery. The fugitives made it easy on me by hiding in my district. It's always convenient to not have to drive to another city or even district.

* * * *

The Mr. Steak chain of restaurants along the Front Range was experiencing a three-month rash of robberies. The M.O. was consistent: three males robbed the restaurants at gunpoint, ordering the employees and patrons to lie down on the floor. In some of the intrusions, one of the bad guys sexually assaulted females by putting his hand into their panties.

The trio had rung up to 27 armed robberies, and a task force was formed by police officers from Denver, Lakewood, Arvada, Westminster, Pueblo, Colorado Springs and the Jefferson County D.A.'s Office.

Acting on a tip, this example of multi-jurisdictional cooperation followed Charlie Hampton for five days, 24 hours a day. He would try to thwart the tails by driving around in circles, racing 90 miles an hour down Federal Boulevard, slowing to 10 mph on the freeway, and pulling multiple U-turns before heading to his target. Despite his evasion tactics, Hampton was observed circling potential target restaurants.

Hampton was a bank robber by trade, but he seemed to have changed his preferences. During one of his previous capers, he and his accomplice put cardboard boxes over their heads before they robbed the bank. He twice shook surveillance, and each time a robbery occurred that matched the other stickups—down to the sexual assault.

On the fifth day, I found out that someone had observed one of the suspects wore wingtip shoes, and I immediately figured it was Angelo Macias. The task force followed the criminal crew down I-25 to Colorado Springs. They stopped nine blocks from the Mister Steak, at Scotty's Motel. The surveillance team watched them cruise the restaurant parking lot several times, park a block away and walk to the target armed with a shotgun and handguns.

They lost sight of the trio, so after a few minutes decided to close in, thinking the robbery was going down. Instead, they met the heavily armed men coming up an alley and ordered them to drop their weapons. A shootout ensued, and numerous shots were fired.

Victor "Skunks" Anaya was killed in the exchange, and the other two robbers dropped their guns and masks, hopped a fence, and ran. Hampton was spotted three blocks away, standing in the empty engine compartment of a vehicle, his legs clearly visible. Macias escaped the scene but was arrested when he appeared for a court date in Denver, in his wingtip shoes.

The crime spree of three of the most dangerous career criminals in Denver came to an end in Colorado Springs, and citizens were safer. The criminals had no known vendetta against the Mr. Steak chain but kept hitting those restaurants because the layout was the same at every restaurant in the chain. Criminals are creatures of habit, and they were comfortable with Mr. Steak.

I was and remain impressed with this investigation and complex surveillance. The policemen involved are to be praised for their professionalism, persistence and calm under fire. I hoped they got their deserved commendations through their respective departments for their bravery, and wish I had participated in the investigation.

* * * *

Another chain of steakhouses was targeted by another gang of criminals. A stickup team was hitting Bonanza Sirloin Pits in the Denver Metro area, using a sawed-off shotgun and a revolver. An informant clued us in that the culprits were Giron and Lloyd, and also identified their getaway vehicle and address.

I contacted the Wheat Ridge Police Sgt. W. Davis and Tech H. Anderson, who confirmed a $3,000 robbery. The Wheat Ridge officers showed a photo lineup to victims in the restaurant and got a positive ID on Lloyd. Another robbery had been perpetrated by a group of whites and Hispanics in Adams County. Det. Roger Simms confirmed $350 had been stolen and had a description of the suspects who brandished a sawed-off shotgun and a revolver.

Our Investigators found out the stickup team and two others had gone to Salt Lake City to cop four ounces of heroin. We had set up round-the-clock surveillance on their home so we would nab them the instant they returned.

Det. Clarence Voyles of the Salt Lake Police called in response to the information we had provided them and informed me that four individuals, including our suspect, were arrested after an armed robbery of a restaurant. A dishwasher had slipped out to call the police, providing a description of the car and suspects. They had robbed the restaurant and its 11 patrons of about $1,200 with a sawed-off shotgun and a handgun.

We had been sitting on a stakeout for three days, and the suspect was arrested about 500 miles due west. Each suspect was charged with 13 counts of armed robbery and held on a $1-million bond. The Dodge Charger the quartet used in the Colorado robberies was found at a Salt Lake City motel—broken down.

Salt Lake P.D. seized evidence based on a search warrant they executed on the motel room and vehicle. We carried out the search warrant on the house, gathering clothing worn in the Colorado robberies, narcotics, two rifles and a quantity of stolen items.

The officers who assisted in the Bonanza bust operation were Wheat Ridge Dets. J. Darlinger, R. Davidson, D. Farley, H. Anderson, Sgt. W. Davis and Denver SCAT Officers Bill Wiederspahn, Dave Abrahams,

Billy Cardenas, Larry Blumer, John Goodfellow and Rick Polok. Darrell Dyer of ATF and Ken Hawkins of the Denver D.A.'s office also assisted.

* * * *

I teamed with Sgt. Dave Michaud and Det. Rich Pfeifer to do surveillance on a heroin ring in Thornton, a middle-class suburb north of Denver. My information indicated that a woman was dealing ounces for her husband, Nick, who was in the joint for selling "weed." She distributed the ounces in 1-gram balloons by tucking them under the A-frame signs at a nearby car wash.

We watched a male leave her house and hide the heroin at the car wash. The buyer arrived with an entourage. The instant he picked up the baggy, we jumped him, retrieving the dope.

I drafted an affidavit and returned with the search warrant. The Thornton Police joined Denver officers Ed Roy, Joe Garcia and Sgt. Truman Leutheuser in kicking down the door. The drug ring was cutting five ounces of heroin and tried to hide it under the bed.

The suspects were building a swimming pool in the back yard, but we found food stamps in the house and suspected the drug dealers were on welfare. They also had a rare high-end offset printing press that could be used to counterfeit money.

* * * *

One autumn day, we were contacted by Agents Jovich and Huggins of the FBI, who had a warrant for one of the Lovato brothers for the bank robbery of the Otero Savings & Loan. Rolling surveillance of one of the brothers took us north to a home in Adams County. We contacted The

Adams County Sheriff's Office and Watch Commander Turner assisted us.

A female was observed leaving the house, and Adams County made a traffic stop on her blocks away. She was the common-law wife of Lovato. After a while, a man with a baseball cap came out to the back yard and began raking leaves. We closed in and arrested Lovato, seizing a loaded .22-caliber handgun from his jacket.

His wife granted consent to search the property, and we seized a number of firearms and a police scanner from his vehicle. Lovato's fall partner "FiFi" was on bond for a robbery he had committed with him.

* * * *

I received information one day that a man wanted for burglary would be attending a funeral. It got even better: our guy would be in the hearse transporting the deceased to the cemetery. I had to ponder this one... how much heat would I catch if I arrested our suspect in route?

I decided that it was better to nab him in the hearse than at the cemetery, where we could get jumped by the assembled mass. So, we pulled over the hearse and told the guy he was wanted. He got out of the car, and we were gone in about two minutes, with no altercation. We lucked out, but I figure we also made the right call on the fly on how to handle a delicate situation.

* * * *

After my shifts, I would go out and work on my projects. As I progressed as a cop, my investigations got more complex and harder to put together. When I initiated them, I never had any idea I would spend years on a case. There were always lots of quick hitters, and I couldn't pass on them. I had to verify a daily flow of information on suspects, houses, and vehicles.

By this point, I had set up my home office with all the forms needed to do my job, most notably search warrants and affidavits. At any time, I could type an affidavits or search warrant, go to the on-call judge to have it signed, and meet the team to execute it. I had my "in-house" ID Bureau of thousands of mug shots, "Daril's bad guys books" and my nickname file. A phone call or two would provide me with all the information I needed from intelligence or narcotics. I called my home office "District Five."

Banner Molinar pulling armed robbery prior to McDonald's murder/robbery.

<u>Career Criminal Unit</u>

L-R Back row
Sgt. Tony Lombard
Sgt. John Thompson
Det. Daril Cinquanta
Det. Bobby Miller

L-R Front row
Det. Larry Subia
Det. James Lebedoff
Det. Steve Barnhill

Chief Art Dill congratulating Daril Cinquanta
in receiving the **Medal of Honor**

Corky Gonzales
Leader of the
Crusade for Justice

DENVER POLICE
71855

My grandma & Uncle Tony

Daril Cinquanta and younger
brother Marc (Junior Police Band)

Daril Cinquanta and John Walsh
"America's Most Wanted"

Sgt. Dave Michaud and Det.
Daril Cinquanta routining
Larimer Street bars

Det. Daril Cinquanta and Det. Larry Subia receiving **Optimist Awards**

Denver Police Academy
Class of 70-1

Daril Cinquanta
Denver Police
Academy picture

Daril Cinquanta
undercover photo

Daril's Piper Cub Special
"Fancy Pants"

District 4 Sub-station
target of bomb plot

The Alpinian Italian Restaurant Riverside, **CA**

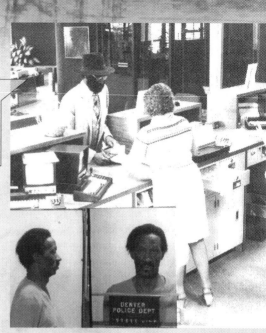

George Benningfield in disguise robbing a Columbia Savings Bank

9 lbs. Heroin seized from **Benny and David Maciel**

Old Intelligence Bureau – 1960's

L-R back row: John Gray, Don Mullen, Willie Norton, Lester Bates, Don Mulnix, Dick Sherwitz, Steve Metros, Mike Dowd

L-R front row: Bob Harmon, Frank "Fat Back" Parsons, Jerry Kennedy, John Hindes, Dwayne "Red" Borden, Larry Britton, Jimmy Jones

Juan Haro - bomber
Crusade for Justice

DENVER POLICE
41125
1 10 73 -E 1300

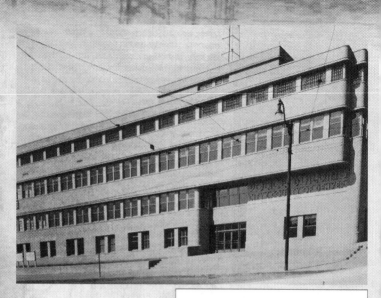

Old Denver Police building,
13th & Champa Streets
(Penthouse on roof)

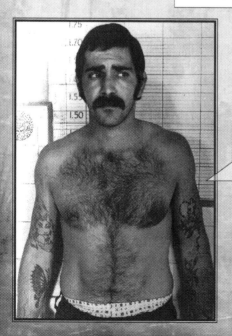

Lawrence Pusateri
who shot me on
Oct. 3, 1971

Lawrence **Pusateri** FBI Most Wanted poster

Special Crime Attack Team
(SCAT) 1981

Superbowl Sting Undercover team

L-R back row: John Thompson, Dave Michaud, Milt Gras, Art Hutchison, John Mulligan.

L-R middle row: Diane Montoya, Terri Hayes, Chris Bridges, Yuda Pringle, Carolyn Rogers (Priest), Steve Carter

L-R front row: Daril Cinquanta, Larry Subia

Vice/Drug Control Bureau **(1975)**

DETECTIVE DARIL CINQUANTA
Crimefighter

Denver Police Department
1331 Cherokee Street
Denver, Colorado 80204   Pager 855-9552

Crime Fighter
Card

Matterhorn Restaurant Boulder,
Colorado

My 57 T-Bird at The Dunafon Castle

My dad

Uncle Joe

Capt. Jerry Kennedy, Capt. Elvis Presley, Chief Art Dill

Denver Police Recruit Class 70-1

Uncle Joe flying at The Matterhorn

L to R: Det.Greg Meyer, Pat. Buster Snider, Capt. Larry Britton, Det. Daril Cinquanta, Sgt. John Thompson

First floor completion of The Matterhorn with a view of the hangar and our airplanes. Behind the restaurant is the cabin I lived in when I left home.

L to R: Photo taken at The Elitch Gardens Theatre in the 70'S.
Det. Mike Ortiz, Det. Daril Cinquanta, Det. Alta Metzinger, Capt.
James T. Kirk of The Star Ship Enterprise, Capt. Jerry Kennedy

CHAPTER 13—
SPECIAL CRIME ATTACK TEAM (SCAT)—
11-77 to 4-81

In October of 1977, I was transferred to the Special Crime Attack Team. This was one of the Denver Police Department's master strokes, at least in relation to me, because it was perfectly aligned with my talents and desires. I was working under Capt. Don Brannan and Sgt. Dave Michaud, whom they obviously had paired with me to try to supervise me. The SCAT unit had very talented personnel.

Brannan was replaced by Capt. Don Mulnix. The other sergeants were Gerry Frazzini, Ed Hansen, and Harold Oaks. The detectives were Bobby Vescio, Gordon Baker, Greg Cross, Brian Deasy, Charles Flos, Steve Fugate, Bob Palfrey, Dan Schreiner, Darrell Wagner, Mark Chavez, Gerry Fitzgibbons, John Goodfellow, Ed Hertzing, Gary Lauricella, Ernest Martinez, Tom Ortiz, George Palaze, Rick Polak, Gary Regan, Steve Tokarski, Ken Vasquez, Tony Ventura, Larry Weant, and Steve Wilson. It was an elite force. Every one of those officers was hand-picked. We filed our own cases and had our lab guys. While in the SCAT Unit, I got my nickname, "C-Q."

The original missions of SCAT were to patrol and investigate neighborhoods that were being hit hard by burglaries and to reduce the overall crime rates in those areas. I immediately asked why—with our crew of hotshot detectives—we couldn't target the burglars based on informant information or on the period of time they had jumped out of the joint?

So, I took that approach. We checked the recent parole list. I gave each ex-con about one month before he would be strung out again and needed to do something rash to feed his habit. Nothing was worse for users than being dope sick and needing a fix to get "straight" again. It worked over and over, and we were aces at following the bad guys.

Our only requirement was that we arrested them when we witnessed them committing the first felony. We also pursued all felony information, and it resulted in many arrests. It turned out my new partner, Dave Michaud, was a first-class investigator and a great interviewer. We complemented each other.

During my time in SCAT, we had two spectacular secretaries, Faye Bradeen and Juanita Lawless. They supported the detectives and the whole unit, and always jumped in to assist us in any request to type a case, search warrant or do research. Faye and Juanita were unfailingly pleasant and fun to be around. They were a valued and crucial part of the team, and we all considered them our friends.

* * * *

As soon as I joined the unit, I contributed several fugitive arrests. Then we picked our first official surveillance targets, Robert "Fiddles" Chavez and Jimmy Contreras. We knew they were shooting heroin daily and had informant information they were pulling burgs.

We were sitting in their house in Five Points and suddenly turn to find them behind us asking, "What's happening?" They were pleasant, and we made small talk, and they were on their way into the house. They got the drop on us, and we were embarrassed. So, we played it off like we just happened to be there, lingered for a while drinking our cokes and then pulled off. One of the other cars took the "Eye," meaning those officers could see the target.

We assembled a six-car surveillance team, then rotated cars so often they would not pick up that they were being tailed. That night, Chavez and Contreras headed north to Adams County. We informed Adams County Sheriff's Office that a couple of career criminal burglars would be in their jurisdiction.

The burglars didn't appear to be particularly scientific, cruising a residential area to find a house that looked like an inviting target. They picked a corner house, which burglars prefer because it minimizes the number of neighbors seeing them committing the crime.

One of the thieves went to the front door and knocked. No answer. He popped open the front door and walked back to the car, and they drove off. We knew they were seasoned thieves, and we knew they were testing to see if any police cars responded to an alarm. They cruised the area for about 15 minutes, circled back around and gained entry.

Most professionals do a three-minute burglary and are gone. They toss the bedroom first because people keep their valuables close to them. Crooks take cash, jewelry, and guns and if they nab enough small valuables, they often leave without taking large items. They had gathered the bedroom booty and were stacking items from throughout the rest of the house when we interrupted them.

This is a very dangerous point in time. If the burglars are armed, this is the moment they might shoot it out with the cops. This duo ran out the back door and Fiddles was straddling the fence and would not show his hands, so

Michaud used his new revolver to shoot him in the butt, knocking him off the fence. We looked over the fence and Fiddles looked up at us and said, "Daril! Dave! You shot me." Michaud almost made an alto soprano Fiddles.

When Jimmy came flying out the back door, he had something in his hand, and I took a shot but missed him. He was caught a block away running at full speed. In court, Fiddles claimed, "Cinquanta shot me and switched guns with Michaud." Nobody in the courtroom knew what he was trying to accomplish because it did not make sense.

* * * *

Det. Deasy and I took on the challenge of finding a true bad ass, Dick Jones. He came out of Long Beach, California, wanted for three armed robberies and a murder. This guy was a violent career criminal with a long rap sheet of felonies. We tracked him over a period of time through known associates and aliases. We surprised ourselves, being unsure that we had found him in a Northglenn apartment under an assumed name.

I listened through the apartment door with my stethoscope to determine if anyone was inside. I could hear rustling around. We radioed for assistance from Northglenn P.D. and arrested Jones in possession of a.32-caliber handgun. He was extradited back to Long Beach, having been arrested while in possession of the suspected murder weapon, based on caliber.

* * * *

Larry Subia and I were summoned to D.A. Dale Tooley's office because they knew we were wheeling and dealing on cases filed on informants. He wanted us to document all of our informants with his office. Tooley's plan was to decide what consideration informants would get for information they provided as to their pending case. We looked at each other, back at the lawyers, and said "no."

Then we walked out. Letting the District Attorney's office control the destiny of our informants would cripple us. As soon as they converted all of our informants to witnesses, they would put us out of business.

* * * *

We teamed with Adams County Sheriff's Office to target a team of burglars, and ended up following them for hours. They were cruising a neighborhood in the Globeville/Swansea area on the northwest edge of downtown Denver. They tried to break into a couple of dark homes but moved on.

At a third house, they attempted to break a window. This is a rash maneuver, and most burglars avoid breaking glass because it's too noisy. Sure enough, they woke up a female occupant, so they bolted. What these guys lacked in technique they made up for in persistence.

They broke into a dark house, and we observed them running back to their vehicle. When they were inside, we had used an ice pick to pierce a hole in their tail light lens. This was a slick trick what we sometimes employed because it made it easier to tail getaway vehicles. Sgt. Michaud checked the house and found that they had made entry through a back window and left both doors open. The bedroom had been ransacked.

The two burglars took off and Adams County Dets. Peterson and Mitchell started chasing their vehicle. One of the occupants was throwing items from the car in the Chaffee Park area, where they lost control of the car and bailed out. We found one thief in the nearby Merry-Go-

149

Round Bar, but the other one got away on foot. We recovered the jewelry from the burglary the next day on a lawn along the car chase route. Adams County SCAT Officers L. Peterson, D. Michaels, R. Blasko, H. Stang, and L. Mitchell. The elusive bad guy was arrested in Raton, New Mexico and brought back to Colorado.

These follow jobs were challenging and fun. Outside jurisdictions asked us to call so they could come and "play" with us. The cops in the surrounding towns knew we had a high success rate and there are policemen everywhere who enjoy doing genuine police work.

* * * *

The SCAT was starting to roll, making arrests for armed robbery, burglary, escape, drug trafficking and forgery. Dave and I made a stop and recovered several pounds of marijuana. We followed up the arrest with a search warrant on their home and a storage locker. By the time we wrapped up the investigation and arrests, we had seized 250 pounds of weed—which went down as my biggest seizure of marijuana.

* * * *

I really liked two Denver Sheriff's deputies, Vito Santangelo and Al Rubio. Their specialty was chasing individuals wanted on *alias capias* warrants. These warrants are issued by the judge as soon as a suspect fails to appear in court to face felony charges. The Sheriff's Office was entrusted with locating, arresting and returning the suspects to court.

When I came upon someone wanted on an *alias capias* warrant, I called Santangelo and Rubio. They were very aggressive and made a lot of arrests. They were a dream team. Vito was a large man, probably pushing 250 pounds,

150

and tough as nails. Al was a smaller guy, built for speed. I always figured Vito did the fights and Al did the foot chases. Together they were awesome.

* * * *

An informant tipped me off that a guy was putting out feelers to find an accomplice to pull some stickups. He was ambitious, but not particularly careful. Before I met him, I disguised my appearance with a knit cap and a fake facial scar. The cherry on the sundae was the leather eye patch that Willie Newman, an ace undercover officer from a northern suburb of Denver had given me.

I met with the bad guy and told him I was on the run after escaping from the joint. I also told him I did not have a gun, and he replied he would provide me with one. His robbery agenda included a Greek restaurant, a bowling alley and a big bar booth game, which is a dice game commonly played for high stakes.

The night of the first slated robbery, he gave me a loaded semi-automatic pistol, as well as a detailed strategy for robbing the bar booth players. He and I were parked outside the game site, where I arrested him. He took a plea and served no prison time.

* * * *

We received information that a "stick-up for hire," David Kendall, was brought to Denver from St. Paul, Minnesota. Occasionally criminals import other crooks to do crimes like home invasions because they are not recognized by local authorities.

Home invasion robberies used to be a rarity. Kendall's designated target was an elderly doctor and his wife in Arapahoe Country. He robbed them at gunpoint in their home. Not satisfied with their available money and other

151

valuables, he brutally beat them with his gun. The stickup artist was bald. My informant indicated that he wore a hairpiece or hat during the robbery and also knew he was an ex-con from Minnesota.

The offense happened in Arapahoe County, so we contacted Arapahoe County Case Det. Roy Taylor. He confirmed the offense had occurred and corroborated the description of the suspect. Det. Taylor contacted St. Paul P.D. and learned that our suspect was from there, and was on parole for an armed robbery of a jewelry store in which he had pistol-whipped the owner.

Det. Taylor received a mug shot of Kendall, and the Denver victims positively identified him as the man who had robbed and beaten them. Det. Taylor obtained an arrest warrant for aggravated robbery, first-degree assault to murder, burglary, and conspiracy. Kendall was arrested in Minnesota and extradited back to Colorado.

* * * *

Acting on informant information, we made two Gallegos brothers and their uncle, Bob Lovato of the Lovato Crime Family, in a series of four jewelry store robberies. The gang had hit retail stores May D&F, The Denver and LaBelle's, as well as Zale's Jewelers.

I phone scammed the trio into meeting me at a downtown bar to sell me a portion of the stolen jewelry. Det. Tyus went in my place because they knew me. They showed up with $40,000 worth of jewelry, we purchased it for $9,000, and they were arrested. Bob Lovato twice had been found to be innocent by reason of insanity for crimes including bank robbery.

Two search warrants were executed at their homes, where additional jewelry, guns and the clothing worn in the robberies were seized. Also, involved in the investigation were Arapahoe County SCAT, Arapahoe County Sheriff's Department, and Lakewood Police Department.

* * * *

I received information that a "weird guy" carrying a large revolver had been hanging out at The El Casino bar at West 8th Avenue and Mariposa Street. We assembled a team consisting of Sgt. Michaud, George Palaze and Bobby Vescio. We set up surveillance and caught him walking mid-block.

We patted the weird guy down and seized a loaded 6-inch barrel .357 Dan Wesson revolver. We ran the serial number and determined it had been reported stolen in an Arvada burglary. At Headquarters, we learned he was wanted for probation violation, third-degree assault, and disturbance. But none of that is what was unique about the pinch.

The guy's record reflected that he had been arrested for extortion and aggravated assault, and was committed to Ft. Logan Mental Health for two years. Then he was arrested for rape and was found not guilty by reason of insanity and was sent to the Colorado State Mental Hospital in Pueblo.

He was a one-man crime wave, having also been arrested for armed robbery, carrying a concealed weapon, and narcotics. Fortunately, in this case, he wasn't doing much of a job of concealing his weapon.

My opinion based on meeting the guy and getting a look at his record of crimes of violence, he should not have been on the street. Ever. Anywhere. He had a long pattern of abnormal violent behavior and was a definite threat to society. The trouble with the "by reason of insanity" determination is it gives a lot of mentally deranged individuals on the street a built-in defense for the next time they commit a crime of violence.

* * * *

A national study about police complaints determined if police officers would remove one word from their vocabulary, they would cut discourtesy complaints by one-third. That word was "asshole."

* * * *

A very dangerous man we called "Shotgun Tommy" was wanted for a series of aggravated robberies and parole violation out of Phoenix. He was a Denver boy, having grown up with his family in the Westwood Projects. I summoned the SCAT Unit to help catch him. Sgt. Harold Oaks and Dets. Gordie Baker, Charlie Flos, Tom Ortiz, Dale Spence, Bob Clair and Mark Chavez showed up.

My informant indicated that he would show up at Taylor's Pharmacy on South Federal Boulevard to pick up some medicine. A perimeter was set up around the pharmacy in hopes of preventing his escape. A Yellow Cab showed up, and a female went into the pharmacy. We spotted a male in the taxi, but we could not see his face. The woman came out and entered the cab. Oaks and Baker said they thought the male was Tommy.

The cab exited the parking spot before we could block it in. As it traveled down Federal Boulevard the two kissed, and we removed all doubt; It was Tommy. Officers Martinez and Ortiz conducted what appeared to be a traffic stop on the cab, and arrested Tommy without incident. That's quite an achievement with "Shotgun Tommy" a six-time convicted felon and six-time ex-con.

A few days later we arrested Tommy's cousin Ricky for multiple armed robberies and grand theft out of

Phoenix. I rounded up Sgt. Oaks, Dets. Charlie Flos and Gordie Baker, and officers George Palaze, Dale Spence, Mike Ortiz and Tony Ventura.

I phone-scammed the occupants of the unit to verify that Ricky was inside, gave the signal and the team hit it. Ricky was inside, and we arrested him and tacked on three additional arrests on other occupants for drug possession. Ricky also was charged in Taylor's pharmacy robbery.

* * * *

The SCAT did a major joint investigation into a stick up ring responsible for ten supermarket robberies, as well as numerous robberies across Metro Denver at beauty salons, banks, and a credit union. I had a spectacular informant into the criminal enterprise. The detectives involved were Dick Shaffer, Denver; Frank Lewark, Westminster; Dave Allen, Boulder; Roger Roundtree, Arvada; Don Brannan, Arapahoe County SCAT; and Mike Powell, Lakewood.

We had previously arrested Patrick Runningbear, the "Beauty Shop Bandit." He had previously confessed to 17 armed robberies of beauty shops in the Denver Metro area, as well as Look Furniture on Colfax, which had a fiberglass giraffe on the roof, and Doyle's Sewing Center. He also confessed to 25 beauty shop robberies in California and eight in Arizona.

Richard "Bucky" Borrego was suspected of 11 robberies with Runningbear and Toby Borrego. When Det. Fitzgibbons and I had previously arrested Bucky on a stickup warrant, he repeatedly threatened to kill me.

We arrived at the jail elevator, the cuffs were removed, and Bucky attacked me in front of two deputies. He suffered some cuts and bruises, and I had a cut and a scrape on my leg where he kicked me, and a cut on my arm. We mixed it up pretty good, and I was able to bring Bucky closer to God during his resistance.

Det. Lewark got a positive ID, and an arrest warrant on Toby Borrego and 24-hour surveillance was begun to arrest him when he returned home. Borrego did return home, and officers closed in to make the arrest. A police vehicle had blocked the front of the vehicle, so Borrego threw it into reverse and floored the accelerator pedal, striking an undercover car that had moved behind him to prevent his escape. Toby Borrego was arrested by Fitzgibbons and Kautz at gunpoint.

The surveillance and arrest team were Watch Commander Fred Stoll, Adams County; Sgt. Bill Spotts, Boulder; officer Al Wilson, Westminster; officer Nick Manfro, Westminster; officer Gail Lutter, Adams County SCAT; and officer Paul Siska, Adams County SCAT.

We executed the search warrant and seized wallets of victims from robberies of an Albertson's supermarket and numerous beauty salons. Also seized were 20 balloons and a bowl of suspected heroin, lactose used for cutting drugs for street sales, balloons, funnels, needles and syringes, cotton balls, marijuana, scales, clothing, a ski mask, checks, and jewelry.

Seized from the backyard shed were four boxes of pharmaceutical drugs bearing labels that read, "Gibson's/Scottsbluff, Nebraska. Scottsbluff Det. Lorentz verified that a lot of drugs was taken in a burglary of a Gibson's Drugstore. We also discovered victims' IDs from the Colorado pharmacy robbery and Engineer's Credit Union.

* * * *

We started including Jefferson County D.A. Investigator Mike Russell in our investigations and arrests. Because Denver County had such a large common border with Jefferson County, many of our cases ended up in JeffCo. Russell was a quiet, detailed, effective cop who enjoyed participating in our "capers."

He joined the newly formed Career Criminal Unit and was a dependable member of the surveillance team. Everyone liked Mike, and at one point the unit honored him with a plaque. I have always considered him a friend.

* * * *

One night we were working the all-star wrestling at the Denver Coliseum. Even though it was more of a stage show than an athletic contest, people tended to get pretty wrapped up in action and tended to vent their emotional on the rasslers. Gary Salazar and I were escorting one of the wrestlers from the ring to the dressing room after a match, and someone threw a coke all over the three of us. We were a mess, and I hate to be sticky.

Salazar and I grabbed the guy who doused us in pop and took him into the dressing room. Salazar had the guy backed up to a partition as he placed him under arrest. I walked to the sink on the other side of the partition to try to wash off some of the pop. The wrestler placed a chair on the back side of the partition and he was reaching over the top, taking swipes at the guy who drenched us. He could never swing low enough to land a shot on the soda-slinger.

About a week later I was called into Internal Affairs, and a sergeant was grinding on me. He said I was picked out of a lineup by the pop thrower, who alleged I knocked him around. He claimed I was wearing a tag with the name "Gallegos" on it.

I told the sergeant I had never touched the guy, so he wanted me to give up the officer who roughed him up. I told him I was at the sink cleaning up and did not see anything. "Here we go again," I thought. The sergeant became agitated, repeatedly accused me of lying, and eventually demanded my badge and ID.

I told the asshole, "I'll get it back tomorrow." I did. I never figured out whether he had the authority to take it in the first place, and I was not about to give up a fellow cop on a bullshit complaint. Nothing ever came of the complaint or the sergeant's attempt to fuck with me.

* * * *

My long-time friend and police academy classmate Det. Brian "Deas" Deasy was involved in three shootings during his career. In the first one, a guy named Garcia had just committed a burglary and was walking from the scene carrying a large bag of loot. Deas and his partner, Stan Flint, repeatedly commanded the suspect to drop the sack and put his hands up. Instead, he put one of his hands in his coat. Deas feared that he was reaching for a gun and shot and killed him. I know that shooting has bothered Brian to this day. In my experience, policemen don't want to shoot anyone.

In the second shooting, a stickup named Sedillos had just committed an armed robbery at the Central Park West Bar at East Colfax Avenue and Pennsylvania Street. When officers arrived at the scene, Sedillos had a pistol pointed at the victim's head when Deas told him to freeze. Sedillos spun to aim the gun at Deas' head, which was only a foot away. Deas fired one shot, instantly killing Sedillos, whose gun was loaded and cocked. Brian Deas should have received the Medal of Honor for this action; he received nothing.

Deas' third shooting involved a bank robber and escapee out of Pennsylvania. The known criminal had been arrested and told the two detectives that he would do a "cleanup" by copping to all of the robberies and burglaries he had done. He conned them into taking him to his elevated apartment so that he could point out the scores from the high vantage point. His hands were cuffed in front of his body.

The suspect snagged a gun he had stashed in the fireplace flue and bailed out of the window, taking a few potshots at the detectives. The criminal made his escape to Colorado, where he immediately embarked on a series of drug store stickups targeting the painkiller Dilaudid.

After one of the robberies, FBI agents Red Nelson and Leo Ford spotted the suspect's car and aired the sighting over the clear channel. However, they lost the vehicle, which had been traveling in the opposite direction. Sgt. Dave Michaud had scanned parking tickets to find that multiple violations were written on the red Ford Thunderbird in a certain city block. The SCAT went to that block and started knocking on doors and asking questions.

A woman was explaining that the suspect lived next door, and suddenly exclaimed, "There goes your guy! He's getting into that cab!" They gave chase, and at Denver City Park the bad guy bailed out of the taxi and sprinted across the park, gun swinging in his hand. Sgt. Michaud, Det. Darrell Wagner and Deas pulled their weapons and took aim.

Deas fired first, and then Michaud and Wagner emptied their guns in an effort to bring down the bandit.

159

During the shootout, the only casualty was the bad guy's thumb. He said he was hit during the first series of gunshots, which meant Deas had shot him.

* * * *

Jaime Quintana was Colorado's undisputed heroin kingpin for years. He was directly importing multiple kilos of Mexican brown tar heroin from Mexico every month. His mule, Benny "Tar Baby" Maciel, was on the run after being arrested at the border with a large quantity of hidden high-grade heroin in his car. I had an ongoing investigation into Maciel's whereabouts. By this point, Jaime also was on the run to avoid heroin distribution charges.

Det. Ron Pietrafeso and I could not agree who was running the organization. Ron and I had an ego conflict. He thought it was two of Jaime's lieutenants and I thought it was Irene Bravo. Ron was in the Organized Crime Strike Force where they worked complex narcotics rings and RICO case and conducted lots of wiretap operations. I knew Ron was a great complex narc, but I felt I was right on Bravo.

The first time I nabbed Irene Bravo, I was accompanied by Dets. Deasy, Steve Fugate, Gary Regan and Sgt. Michaud. We seized two ounces of heroin and stolen goods, but it fell short of the kilos I sought. The bust snared career criminal John Baca, who was on parole for armed robbery and out on bond for pending possession of narcotics charges. Louie Bravo was out on an appeal bond for a murder and robbery conviction, and an at-large warrant was issued for him.

We executed a second search warrant on a Bravo associate and seized only a small amount of heroin. The guy didn't lack for imagination when it came to choosing places to stash illegal narcotics. He had put two syringes loaded with suspected heroin in liquid, ready-to-inject form into a clothesline pole. Then we found a coffee can with a plastic top containing heroin buried in the dirt.

Hiding places in the lawn were revealed only when we pulled up on the grass with our hands. He had placed the drugs under a buried shovel blade incision which was covered with sod. A passerby could have stepped on the cache and never known it was there.

The second time I winged one in on Irene Bravo was with Det. Gary Salazar, Greg "Trapdoor" Cross, Rich Mahoney and J.J. Cartwright. Before our arrival, an unknown individual had pulled into her driveway in a truck loaded with pinon nuts. We cut into the burlap bags to recover 20 ounces of high-grade heroin. We also found a gun in the truck.

The house yielded several stolen diamond rings. The drug mule was identified as Frank Chavez, aka Joe Gomez. The heroin belonged to the Jaime Quintana drug ring. Jaime was on the run when I hit Irene, and the bust confirmed, in my opinion, that she was running his operation in his absence.

Getting really big busts, and busting really big felons, often involves a lot of interdepartmental cooperation—and patience. In the early '70s, the number one heroin kingpin in Colorado and the western United States was James O. Quintana. He and Henry Gutierrez ran an organization that directed about 50 dealers. In 1972, they got caught bringing $650,000 in heroin back from their supplier, Marcelino Velasquez in Juarez, Mexico.

F. Lee Bailey—the attorney who was brought in as part of O.J. Simpson's defense team, represented Quintana, but he got a 10-year sentence. He was released in 1975.

A year later, Henry Gutierrez and Quintana were arrested selling a pound of heroin to DEA undercover agents. While on bond, Quintana fled but was arrested in San Jose, California in 1980. He was convicted there for dealing heroin and attempting to bribe two DEA agents after offering them $50,000. Quintana was convicted and released on a $250,000 appeal bond.

U.S. District Judge Fred Winner revoked Quintana's bond when he and his girlfriend, Irene Bravo, were observed dealing heroin in their hometown of Las Vegas, New Mexico. Because the goal was to drive a stake deep into the criminal enterprise, they were followed back to Denver, where agents seized a pound of heroin from the home of Quintana's parents.

Bravo testified against Quintana, admitting she sold Quintana's heroin for $4,000 per ounce. Quintana's narcotic trafficking network had tentacles through Colorado, New Mexico, California, and Arizona. Irene's testimony sent Quintana to Leavenworth, Kansas for an 18-year prison sentence.

In exchange for her testimony, Irene was removed from the women's correctional Facility in Canon City, Colorado, and placed in community corrections. Det. Tom Fischer spearheaded the operation, and D.A. Dave Thomas was the prosecutor. They were exceptional at their jobs.

In September of 1984, James Quintana was being transported from Leavenworth to Colorado by Deputy Sheriff Sam Lucero out of Kansas to attend a civil trial against his former attorney, Joe St. Veltrie.

St. Veltrie was one of Denver's most respected defense attorneys—high-powered, and talented.

A vehicle containing four armed men ran the transport vehicle off the road in Kansas. They beat and handcuffed Lucero, then locked him in the trunk of his vehicle. Lucero said he heard the sound of a shell being chambered in a shotgun. Lucero testified that one of the four thugs said he was going to kill Lucero, but Quintana said, "Lucero, he's OK. Leave him alone." Deputy Sheriff Sam Lucero's life was spared.

Authorities issued a description of the suspects who carried out Quintana's escape. One was described as wearing a straw hat, and I knew immediately it was Louie Newton, whom I had contacted in The Jolly Roger Bar in Denver.

I sent Newton's picture and history to Kansas, and they confirmed I was right. Police in Kansas City was tipped off about a quartet of people who had just moved into a house in a suburb, and they placed it under surveillance. Officers telephoned Quintana, who was in the house and who proclaimed he would not be taken alive. His three accomplices, Louie Newton, Jaime's brother Joe Quintana, Lloyd Tafoya and Patricia Manzanares surrendered.

Quintana issued a note from the house to the press. It read: "Crime doesn't pay... I wish I never got involved... I feel terrible for all the lives I've screwed up by selling heroin." When Kansas City Police entered the home, they found Quintana dead of a self-inflicted gunshot wound to the heart. He told police he didn't want to mangle his pretty face.

Quintana had lived a lot of miserable years, and had done unconscionable things, but he spared a cop from execution, and ultimately had a conscience.

* * * *

One of my search warrants raised eyebrows. I had gotten informant information that an elusive female heroin dealer was dealing heroin again. The informant told me why no policeman had been able to catch her. He said she packaged the heroin in balloons, and when cops closed in on her, even if she was in the act of selling drugs, she would "box them"—stuffing them up her vagina.

Some men were known to package their drugs in condoms, then "keister" them up their ass for transport in cars, trains, buses or airplanes. I decided to do a search warrant that had never been done before, calling for a cavity search on our dope peddler.

I wrote the affidavit, took it to a judge and hoped he wouldn't read it before he signed it. This particular judge did read the affidavit, took off his glasses, squinted at me and stated, "I hope you are right detective because if you are not, we're both in trouble."

I hit the streets to scoop her up, brought her to Denver General Hospital and gave a copy of the warrant to a doctor. He read it and said, "No." I reminded him the warrant was signed by a judge and he was legally required to conduct the search. The doctor left for a while and returned, saying, "Okay, let's get this done."

He closed the curtain and began the search for the heroin, while I remained on the other side of the curtain. He said, "It's not in here, Detective," at which time I told him, "Go deeper." After a short time, he said, "I'll be damned! I got it!" Our suspect had twenty balloons of heroin wrapped in cling wrap, stuffed up her vagina. Thank God I scored. I didn't want to imagine the headlines if I had struck out.

* * * *

In October of 1977, I made detective. It had been a long climb, and I was proud I had finally achieved my goal. The detective and technician jobs were not Civil Service rank but should have been. Detectives served at the pleasure of the chief of police and could be bounced back to patrol without explanation.

Plus, I made about $200 more each month as a detective. This setup gave the chief a lot of power he should not have had. Most guys and gals who made detective did not want to go back to the street to be exposed to the daily threat of being hurt or shot, suspended over a split-second decision in the field, or sued by some dirtball who wanted free money based on a false allegation.

* * * *

The quality of the experience a cop had when working with the FBI depended on exactly which FBI agent the cop was working with. The problem with the Feds was the guidelines they had to work under. Federal agents had to document every informant and the rule was every informant was either a "defendant or a witness."

Although real life is much more complicated, and real people with very messy lives were involved, there was nothing in between for the Feds. I could never have worked under their strict guidelines on conducting investigations. Consequently, I could never let Federal agents meet my informants. I used to tease them, saying, "You couldn't find a corpse in a phone booth without the locals' help." They would laugh knowing I was busting their balls.

One time I invited the FBI to come along on a bank robbery arrest. The agents were late, and when they arrived, I told them they were prima donnas. One of those agents made a verbal complaint against me, and I got my ass chewed out. So much for interdepartmental cooperation and camaraderie. By the way, the FBI agents somehow kidnapped my bank robber pinch and took him to the Federal Building in Denver to book him.

Denver cops loved Red Nelson because he was an old school FBI agent who understood old-fashioned police work. We had done a number of federal arrests with him and his team. Don Gunnerson, Reggie Powell, and Bill Malone were the agents I personally worked with, and they were good.

Red was famous for helping break the 1960 Adolph Coors kidnapping murder. Joe Corbett had confronted Adolph, who was the grandson of the original Adolph Coors and heir to the brewery fortune. The crook intercepted the wealthy young man on a bridge in an attempt to kidnap him for ransom. However, Adolph resisted, and Corbett shot him twice in the back. Coors died, but Corbett took the body in hopes of still collecting a $500,000 ransom.

This landmark case put forensics on the law-enforcement map. The FBI developed Corbett as a suspect based on sightings of his canary yellow Mercury in the area of the kidnapping. The vehicle turned up eight days later in New Jersey—in flames. Corbett had bragged to fellow employees at Benjamin Moore Paints of an impending "big score" of half a million dollars.

Authorities seized the scorched Mercury and matched the dirt on the vehicle to that of the Rampart Range, where

Adolph had been kidnapped. After the murder and botched kidnapping, the car was transported from Colorado to New Jersey and Canada. Federal authorities were comparing blood and other physical trace evidence to crimes in the United States. Corbett was arrested in Vancouver and convicted. Adolph Coors' remains were found in a Douglas County dump nine months later.

Corbett was an ex-con and escaped in 1955 after serving two years for the murder of an Air Force sergeant during a fight in 1951. Corbett was freed in 1980 after serving about three decades for the Coors murder, and soon after committed suicide.

* * * *

Michaud and I developed some heavy information on a Cheyenne, Wyoming felon who had put out a contract to kill the Cheyenne County Attorney, Tom Carroll. Carroll had convicted him of heroin possession, which provided a revenge motive. The bad guy had been tracking Carroll, finding his home, charting his daily routine and sketching out a diagram of his home.

He wanted to murder Carroll during lunch at a Village Inn. The felon had a 9mm handgun and a 30-06 rifle that was fitted with a scope. He had tried to recruit several men to murder Carroll for money and or drugs. The murder plot was exposed, and the bad guy was arrested on a warrant, convicted and sent to prison.

* * * *

Longtime escape artist and super-burglar Ricky Ellis had been on the run for two months after yet another escape following yet another stay in the Colorado State Hospital in Pueblo. He had escaped by crawling through a vent in the ceiling. This sounds like the kind of crazy stunt that works

167

only in a movie or a bad mini-series. However, Ellis had already been adjudicated and declared insane four times.

Denver cops looked at Ricky as one of the slickest and most prolific burglars in Colorado history. His lifetime and lifestyle were mostly centered on hundreds of home and ranch burglaries. I had been chasing him with full knowledge that he was being pursued by detectives from most of the metro area police departments. Ricky Ellis was a big fish, and I had told all of my informants to be on the lookout for him.

We received information that Ellis was holed up in a Lakewood residence. I assembled the SCAT Unit with the intention of kicking the door down but was told we had to contact Lakewood P.D. to let them in on the arrest. We met with Lakewood, and I explained that if Ellis' van was at the residence, then he was there.

A car did a drive by and the van was there. Lakewood called in the SWAT team, and they were going to take the "high ground." That meant they were assuming strategic points on surrounding buildings to get to the drop on him when he came out. I thought they had the place surrounded, but I would learn hours later that they had hit it based on our willingness to give them a courtesy call, and the van was not present. We missed him.

Ricky immediately called the press and told them he was having breakfast in bed while he listened to the radio reports about his imminent capture. In the newspaper article, he referred to me as an "egotistical creep." He added that he had left the Lakewood residence an hour before we arrived. Keep in mind that he had been placed in the state Mental Hospital by the courts four times, but Ellis boasted that he had committed 5,000 burglaries.

Ricky told the reporter he did not do that any longer. He bragged that this was his seventh escape from jails in two states, and was not going to be incarcerated again after being locked up for 13 years. Ellis proclaimed he would continue matching wits with the SCAT Unit—or anyone who thought they were smarter than he was.

Ricky Ellis said when he carried a gun—which we knew was all of the time—he carried it as a defense against criminals and creeps, not to use against legitimate citizens. Ellis also claimed he would not shoot the "man," a term used in the streets for the police.

In his focused but rambling conversation with the reporter, he denied being a psychotic killer but admitted that he would kill someone before he would go back to the joint. Ricky stated that when he escapes and is on the street, he is giving the cops work, something to talk about, thus building up our egos, and this is the gratitude he receives.

Ricky added he has never taken a hostage or hurt anyone. Ellis boasted in the past of being a locksmith and safe cracker, but authorities could never find evidence of those claims. True to form, Ellis was all over the place in his interview with the press.

Acting on informant information, Rick Polak, a talented and thorough detective in the SCAT, and I saddled up the unit. We went to and surrounded a southwest Denver house, and were about to take him down when a sergeant on the scene told me I had to knock before entering. I figured this was a lousy idea in light of our knowledge that Ellis almost certainly would be armed, and the additional knowledge that giving an armed fugitive a warning might not yield positive results.

So, I sneaked up to the door, knocked one time and instantly kicked down the door. Ricky leaped up from the couch and ran down a hallway with us right behind him. He threw one gun down the hall, screaming "Don't shoot me!" He opened the back door to see many cops waiting for him, guns in hand. Ellis then ducked into the bedroom where he and the other four occupants threw their guns in a closet and gave up, hands above their heads.

Ricky was a challenge and liked the publicity, drama and the "chase" as I did. Years later, Ricky Ellis somehow got released and called me to reminisce about our true life "cops and robbers" days of playing cat and mouse. Ricky Ellis and I frequently talk to this day.

* * * *

While working off-duty at Elitch Gardens, a landmark amusement park in North Denver, Det. Dennis Cribari received information as to the whereabouts of a dangerous escapee from Folsom Prison in California. After our shift, Det. Greg "Trapdoor" Cross teamed with us to go to the apartment on a ruse of child abuse complaint. We were all in uniform.

The assembled cops saw the escaped convict in bed with his arms under the sheets and suspected he had a gun. We regrouped to cut off all avenues of escape and hit the house. He was gone through the bedroom window. We believed he had not entered the alley, and we knew the area between the window and the next building was a dead end.

We stood talking, scratching our heads when officer George McCutcheon observed the ground breathing. The con had buried himself and was breathing through a tube. He was wanted for escape after being convicted of a $39,000 bank robbery. We had arrested a high-ranking member of the Mexican Mafia, and he didn't hesitate to threaten he would have us killed.

Cops work off duty to supplement their incomes. We called it "moonlighting." I worked Denver Broncos games, concerts at Red Rocks, All-Star Wrestling matches, Currigan Hall events, and weddings and parties at Potenza Lodge.

I got my first off-duty job when Jimmy Egan, whose real last name is Mancinelli, walked up to me, looked at my name tag and asked, "Are you Italian or Mexican?" I responded, "Italian." He smiled and asked, "Do you want an off-duty job?" I began working at Potenza Lodge, which rented the hall to Italian weddings and hosted the yearly feast of St. Rocco.

I had the privilege to work with Red and Rose Villano, who bartended and were fine people. They made the best sausage sandwiches at the feast and offered games of chance in which contestants could win a salami, olive oil, cheese, or capocollo. Every year I ran into people I hadn't seen since the previous year's feast. "Working" at the Potenza Lodge allowed me to meet many Italian families who became my friends.

Elitch Gardens security was a fun off-duty job. For many seasons I worked with Alta Metzinger. She was not only tall, blonde and pretty, but she was easy to spend time with walking around the park. Alta was smart and had a sense of humor. One night an offensive man poked her, and she kicked his ass properly. Every time he pulled himself up the Elcar chain-link fence, she would knock him down. I stood there in awe as to how tough she was for such a feminine gal. I think she had some pent-up emotions. Alta and I shared a philosophy: Don't take any shit off of anyone.

Sometimes I cruised the parking lot and parked in the Elitch car. I would drive a couple of blocks and go harass my friend Rick Nicoletti, who was studying for the bar exam. He, Joe Black and I buddied around on occasion. Nicoletti was always a fun guy, but he had this cat from hell, "Nukey." Nukey shed everywhere, and I couldn't sit anywhere in his house without trashing my uniform.

One time after the park closed, John Gertler, part of the family that owned the park, put all of us on the Twister for a ride. John was a fun guy who liked the cops, and we had drunk a few beers with him.

The Twister was a big, tall wood-frame coaster and had plenty of balls for its day. We spun out and rolled back around, and then John pours on the coal, sending us around the circuit again and again and again. I almost threw up, and John was laughing his ass off. When we finally got off, we were too queasy to load John onto the Twister for a few spins. But we ended up laughing with him.

He also let us drive the electric bumper cars, which we all liked because we were competitive and could get physical. Then we would shoot some hoops. Sometimes we stayed after hours at Elitch's for hours.

* * * *

During the '70s and '80s, criminals did not want to lay a hand on a cop, spit on us or in any other way disrespect us or put our lives in danger with a weapon. There was a disincentive to bad behavior because if they did, they knew they would probably get their licks or even be shot immediately. They rarely complained because they knew they had it coming for being stupid.

In the late '80s, I saw a bad guy accompanied by three other men spit on a patrolman. Another detective and I waited for the officer to nail him. He didn't, so I did. Not doing something about being disrespected is setting up the next cop to be assaulted in a worse fashion because criminals' natural inclination is to push the limits even further every time they get away with bad behavior. We had to exact street justice for our survival.

* * * *

One night when I was working a feast at the Potenza, I spotted an Italian gal wearing a leather top with beads, skin-tight blue jeans, and red high heels. Her nails and toe nails were painted red, and she wore gold jewelry. I had to meet this dish. We ended up dating and hung out with the SCAT.

She had an unbelievably charismatic personality and was fun beyond belief. Everyone liked her, we dated for years and became lifelong friends. She had a great old North Denver family. There were many feasts at Little Italy churches such as Mt. Carmel and Holy Family.

* * * *

Frank Dardano was an old North Denver Italian who had a "pot lot," a small private car lot, on West 38th Avenue. His wife Vita was a saint and treated me very kindly. One day when I had stopped to say hello, Frank told me he had made a batch of super sot, homemade dried Italian sausage, and hung it in his shed to cure. He said it was almost ready and he was looking forward to eating some. He did not offer me any. So the next morning at about 3 a.m., I dropped by to peek at his stash of super sot and took two to sample. It was delicious. A couple of days later Frank was complaining that he thought someone had taken some super sot from his shed.

I was at a Sons of Italy meeting years later, and there was a paper plate on the bar with slices of super sot. I tasted one and said, "That's Frank Dardano's recipe." Larry and Kenny Dardano asked how I knew that. I told them the story of me snatching some that day.

* * * *

Jefferson County was experiencing a rash of burglaries in mountain towns like Evergreen, Lookout Mountain, Indian Hills, Conifer, and Pine. The mountains were a great place to commit home and garage burglaries because the residences tended to be isolated, often with no line of sight to any other home.

All of the thefts were committed in the daytime hours. The thieves knocked; if there was no answer, they would break in. They usually took a fairly typical array of burglar booty: TV's, stereos, guns, cash, and jewelry. Acting on informant information, SCAT executed a search warrants, seizing many stolen items.

In the end, we solved about 130 burglaries with a stolen property loss of $175,000. We also cleared four armed robberies and four street robberies where they took bank bag deposits at gunpoint from the victims as they entered the bank. Six individuals were arrested and charged in those brazen heists.

* * * *

The SCAT was always proactive and productive, and made numerous arrests of serial burglars, stickups, rapists and auto thieves. When we arrested perpetrators, and they knew they were "had" we offered them a "cleanup." It was a great way to leverage a single arrest into a huge bust and solved a lot of crimes that might otherwise have remained on the books.

The arrested criminals would cop to all—or at least many—of their crimes over a period of time, and we verified their M.O. and details about individual crimes that only the perpetrator would know. We cleared "inactive-not cleared" cases while filing only a few of the new offenses. That's what went down with newspaper articles that stated we had cleared a hundred burglaries with one arrest.

While some criminals are ingenious, most are unimaginative. They do the same type of crime the same way, over and over again, down to the point of entry and type of tools used. When they copped to a string of crimes, it also helped us down the road when they were released and went back to doing bad deeds exactly the same way as before.

Whenever we arrested someone who was dumb enough to have his or her address book, I took it and duplicated it. Depending on the criminal, we figured out who the telephone numbers and addresses belonged to if we could not tell by the notations next to the numbers.

I often cold called these individuals to ask them to meet me to sell me drugs. I often checked their Intelligence Bureau cards to see if any of their friends were in the joint. Again, this was so I could drop their names in a conversation with a convict, often pulling off a black or Hispanic accent to make my scam even more convincing.

* * * *

On one of my deals, I called the girlfriend of a career criminal, Russell Billings, who was in the joint. I told her that Billings had recommended I call her because he thought we could make some money together. She agreed.

Det. George Fortunato and I met her and a second girl, whose boyfriend Solomon Vigil also was in the joint, at a southwest Denver bar.

The women said they had some scores that they could use some help on. We would split the money evenly. We told them we did not have a gun or masks. They responded, "We can get a gun."

So here are the four of us in my Dodge pickup, driving to pick up a gun and some masks. We went to a house in Ruby Hill where she grabbed a loaded gun and nylon stockings. We were then going to case their prospective scores, but when Billings' girlfriend got in the truck, she pulled the gun, laughed and pointed it at George's head.

I had my semi-auto stashed on the left side of the driver's seat and was coming up to shoot the bitch when she lowered her weapon and laughed—just in time. George was smiling when she put the gun to his head, and I wondered what in the hell was going through his mind at that moment. I guess it makes sense because that guy was always smiling.

We drove a short distance to District Four and arrested them for conspiracy to commit robbery. George and I never worked together again, but I never could figure out why. He was a great detective and had big balls. He became a pastor after he retired and I cannot help wondering if that close call brought him closer to God and pushed him toward the ministry.

* * * *

Sometimes a cop doesn't know what's inside a caper until he unravels it. One afternoon I cold-called a Hispanic gal and told her that an informant told me was trying to sell money orders taken during a series of convenience store robberies.

I name-dropped her associate and told her I heard she wanted to dump some paper. When I told her I was interested, she blew up and said it was her paper, not her friend's, and made it clear that she was selling them. I said, "Okay, how much?" We settled on a price of $300, and she agreed to meet me at a parking lot on West 38th Avenue.

The SCAT Unit headed that way, planning to set up a perimeter. We had no idea who she would show up with and if they would be armed. However, officers always assume everybody is armed.

We spotted the vehicle cruising the parking lot and moved in. Like some kind of clown car, a stream of known stickups and other career criminals bailed out of the vehicle. We immediately captured and arrested all of the bad guys except one, who ran down an alley. A detective caught him and brought him back.

We could not find the money orders that inspired the entire wild chase, so we retraced the runner's route. A neighbor had found the discarded stolen paper. The 40 seized money orders were traced to three armed robberies.

Some of the arrested parties were from the Bueno crime family, which had previously made a phony complaint to Internal Affairs that I had stolen money from them while executing a search warrant. Bueno means "good" in Spanish, but in this case, not so much.

The Buenos and I didn't much get along, and over the years I put every one of them in prison. They didn't seem to place any limits on the types of crimes they committed, and if an opportunity presented itself, they "took" it. So I just waited for each one to screw up, and then nabbed him or her.

One of the Buenos was wanted for armed robbery, and another was a career criminal. We could not find some of the money orders, so we removed the female from the back seat of the police vehicle, thinking she may have dumped them behind the seat. Instead, we found a loaded .22-caliber pistol that she had stashed there. Because it's S.O.P. for all police officers to inspect their vehicles, including the back seats, every time they come on shift, we knew she was the one who dumped the gun.

Our surveillance team consisted of Sgt. Michaud, Dets. Deasy, Reagan, Wessels, Mueller, Cuthrell, and Blumer. We executed a search warrant on the Buenos and found a sawed-off shotgun in their home and the missing money orders in their vehicle.

* * * *

In one case, I suspected an escapee, Alan Vigil, was staying at a woman's house. However, I was not sure, so I did not hit it. I cold-called the house's landline and a woman answered. I told her in a panicked voice that I was picked up for narcotics use and that I overheard detectives say they were going to arrest Alvin Vigil at a north Denver house.

I told her to tell Alvin to get the hell out of that house and hung up. Seconds later Alvin flies out of the house into the waiting arms of the SCAT Unit. After that ruse, Michaud came up with, "You did the Duke and the double Duke and tricks unknown to the common puke." I got a laugh at that one. Dave was the only guy I ever knew who could recite "Casey at The Bat" from memory.

I did another phone scam on a guy called "Popeye." My informant described Popeye as having a military look, clean-shaven with a crew cut, and dressed like a preppy. The informant said Popeye golfed at City Park, where he sometimes dealt heroin. The suspect went to the health spa daily and frequented country clubs.

I got Popeye on the phone and talked about buying dope from him, including details about price and quantity. I was reluctant to go undercover with this guy, not knowing if he had Hispanic connections. I met with Sgt. Dino DeNovellis of the Major Peddler Unit and he put Det. Tommy "Fuji" Sanchez "under" with Popeye.

I hooked up Tommy with Popeye on the phone. Tommy was a great undercover narc and really took Popeye down the path. Tommy made several buys from him, and on the final buy, Popeye tripped to his home with Tommy because Tommy wanted more heroin than was negotiated.

Once there, Popeye showed the dope, and we busted him. We seized seven ounces of high-grade heroin from the house. He was obviously a major player, yet was unknown to us until the informant tipped us off.

Newly arrived criminals had the advantage of us not knowing them, but the disadvantage of them not seeing us coming, either. Tommy deserved a commendation for the excellent detective work, but nobody involved with the case received one.

Doesn't matter what kind of work someone does, or what he or she says about recognition. "Atta boys" are nice and give you a morale boost for doing a good job. Commendations went in a cop's file and sometimes made a small difference in a disciplinary hearing. A lot of officers and detectives I worked with over the years should have received medals for acts of heroism and major arrests, and there wasn't as much as a kind word or a pat on the back. I never could figure out that thankless dynamic in the Denver P.D. hierarchy.

I used address book contacts to follow up with many blacks. I'd drop the name of some guy who was in the joint, and my targets often agreed to meet me at a location, bringing balloons of heroin. When we confronted them, the fight usually was on.

We'd have to figure out where the dealer had the dope. Is it in their mouth or pocket? Or did they lay it down on the ground somewhere nearby? They were always pissed and wanted to know who the black guy was who had called them. There was no black guy. It was me. I derived a lot of satisfaction and amusement out of pulling off phone scams.

Sometimes a dope dealer would swallow the balloons he was selling. If he could not choke it from their mouth and they succeeded in swallowing them, we were off to DGH. One of my fellow officers would sit with the suspect at the hospital, while I went to get a search warrant for their stomach contents signed by a judge.

The doctor would use Epicac to induce vomiting or diarrhea to get the drugs from the suspect's body. Once I got the stomach contents, the dope dealer or user was off to jail for possession of narcotics. I had to do this procedure several times in my career. Some doctors at DGH would go nuts when they saw me enter the ER.

Working undercover is dangerous. The smallest detail can spook the bad guy, leading him to question the undercover agent and initiate violence. Undercovers need nerves of steel and have to be very mentally agile to be able to fire back verbally with lightning speed during a confrontation or accusation.

In most cases, the backup will never get there in time, so the undercover is going to have to fend for himself or herself for a while. The cop could be buying heroin from a bad guy, who wants to see the undercover shoot some dope to prove he's not the man. What do I say? What do I do? Or the bad guy tokes up a joint and offers the officer a hit.

Undercovers need to be flexible, creative and credible. In non-drug related undercover investigations, rule one is the cover story has to be believable. That means the officer better know a lot about the profession or story he or she is laying down. I had my undercover IDs made at DMV because they had to be flawless. What beef can a crook have with the real thing? Some undercover narcs went to DGH to have needle "tracks" put on their arms. When it's going down, a cop better have his shit together.

* * * *

The SCAT Unit spent two months trying to identify and arrest a burglar we dubbed "The Stamp Man." He was far-ranging, having hit Boulder, Lakewood, Arapahoe County, Aurora, and Limon. The Stamp Man would hit between midnight and 6 a.m. at office buildings that had no alarms. We estimated he had burglarized 300 offices in 50 buildings, focusing on stealing postage stamps, dental gold, petty cash, and coins.

Sgt. Michaud and I got a break in the case when a homeowner reported a suspicious car was parked on her street at 3:40 a.m. The vehicle was a decommissioned police car and its plate listed to the address of a motel on West Colfax, but the man had moved out. The owner of the motel said she frequently bought stamps from him, so we figured we had our guy.

We arrested him at his home. He was melting the dental gold in a small pan on the stove. The suspect talked to us about his string of crimes. Looking at him, nobody would have pegged him as a burglar. He was balding, round, dumpy and unassuming. I think he wanted to be a cop.

He told us he often had coffee with the local police at their hangouts, then went to hit a building. The damage he caused to gain entry far exceeded his take. We interviewed his wife of three weeks, who said her husband had led her to believe he was an insurance agent who worked from midnight to 8:00 a.m., investigating burglaries. It was the perfect cover. Because no offense to insurance agents, this guy certainly didn't look like a burglar.

* * * *

One day the SCAT assigned a case in which someone was hitting parking meters along Broadway by using a key. The thief was stealing hundreds of boxes loaded with coins. The estimated loss was $10,000 when we received the case. The thieves apparently had been on that trail for months, at a rate of five to ten meters per day.

The previous year about 1,000 meters were hit. The Unit began investigating locksmiths, checking banks for large deposits of coins, and of course working the informants.

The big break came when the Unit interviewed a locksmith in Boulder who stated he had made a circular key for a Boulder resident. He named the buyer of the key. They got a key by removing parking meter head with a pipe saw. They battered the meter until they could get the box out, then took the box to the locksmith and had a key made. That key fit all of the pop machines in a certain, sometimes wide, geographic area.

Now the crooks were off and running. They traveled to Nebraska, Kansas, Missouri, and Wyoming to hit meters, and their take was steadily growing. We hit the suspects at their Boulder home and scored the keys, 123 pounds of pennies from Boulder meters, and a large quantity of other coins. The three perps were put in chains, and the "Parking Meter Mystery" was solved by the SCAT.

* * * *

Another one of my high-profile cases was a "who done it" involving one of the Leprino brothers. Mike Leprino and his family owned Ridgewood Realty and The Leprino cheese factories that produced the bulk of mozzarella cheese in the United States.

At 6:30 p.m. one evening a knock came at their door, and two men identified themselves as census takers. They had official-looking badges, clipboards, and briefcases, but this was the beginning of a home-invasion robbery.

The Leprinos invited the "census takers" into their home. A third man entered, and one of the intruders pulled a gun and ordered the family onto the floor. One of the robbers stated that if Mike's wife, Joan, did not get the expensive rings off of her fingers they would simply cut off her hand. The family was terrorized and thought they were going to be killed. The robbery netted $200,000 in jewelry and cash.

Det. Gerry Fitzgibbons and I learned through an informant that the suspects, Richard "Sandman" Sandoval and David Davalos were U.S. Census takers months before. Sandoval was a former youth counselor at The Lookout

Mountain School for boys, but his life transformation apparently didn't take. Sandoval really was a four-time ex-con with convictions for three armed robberies and one burglary. After the robbery, I found that Sandoval had rented a car and headed for New Mexico. I learned that he and Frances Sanchez pawned a large quantity of the jewelry, and Denver Police recovered it for the victims.

When Sandoval and Sanchez returned to Denver, we executed three search and arrest warrants, nabbing Albert "Blackie" Nunez, Davalos and Sandman. We recovered jewelry, census taker IDs and other evidence that had been used in the Leprino robbery as a result of the search warrants.

We later learned that Peter Iacino, a friend of the Leprino, had set them up. Mike had played cards at Rolling Hills Country Club with Iacino who "dropped a dime" to his "crew." Yes, there was a time when there were pay phones, and it took a dime to make a call. Iacino had told Sandoval that Leprino would have a large amount of cash and jewelry.

Iacino also told the conspirators that Leprino's son would have a kilo of cocaine. There were no drugs in the house. The SCAT came to believe Iacino was going to receive a cut of the proceeds from the sale of the jewelry. I think the cocaine fabrication was the "hook" to convince them to do the robbery because they were all addicts. They would have made more money from the "key" of coke than from the jewelry. The whole lot of them was convicted and sent to the joint.

The Leprino family became my friends after the investigation, and I received a cheese basket from Frangi's every year that included a cheese log spun through with red pepper. I dated Lori Leprino for some time. Like the rest of the family, she was very smart. She loved to support political candidates. We had a great time together and remain friends.

The moral of the home invasion story is the same thing I tell all of my friends and family: "Do not answer your door unless you know the person on the other side."Nobody thinks it could happen to them until it does.

People don't realize until they are victimized that one encounter with a predator can destroy a life. What could that person at the door possibly say that is that important enough to open the door and let a bad guy enter the home and control the family's fate? I believe in security doors and peepholes. Most home invasion robberies occur after the victims open their doors and let the criminals in.

* * * *

My partner Larry Subia and I received a tidbit of info from one of my best CIs that Freddie Diaz was pulling burglaries while carrying a gun. That was all the info the CI had. During this time, many wealthy families throughout the Denver Metro area were experiencing home invasion robberies.

In Boulder, three males knocked on a door in the early morning hours and the victim opened it to be met with a gun-wielding bandit who had never had any acquaintance whatsoever with the homeowner. Three males forced their way in and tied up the victims. Freddie Diaz was a career criminal who served time and was on parole for attempted murder for stabbing a woman with a pair of scissors in Utah.

In Colorado, he did time for burglary and criminal mischief. He was also incarcerated for first-degree aggravated motor vehicle theft, which means he attacked or threatened people while stealing their car. Diaz had a long, earned reputation on the street as being very violent. He was only 5'3", but was stocky and powerful.

The SCAT began looking for Diaz in the Globeville industrial and residential neighborhood north of downtown Denver, where his family lived and immediately spotted him walking with his girlfriend. We contacted the couple, noting he was wearing a sweater with ducks on it that hung over him like a circus tent. His girlfriend was wearing jewelry that looked expensive.

We arrested him for not reporting to his parole officer and took them downtown to Headquarters. We got on the phone because we had not yet received the "squawks" (offense reports) from the Greenwood Village, Jefferson County, Cherry Hills, Bow Mar and Boulder Police Departments.

The SCAT found that the sweater and hat worn by Freddie were stolen in the Greenwood Village home-invasion armed robbery and rape of the victim's nanny by two of the robbers. The jewelry being worn by the girlfriend was also stolen during the home intrusion. We executed two search warrants, recovering more jewelry and other items that further tied them to the home intrusions.

The other affected jurisdictions presented photo lineups of Fred Diaz, Diaz' nephew Isaac "Ike" Montoya and Arturo Guzman to the victims, who were subsequently identified as the perpetrators. Another rape occurred in the Cherry Hills offense. The victim identified Diaz and Montoya as sexually assaulting her after threatening to kill her with a gun.

We went to trial on one of the most clear-cut and provable cases of my career. Based on rock-solid evidence from numerous law-enforcement agencies and testimony of victims, Diaz received 11 life sentences, with five to run consecutively, in the Greenwood Village home-intrusion armed robbery, first-degree burglary, and sexual assault.

Diaz was sentenced to 115 years in the Cherry Hills home-intrusion sexual assault, second-degree kidnapping, aggravated robbery, first-degree burglary and aggravated motor vehicle theft. Freddie will not be eligible for parole for 257 years.

Freddie Diaz was a real predator, who along with his co-conspirators was escalating in the violence during their home intrusions and sexual assaults. It was just a matter of time until they killed someone during a home invasion. In 2012, Diaz pushed the authorities for DNA testing in the 1988 Greenwood Village rape.

All the testing did was to further prove his guilt, which already was proven beyond a shadow of a doubt. This was one of the most satisfying investigations for Larry and me during our careers. We solved another "who done it," giving the victims some calm and sense of justice.

* * * *

Sgt. Michaud and I stopped a vehicle that we thought was driven by a heroin dealer. I approached the driver's side of the car and realized that it was not the dope dealer. The driver rolled down his window about four inches and was looking straight ahead.

When I asked him for his driver's license, he dropped his right hand from the steering wheel and reached across his body putting his right hand inside his coat. Simultaneously, his left hand came down to his lap. He was still looking straight ahead. I pulled my gun from the holster on the right side of my body and put it to the man's head, ordering him to take his hand out of his coat. He complied and was taken out of the car and patted down for weapons.

His movements indicated he might be pulling a weapon. The man identified himself as a private investigator, but I didn't know him. Michaud and I apologized, let him go and went about our business. Weeks later he sued us and asked that I be charged with aggravated assault.

His version of the mostly routine traffic stop was that I approached the car with my gun drawn, put it to his head, and verbally threatened to kill him. He claimed I called him a "pest." He said he could hear my pistol's hammer making a clicking sound. What he actually heard was me taking off the safety, preparing to defend myself.

When I stopped the vehicle, I had no clue who he was. The guy claimed he had testified in a court case against me and said he called me by name when I approached the car. Neither allegation was true, and his three lie-detector tests were all over the board and inconclusive. Polygraph tests are not admissible in a court of law because they are not always accurate and can be defeated by some suspects, experts, and techniques. Regardless, thought processes such as lying or being deceptive often trigger a bad result.

My episode was not the first time that same P.I. was on the other end of a policeman's gun. An Aurora cop had to pull his weapon when the P.I. would not stop advancing on him. He refused to obey repeated orders from the officer. The Aurora policeman testified in my case. However, that cop did not get sued and the P.I. did not get shot.

The jury found that I acted in self-defense when I pulled my gun. Sgt. Michaud was found not guilty of negligence. District Attorney Dale Tooley declined to charge me with assault. The P.I.'s fabricated story was all about "free money," and he got none.

Ted Hallaby was the attorney for the city and is probably the best I ever saw in police defense cases. Attorneys Ed Geer and Bob Goodwin protected our interests in the case. Attorney Ken Padilla is no friend to the police and represented the private investigator. As soon as the bad guy embellishes or lies about the facts of the case, I know I am going to win.

* * * *

In another case, the Denver Dry Goods store in Boulder was targeted in an armed robbery, and the two bandits got away with $200,000 in jewelry and cash. My informant indicated Frank E. Bueno and George Archuleta were the stickups.

I passed the info on to Boulder Det. Dave Allen, whom I had worked with on a number of earlier cases. Dave was a really good detective, and he and his wife Kim, a Boulder dispatcher, were my long-time friends. Dets. Allen and Julius Toporek showed a photo lineup of each suspect and obtained positive IDs from the store employees. Arrest warrants were drafted and the duo was swept up.

During pre-trial hearings, attorney Tom May, representing Archuleta, argued that my informant had to be disclosed because he was "eyes and ears' to the robbery. This claim was bullshit, and I refused to reveal the name of the informant.

Judge William Neighbors had an issue with me being controversial in Denver and dismissed the case. My informant did not participate in the heist and was nowhere near the scene. The Boulder District Attorney appealed the decision by Judge Neighbors. The Colorado Supreme Court overturned Neighbors' ruling, and we were headed for trial again. I celebrated that night.

* * * *

Det. Brian Deasy and I were partners for a period of time in the SCAT Unit and made a number of quality arrests on burglaries in progress, escapees, stickups and wanted parties. He is one of my best friends and one hell of a detective, and he has always defended me in every way. Deas was from New York and would not stop talking, but at least he was funny. He was a military veteran and was tough as nails.

The SCAT usually made pinches as a Unit so everyone could have some fun. Our Unit liked to put criminals in jail. We had varied personalities and talents, but it came down to every cop being a good cop.

We arrested a guy who was brandishing a machete and had to fight him. We got him to the basement level, B1, in the downtown Police Headquarters and walked him to the elevator to take him upstairs to the jail. Every step of the way he was defiant, threatening and disrespectful. Machete man insisted if he was not cuffed, he would kick our asses.

At the elevator, we removed the cuffs, and out of the clear blue, to me at least, Deas holds his hand above his head and asks the dummy, "Do you see that ring?" Machete man looks up at the ring on Deas' hand, and in an instant, Deas knocks him out with one punch. I had never laughed so hard on the job. Maybe Deas was referring to the ringing of the bell at the end of a boxing knockout.

* * * *

One informant told me for years about a thief who stole only artworks. We tried and tried to get the crook's address, but never could. We knew who he was, but none of our informants could give him up because none of them knew his address.

We received information that he had stolen a high-dollar vase from an antique store on South Broadway Boulevard. He then sold it to a fence who bought stolen art. We knew the identity and address of the fence, but couldn't get through his door because we did not have an offense report number to put into an affidavit for a search warrant.

I still revel in a lot of the spectacular cases we solved and the drama that went into the chases and the busts, but a lot of police work is just paperwork and drudgery—like most other jobs. However, in this case, it all made sense because we couldn't go after a guy on a theft that had never been reported. Det. Jim Lebedoff and I decided to walk Broadway in an attempt to find the shop from which the vase was stolen.

Eventually, we found the store, made the offense report, drafted the affidavit and got the search warrant signed by a judge. We invited Wheat Ridge Police, Jefferson County D.A. Nolan Brown, and the Tactical Support and Intelligence bureaus to the search warrant execution party.

Upon entering the residence, I observed two bronze statues listed as stolen in the DPD daily bulletin. The vase was found on the dining room table, and several pieces of suspected stolen art also were seized, along with guns and electronic equipment. Items nabbed were linked to about 25 burglaries.

The I.R.S. seized a large amount of cash from his car trunk. Numerous Salvador Dali signed and numbered prints were found, but an offense report showing them as stolen could not be located in the United States. In the hallway, we observed a picture of the suspect with Denver Mayor Federico Pena and other politicians.

Discovering the suspect was connected did not give us a warm feeling. He did no jail time and received some sort of disposition.

* * * *

The unit conducted many surveillance operations and follow jobs. One night we were sitting on two wanted guys. I looked over at our undercover van, and it was rocking side to side. At first, I thought the engine was probably missing on a couple of cylinders, but I later learned that an unknown sergeant was deep undercover inside, bopping some girl.

Another brave cop apparently brought a female into the SCAT office after hours. In the morning, Capt. Brannan observed butt cheek marks on the glass on his desk. This was a room full of detectives, but figuring out what had happened didn't require credentials. That one didn't go over well. The rank and file joked that Brannan had the lab techs take butt prints.

Cop units are highly charged with testosterone and sex. One unit detective was having some afternoon delight at a gal's Victorian style home. A sergeant was in the next room with a female friend.

As the story goes, the detective saw an eyeball looking through the skeleton key hole. Who would have guessed that a sergeant who is in a position of power and a supervisor would be a voyeur in the classified service? He was referred to as "Sergeant Keyhole" by the detective from that day forward.

One SCAT detective occasionally missed roll call. Capt. Brannan would tell a couple of officers to go check the house of "Sweet Thing" for him. We knocked on Sweet Thing's door, but there was no answer, and it was unlocked, so we walked in. Candy, chips, and cookies were in bowls and trays all over the place.

We found our fellow cop and Sweet Thing laughing in the tub as they enjoyed a bubble bath and several cocktails together. We told him that the captain wanted him to come in when he was done with his business.

* * * *

The Arapahoe County Special Crime Attack Team contacted our SCAT Unit to assist them with surveillance as part of a drug investigation. Denver SCAT had done many investigations with Arapahoe County SCAT, and they proved to be highly effective detectives.

We followed their suspect to a parking lot where he exited his vehicle and placed a bag in the back of a truck. The assembled police force descended on the truck and determined the bag contained marijuana.

After the arrest, an Arapahoe County SCAT detective seized the evidence from the truck. I was asked to prepare the search warrant, so I left with one of the Arapahoe SCAT detectives. We dictated the search warrant to Det. Gary Salazar, based on information from the Arapahoe detective and my observations. The Arapahoe detective dictated to Salazar that he also saw the bad guy dump the narcotics into the truck bed.

This was not my investigation; I was just assisting those detectives in theirs. In fact, I had never met the

Arapahoe detective. Not once during the drafting of the affidavit that Det. Gary Salazar typed did the Arapahoe County detective contradict my observations or say that he did not see something I reported. We executed the search warrant, Arapahoe SCAT took their bad guy and the evidence, and were gone.

Days later the headline in the *Rocky Mountain News* reads, "Denver Narc Accused of Planting Evidence." The detective I rode with from Arapahoe SCAT suddenly claimed that I had falsified an affidavit by stating I saw the bad guy dump the drugs.

It turned out he really did not see the suspect place the marijuana in the truck bed because it was dark. Also, the time period in which their informant had purchased drugs from the bad guy was inaccurate. I didn't make it up; the Arapahoe SCAT supplied the information.

No one can say what another person saw or did not see. Their detective also claimed I planted the pot, which was a total lie witnessed by at least five other detectives. I did not find the dope but merely acknowledged I had seen another cop take it from the truck.

Their detective asked a lot of basic questions that evening about search warrants and police work. The Arapahoe County detective's allegations as to what I had related to him were completely taken out of context probably due to his inexperience. I had relayed informant information supplied by the Arapahoe SCAT during the writing of the affidavit.

The matter was taken to a Denver Grand Jury by D.A. Dale Tooley, with me being singled out as the "target." I talked to my seasoned attorneys, Ed Geer and Bob Goodwin. I told them I was going to testify, despite the knowledge that targets of grand jury inquiries virtually never testify. My lawyers were totally against it, but I explained to them that if I did not testify, the grand jury would indict me and then we would have to fight a criminal case.

So, against the advice of counsel, I testified. Assistant D.A. Dick Spriggs led the grand jury. As I began to address the panel, Spriggs repeatedly interrupted me, apparently to knock me off track. Eventually, I had to tell him to sit down and be quiet because I had a lot to tell that grand jury.

My attorneys were allowed to sit in, but could not speak to the panel. I walked them through the evening in question, the drafting of the affidavit and subsequent execution of the warrant and seizure of the evidence. I also described my interactions with the detective I had accompanied that evening.

I asked the grand jury to take testimony from every officer who participated in the investigation and told them they then would realize that I was telling the truth and that I had neither falsified the affidavit, nor planted evidence. The problem with grand juries is that the assistant D.A. leads them, hence the saying, "You can indict a ham sandwich in a grand jury."

The grand jury returned a "no true bill" finding, and that was the end of the criminal case. Dick Spriggs put his arm around me and said, "I had to do that Daril." I looked him in the eye and sneered, "Bullshit!"

Geer said, "Daril, let's go to Homer Reed so I can buy you a tie." Goodwin added, "You have big balls, Daril." I received several ties from Ed over the years. Ed Geer loved his thoroughbred horses and practicing law. He was once manager of safety for the City of Denver. Goodwin collected Russian art and was just a cool guy to be around. Hell, it felt like an adventure to go to lunch with those guys. But it was better having the peace of mind that they were there to represent me.

I was exonerated as the result of my own bold stance, but now I had to deal with the Monster. No departmental embarrassment goes unpunished. I would have to feed the Monster its pound of flesh. Even though I essentially proved I had acted honestly and honorably, I was suspended for 15 days without pay and demoted from detective to patrolman. They also transferred me to District Four for "violations of rules and regulation in the operations manual." The punishment was excessive.

Shortly after receiving the news that I was busted down and fined, I granted an interview to Sharon Stewart of the *Rocky Mountain News*. I was pissed off. The headline read, "Cinquanta Undaunted by Department Discipline." I gave the interview in my attorney's office.

My pager kept going off during the newspaper interview because informants were trying to get a hold of me. I wrote the information on the back of my hand so I could transpose it later. Fellow cops teased me for writing on my hand and carrying around my "project" files. When my pager went off, Michaud taunted me by saying, "It's the big one! It's the big one!"

That newspaper interview gave me the opportunity to vent about the constant attacks on my credibility by defense attorneys. I also got to talk about my ethics, my use of informants and the joy of chasing criminals. All said and done, I thought Sharon Stewart did a fine job of allowing me to tell my truth.

I felt that I had been beat up, but I wasn't nearly ready to toss in the towel. I filed suit against the Arapahoe County Special Crime Attack Team, specifically the director and the detective who made the false allegations against me. The lawsuit was filed but did not go to trial. I had made my point. The press had dragged me through the streets. They truly are a double-edged sword in that one day you are the hero and the next a criminal. The Arapahoe SCAT and the press made me look bad and embarrassed me. I would not forget it.

* * * *

The next allegation against me came from a gal who had a checkered past as a long-time member of the community of career criminals. Sam Neumeyer and I stopped her for driving under suspension. She copped an attitude, and I arrested her and put her in the police vehicle.

She later claimed I struck her head on the door, entered the car to backhand her, and grabbed her arms. None of that fit my M.O. I never beat up a handcuffed prisoner, which is a civil rights violation. She did kick me on the way into the police car, but her so-called witnesses testified only that I had struck her. She also accused me of using vulgar language. What I said to her was, "Don't act like a bitch."

At Headquarters, she explained that she would be fired if she did not go to work. I felt sorry for her and took her to her home, rather than to jail. If the altercation had gotten physical, she would have ended up in jail. Here is a suspect embellishing and lying, not only setting up a defense, but also a lawsuit to grab some "free money."

She went on trial, defended by my favorite cop-hating defense attorney, Ken Padilla. She was acquitted. The odds of me arresting her again were high because she ran with bad guys.

* * * *

Defense attorneys continually tried to chip away at my credibility, claiming I lied in affidavits, planted evidence, and entrapped their clients. They attacked my use of informants, alleging they were eyes and ears to crimes or that I had entirely fabricated an informant.

My priority was protecting the identities of my informants and not "burning" them. I always cut them out of the investigation before I executed a search warrant or followed someone on their tip. In most cases, my informants were miles from the scene and not eyes and ears to the crime. In three cases, an informant had told me that specific bad guys were strung out on drugs and pulling burglaries to support their habits.

When we had sufficient time, we targeted the crooks without informing the CIs. Guess what? The CIs showed up with the crooks pulling the burglaries. We caught them, and in each case, I sent my CIs to prison for double dealing me and mainly for participating in the crimes. "CIs are like buses—there is another one coming every 15 minutes."

* * * *

The Denver SCAT Unit started a decoy program in which undercover cops dressed like winos and laid down along Santa Fe or Broadway, appearing to be drunk or passed out drunk. The phony winos had "bait money" in their vest pockets and stank of alcohol. Charlie Flos was perfect for the assignment because he didn't have to stretch his natural unkempt look very far.

The low-level street predators would hit on Flos, and the troops would move in for the arrest. One suspect ate the money, and another took off running when officers were closing in on him and was hit by a speeding car. Most of the guys in the unit served as a decoy at one time or another. Every one of the decoys was "robbed," and lots of good arrests were made.

* * * *

Our cop bar was The Parlor on Broadway. The Parlor was owned by Shilo. She was a great gal and a friend to the cops. The Parlor had good food and drinks, and there was always the added bonus of talking with Shilo. Her employees were friendly, and cops and employees got to know each other on a first-name basis. We met at The Parlor after work.

Women throughout Denver knew if they wanted to meet a cop, The Parlor was the place to go. So many gals and so little time… Shilo opened a second, larger place called Copperfield's that featured a dance floor. Copperfield's was on East Colfax Avenue and became a second hangout for off-duty cops. Gary "The Sal" Salazar sometimes spun records and was the unofficial D.J. A long roster of Denver cops has fond remembrances of the two bars.

All of my memories of The Parlor are not bright and happy. One night I arrived there sick as hell. I thought I might have the flu. I walked a gal to her car and went back in. I was drinking a cranberry and lime at the bar, and I could not figure out why I felt so horrible.

I went to the bathroom and sat on a stool for a while watching the lines in the bricks double. I returned to my seat at the bar, not knowing that I had just been given a visual warning that something bad was about to happen.

I woke up in the emergency room of DGH with doctors and nurses attempting to stick a hose down my nose. That woke me up. They admitted me and said I had a transient ischemic attack, commonly referred to as a mini-stroke.

When I was released from the hospital, I noticed my right leg was still bigger than my left and thought that was odd. I called my specialist, Dr. Donald McIntyre, and he sent me to an imaging center for a veinagram. They determined my leg was full of blood clots that might have caused the TIA or stroke. They immediately took me to Lutheran Hospital and put me on a blood thinner.

I was released a couple of days later. While I was in the hospital room, Bobby Quintana and his wife Paula brought me some needed Italian food from their restaurant, Little Nicks on Kipling. When you are down and nearly out, good friends come through.

* * * *

One day I spotted an organized crime guy crossing East Colfax Avenue. I contacted and cleared him, meaning I radioed in his ID and dispatch told me he was not wanted. I tossed his van and found nothing, so I let him go.

He ends up making a complaint on me for an improper search and harassment. So I made him a project. I had never worked the Smaldone Organized Crime Family in the past, but a known mobster filing a harassment complaint pissed me off. Dets. Deasy, Bobby Simmons, John Dore and Dan O'Hayre of the Organized Crime Strike Force began to follow him.

We determined he was picking up the proceeds from bookmaking operations. We nailed him at the end of his circuit with the cash and his "book"—the list of bets. The

OCSF filed professional gambling charges on him in Federal and State District Court. He was bringing in $20,000 per week. We followed up by arresting some bookies on his route.

I then secured a search warrant for The Dahlia Lounge, a major bookmaking center for the Smaldone mafia family. They had a buzzer system to alert the downstairs, where the lucrative betting business was being transacted. We seized a clothes dryer box three-quarters full of betting slips.

They had gotten fat and lazy and were not shredding the betting slips which showed the names of the bettors. I went through about a hundred slips and found some very prominent citizens among the bettors. I sealed up the box and placed evidence tape all over it.

When the court date came, I went to examine the evidence. The box containing the betting slips was missing. A box the size of a clothes dryer had just disappeared. We could not find those slips anywhere in the evidence room. Someone shrugged his shoulders and said they might have been thrown away by mistake. Maybe I had not put enough evidence tape on the massive cardboard box.

Days later I got a phone call from Clyde "Flip Flop" Smaldone—the capo of the Denver organized crime family. There were three brothers, Clyde "Flip Flop," Eugene "Checkers," and Clarence "Chauncey" Smaldone. They ran rackets and were implicated in crimes including loan-sharking, car theft and cargo high-jacking, gambling, bookmaking, income-tax evasion, assault, jury tampering, and narcotics distribution.

The Smaldones were accused of carrying out murders, but never convicted. They served some time in the state penitentiaries and ran out the string on Mafia crime in

Colorado, with their family dying with a whimper with the old-age death of Chauncey in 2006.

The way it went down in the bigger Mafia circle: "Flip Flop" Smaldone paid tribute to Canelli in Pueblo, who ran the state; who paid tribute to Joseph "Joe Bananas" Bonanno in Arizona, who paid tribute to the Gambino family in New York.

In the phone call, Flip Flop asked me, "What did I ever do to you, Daril? You never screwed with the "Dags" why now?" He was referring to "dagos," a formerly derogatory word for Italians that lost its sting over about a century. I told Clyde, generally regarded as the brains behind the organization, what his Mexican "bagman" had done to me in lodging the complaint. I asked him why there were so many whites and Mexicans in his family, to "tune him up" like a fiddle to be played.

He said all I had to do was call him and he would have taken care of the problem with the complaint. A short time later I got a phone call with an apology from the Bag Man, and I never heard another word about the complaint. Sometimes you get strange solutions to strange problems. Young Gene, the next generation of Smaldones, brought considerable heat on the family, and their ultimate demise, when he was convicted of importing large quantities of cocaine.

* * * *

The SCAT had an annual "Barbaric Arts Seminar" where we could party as a Unit. Our secret party was at a warehouse in east Denver where antiques were stored. Blackjack and craps tables were set up, and there were food and booze.

Some of the guys brought gals, the couples would disappear, and when they returned, they were asked, "Where have you been?" They replied, "Reading scripture." The theme of the Barbaric Arts Seminar one year was, "A Penny for Your Thoughts." We laughed all night long.

* * * *

Dets. Ken Vasquez, Officer Dave Murphy and I arrested an unknown burglar named Ronnie Lee Boltz. He was an athletic individual who wore shorts, knee high socks, tennis shoes and a t-shirt. He was like a thousand guys I saw on the beaches of California a few years before, with blonde curly hair, a light complexion, and blue eyes. His appearance offered him a competitive advantage in the ritzy neighborhoods he targeted because he looked like the handsome boy next door.

When we arrested him, he cleaned up about 20 burglaries. Unlike most burglars who stick to one formula and M.O., he told us he entered homes in various ways after seeking out each home's vulnerability. He claimed he could disarm alarms and pick locks. He said, as a rule, he only took what fit into his pockets, and focused on jewelry and cash.

He always parked a few blocks away, then walked to the target house. He specialized in the three-minute burglary. Littleton indicated that in their 18 burglaries, Boltz nabbed about $87,000 in property.

The next thing we know, an armed robber hit Georgetown's assay office, taking off with gold nuggets and cash. The description matched Ronnie Boltz. I supplied information to Georgetown police, who obtained a positive ID on Boltz.

I secured a search warrant for Boltz' home, and we hit it. In the search, we couldn't find the gold nuggets, but we kept searching. Finally, one of the team found the nuggets hidden in the knots of a ceiling-mounted macramé flower pot hanger.

This was Georgetown's first and only armed robbery. D.A. Terry Rucreigal made the prosecution of the case enjoyable and later became a judge.

Sometime down the road Boltz escaped from jail and officers and detectives caught him at Sloan's Lake. He jumped in and tried to swim to his freedom. Sloan's lake is about 6 feet deep all the way across, and Michael Phelps couldn't swim fast enough to escape anyone there.

One of the officers grabbed a fishing pole out of his car and had a photo shoot with Boltz appearing to be a caught fish, handcuffed on the ground.

* * * *

Don Brannan and Don Mulnix were the SCAT captains. Brannan was a cross between John Wayne and Clint Eastwood. He was a born leader who backed his men. Mulnix also was a good commander. They organized a lot of activities.

When a blizzard rolled in, we locked the doors to the SCAT unit, broke out the booze and played a card game called "Guts." One time Brannan took the unit to the movies to see a newly released cop flick. The SCAT Rats, as they were called, went to skydive. I could never figure out why anyone would want to jump out of a perfectly good airplane and trust a parachute.

We played softball and football against other teams and departments. The work was challenging and fulfilling, and the play was an absolute blast.

* * * *

A couple of gals were nicknamed the "Bathtub Queens." They each were dating a member of the unit. One day they said they wanted us to come to their apartment. A half-dozen cops showed up to a spread of food and cocktails, and a huge jetted hot tub.

We partied and ended up naked and in the tub all together. They were good-looking fun-loving gals. This would not be the last time that we partied with them. They became legendary.

My years in the SCAT were the best. Working in a small special group can create a tight-knit unit. The officers knew a lot about each other and everybody has everyone else's back. We shared a lot of laughs, teasing and good times.

I was involved in countless investigations and quality arrests with great cops. It was a sad day when I had to go back to patrol. Brian Deasy always had my back. He and The Unit awarded me a plaque in appreciation for all the hard work and the fun times we had shared together. It was inscribed "A super cop that no one can stop."

* * * *

An informant tipped me off that a guy was putting out feelers to find an accomplice to pull some stickups. He was ambitious, but not particularly careful. Before I met him, I disguised my appearance with a knit cap and a fake facial scar. The nice touch was the leather eye patch that Willie Newman, an undercover machine from the northern suburbs of Denver, had given me.

I met with the bad guy, Blackie, and told him I was on the run after escaping from the joint. I also told him I did not have a gun, and he replied he would provide me with one. His robbery agenda included a Greek restaurant, a bowling alley, and a big barbooth game. Barbooth is a dice game that often involves huge stakes.

The night of the first slated robbery, he gave me a loaded semi-automatic pistol, as well as a detailed strategy for robbing the barbooth players. He and I were parked outside the game site, where I arrested him. He took a plea and served no prison time.

CHAPTER 14—
DISTRICT FOUR—
5-81 to 7-83

The allegations that arose from our cooperation with the Arapahoe County SCAT came down when Lyle Hesselroad was our unit captain, as did the order for my transfer to District Four. When I was due to report to District Four, I realized I would work under Capt. Don Brannan. I figured out he had requested my transfer to his department, which removed some of the uncertainty from a miserable situation.

I knew Capt. Brannan would offer me some backing and protection. When I met with him at District Four, he told me to just keep doing what I do best, "Put assholes in jail."

Capt. Brannan and his long-time partner, Lt. Lou Lopez, were legends among the police and criminal element. Capt. Brannan has since passed away, and I asked Lt. Lopez to write about our special friend, and Lou wrote the following:

Don and I served as partners in the Denver Police Robbery detail for eight years. During that period, we were involved in a multitude of armed-robbery investigations and arrested dozens of street-wise, cunning career criminals. Don died in 2003 and on the last day of his life, I visited him in a hospice. Don was asleep, and I sat alongside his bed reminiscing of our years as partners. Don woke up stating, "Louie, Louie." We spoke for a few minutes, and as I left, I told Don, "You were a hell of a partner," at which time Don said, "Louie, we were the best." This pretty much emphasizes what this legendary cop felt. Don died the next morning. These were the last words Don spoke to me.

We were involved and solved many notable armed robberies, including the Fairplay bank robbery committed by a former Denver cop, the Lowry Air Force Commissary committed by a gang of ex-cons who also robbed many supermarkets. Don and I hold the record for armed robbery clearances. When we arrested a California ex-con, who pulled 12 Denver area stick-ups and 40 stick-ups in California. As a result, we freed an innocent person who had been convicted of pulling one of those robberies.

We solved all types of robberies, jewelry stores, bars, drive-ins, and private home invasion robberies of prominent citizens, Henry Van Schaack and Temple Buell. We were renowned for our interrogation techniques, and why so many "copped out" still baffles me today, but maybe it was because of our no bullshit approach and our honesty and fairness. We had the respect of the cons, who always referred to us as Mr. Lopez and Mr. Brannan. The cons in Canon City published a weekly newspaper featuring a comic strip called "Brandon and Gomez." A real show of respect.

Don and I were so successful as detectives that when we were promoted to sergeant, we were kept as partners, still conducting robbery investigations. That was the only time in the history of the Denver Police Department. I wrote a book about our involvement in robbery investigations, consisting of 190 pages with photos and newspaper articles. Don and I even starred in a Hollywood-produced TV series called, "Lee Marvin presents the law breakers". Yes, we had a great ride.

I knew I would survive the transfer, as I had always done. I had the backing of the captain, I still had all of my informants, and I was confident that I would expand my informant roster in District Four. I already had the mug shots of most of the bad guys in the district.

One day Capt. Brannan granted my request for the Westwood projects car. That precinct had a high concentration of career criminals. The first thing I did was meet the director of the projects to obtain a list of tenants. The list showed who signed the lease, but did not show all of the occupants.

* * * *

Early on in District Four, I did a joint investigation with Det. Mike Powell and Steve Evans of the Lakewood Department of Public Safety. They would always throw down with me when I called. This was one of many investigations and arrests I did with that duo over the years. They were "old school" detectives, and that always gave me a sense of calm.

I had just gone to District Four when a pharmacy robbery of a large amount of pure cocaine was aired. We located the getaway vehicle in east Denver and secured a search and arrest warrant. We arrested the men inside their house and recovered the gun and a large quantity of the stolen pure cocaine.

* * * *

One afternoon, I was driving back to the District Four station, and I saw an officer making a stop. I noticed the car was smoking really bad. I saw a family with two small children in the car. I parked and approached the officer to ask, "What's up"? He replies, "I am writing a mover on this piece of junk." I shook my head and asked him, "Are you crazy? This is a poor family. This father cannot pay a ticket, let alone feed his family. You write the ticket, he will probably FTA (fail to appear) and be put in jail, and then his family is really screwed. I would not write that ticket if it were me."

He thought about it and told me I was right. For every case of police brutality, there are dozens to hundreds of cases of police common sense and compassion.

* * * *

A state prison inmate, Danny Medina, who was considered an escape artist, broke out of a Jefferson County Sheriff's van that was transporting him from the penitentiary to Jefferson County Court for felony theft charges. Beyond the escape risk, Medina was considered violent.

The sheriff's deputies failed to read the memo. Medina somehow got free of his handcuffs and then slipped his belly chain. He unlocked the door by reaching the outside handle. When the van slowed, he jumped out. Medina had attempted several escapes in the past. One Pearl Harbor Day, he freed himself from the Denver County Jail by jimmying the lock of a holding cell. He was re-captured one day later in a northeast Denver motel.

Three days later he tried to escape again by slipping handcuffs and kicking out a partition between the prisoner compartment and the back door of the van. His attempt was blunted by a door he was unable to kick down.

Dennis Dickman and I developed information that Medina was hiding out at an east Denver apartment. We staked it out, and he came out with two women and entered a car. We watched as he laid down in the back seat and was covered up by the females.

We followed him and blocked in the vehicle with the help of other officers. After his arrest, he vowed to escape again. We noted that he was still wearing his joint shoes, which have a notch cut out of the heel to aid in tracking fugitives.

* * * *

Dennis and I were working together again near West 8th Avenue when a stickup came out at the Ironworker's Union Hall at 501 West 4th Ave. The APB indicated the stickups were both armed with guns and I estimated about four minutes had elapsed since they left the scene.

Every time a call went out after a robbery, I calculated how far the perpetrators could have gotten in a vehicle. This was more than guesswork for me; it was science. One time I took a stopwatch to see how far a vehicle travels at various speeds. I figured out someone could be a mile from the scene of a crime in just two and a half minutes.

As we approached West 8th Avenue and Bannock Street, we observed a lone male who matched the description of one of the suspects. We bailed out of the car and ordered him to stop at gunpoint. He who hesitates is lost or dead. A pat-down search disclosed a loaded gun, $400 in cash and checks were stolen from the Ironworker's Union Hall. Even the best cops rarely catch bad guys within five minutes of the crime going down.

* * * *

I loved analyzing surveillance photos of people robbing banks. Joe Black and I looked over a photo of a robber as he exited the bank, taking his mask off and exposing his face. It was Joe Romero, so we went out and found him. He possessed narcotics, and we also put him in jail for parole violation. Det. Chris Erickson of the Robbery detail and the FBI cleared two bank robberies with the Romero arrest.

John Chavez was another widely known bank robber. Joe Black, Larry Subia and I correctly identified Chavez from a bank surveillance photo and consequently cleared seven stickups in Portland, Oregon and some in Denver. The best cops not only get a charge out of the thrill of the chase but also get satisfaction out of solving a mental challenge.

I would not hit on all of the photos, but I often knew who they were. I IDed Olguin and Flores, two badasses who were hitting convenience stores. Their photos were snapped in one of the heists. The convenience store cameras initially were of poor quality but improved over time. When I couldn't make out the culprits, I often showed convenience store burglary photos to my CIs, and they often cleared up any mystery.

* * * *

One day I returned to District Four station after court and shared with Capt. Brannan that I was again attacked in court as a racist. The captain responded, "Hmmmm... Well, let's see, "You eat their food, date their women and put their men in jail... So, you are not a racist." He made me feel better and made me laugh, so I went out and arrested a bad guy.

* * * *

I was working the day shift, cruising around the district looking for a bad guy. Instead, I found a sad guy. I went down an alley, and I saw a hose traveling from an exhaust pipe into a window of a running truck. I observed a man with his head slumped forward, unconscious and drooling foam from his mouth. I dragged him out of the truck and began performing CPR because he was not breathing. I had called for the paramedics and was never as happy as when they arrived to take over. I thought the man was a goner, but he came back to life. That was the first person I had ever saved, and it was a good feeling.

A few days later I delivered the baby of an Asian gal who would not go to the hospital until she had her baby. It took about two minutes but seemed like an hour. I thought it was one of the more frightening things I had to do as a cop. The paramedics were tardy and didn't arrive until after the baby arrived. I delivered more babies later in my career.

* * * *

One night after my shift I was traveling home when I observed a female I recognized as the girlfriend of a dangerous fugitive wanted for a stickup. I followed her to the Valley Motel, where she parked and entered an unknown room. I called Adams County to request their assistance.

As I awaited their arrival, I went to the office to find out what room they were in. Adams County Sheriff's deputies arrived, and we surrounded the room and hit it with a key. The bad guy bailed out the bathroom window and was met by waiting officers. His loaded revolver was recovered along with a quantity of stolen property.

My strategy was to maintain the element of surprise, surround the house and always have my gun in my hand when I come through the door. I lived by this, every time I kicked a door. I always wanted to get off the first shot. Policemen have a saying, "It is better to be judged by twelve than carried by six."

* * * *

Despite my initial disappointment in being bounced from the SCAT Unit, things were going pretty well at District Four. I was knocking off some good felons and making seizures of dope and stolen goods. I had some projects in the works, including a series of pharmacy armed robberies throughout Denver.

One day, Sgt. Byron Haze showed up at District Four. I did not feel good about this new arrival, getting the sense he had no love for me. I was right. He told me if I drove beyond the boundaries of my precinct or district he would file on me. I immediately wondered who blew in his ear.

I got a tip from one of my CIs that an escapee was at a house in north Denver, which is District One. I knew if I slipped over there Haze would make good on his threat. I went to him and told him he needed to go with me to Colfax and Irving Street where an escapee is in a stolen car. He agreed, which shocked me.

We arrived at the scene and took a position down the street. Not five minutes passed when the suspect came out and entered the stolen Honda Civic. The chase was on, and boy did I love chases. We were on his ass, and I was tapping the corner of his bumper in an attempt to throw him out of control, but I could not get the proper angle.

Sgt. B.J. Haze kept reaching over from the passenger seat, trying to turn off the ignition, and I kept grabbing his hand and pulling it away. Finally, I told Haze to call out the chase. We hit speeds up to 50 mph. Other cop cars converged, and we got the Civic boxed in. One of the police cars cut off the bad guy's vehicle, he slammed on his brakes, and I slammed into the rear of the suspect's stolen car.

We attempted to take him into custody, but he was not happy and resisted arrest, therefore got roughed up a bit in the scuffle. In our day, the bad guys knew if they took us on a high-speed chase and we caught them, they would get their asses kicked if they compounded the nonsense by resisting arrest. He had been on the run for a month. He was doing time for auto theft.

I think Sgt. Haze enjoyed the adrenalin rush; I know I did. He got his name in the paper the next day. He was really hard to read or understand. Sometimes he would go after homicide cold cases, and I believe he solved some of them. He was a decent investigator.

* * * *

While on patrol one day I observed three males in a car who seemed very concerned about me. They pulled over, and one occupant got out and hurried into a house. I contacted the driver, who identified himself as Joe Lujan. He told me he had no ID, and the guy who went into the house was his brother Jimmy. The vehicle listed to Ed Johnson, whom Lujan said was his friend. When the guy came back out of the house, he claimed his name was Jimmy Lujan.

People inside the house verified the name and said he was visiting from Salt Lake City. I noted that he had joint tattoos and the initials "W.L." on his shoulder, which did not correspond with the name "Jimmy Lujan." Cops called these identifying tattoos "monikers." Neither had an ID, and both claimed they lost their wallets at a party.

I knew they were lying and were going downtown with me so I could attempt to gain their true identities. The third guy had ID, and I kicked him loose. I patted the other two down for weapons and cuffed them and off we went.

At Headquarters, I removed every item from their pockets and practically strip-searched the two men. This was always a good practice after an arrest, in case a suspect was hiding proceeds from the crime, dope, or a weapon.

In one of their pockets, I found a phone number with the name "Aunt Rose" on a small piece of paper. I called Rose and identified myself and asked her if she had any male relatives in their twenties in Colorado. She said she had several nephews and provided the names Edward Johnson, Joey Lettig a.k.a. Joe Lujan, and William Lettig a.k.a. Jimmy Lujan. Bingo! "W.L."

Salt Lake City P.D. indicated that all of Aunt Rose's nephews had prior arrests for burglary and narcotics. We figured out William Lettig was wanted for felony escape, carrying a concealed weapon and parole violation. Whenever a moniker does not match a suspect's ID, the odds are that person is a fugitive.

It's now standard police protocol to catalog and photograph a suspect's tattoos during booking and to ask the suspect where the tattoos were put on. It's surprising how often they defiantly and proudly give themselves away by bragging about their criminal roots.

At one time, I could immediately tell if a tattooed suspect was from New York, New Mexico, California or Colorado by the influence in their tattoos. Each style was very distinctive. When tattoo artists started bouncing from prison to prison, it screwed up our cataloging system somewhat. However, today's criminals, especially gang bangers, tend to emblazon their bodies with the name of their gang and the zip code of their city.

The Lettig/Lujan case was a classic example of simple, thorough police work. I followed the only physical lead I had in the case right to several felony arrests.

* * * *

District Four had its share of "Choir Practices"—parties attended by guys and gals. They were fun and sometimes the partiers would end up with someone they did not anticipate being with. I liked the policewomen. They were fun, and we had a lot in common. Some guys were single, and some were married and never fooled around, and some had "chippies," which is to say cops are humans.

* * * *

One day while I was working solo, I observed a male and female walking across a street. It appeared he had a gun under his shirt. The pair made it into a sports car they were driving, but I got there in time to get him out of the car.

I could see the butt of a revolver under the seat and began to cuff him when he exploded and punched me in the face. When he tried to take my gun, there was no doubt in my mind what he wanted to do to me, which was blow my ass away. I finally won the fight by beating him into submission with multiple blows to the face.

I got him cuffed as his female companion took off running. With the gun was 14 balloons of heroin. You never stop fighting, or you die. That was one hell of a close call. The last thing I wanted was to be shot again. A black will tell you that he isn't going to jail or is going to kick your ass. But the Hispanics are sneaky and will jump or sucker punch you. I have always found Hispanics to be tough.

* * * *

A who-done-it armed robbery was perpetrated at a Lakewood convenience store by a lone white male. He shot the female clerk in the chest when she was not able to open the cash drawer. The Ford Mustang used in the robbery was stolen by the gunman prior to the robbery.

I contacted Mike Powell and Steve Evans of the Lakewood Police Department and gave them the information on Ricky White. They showed the victim a photo lineup, from which she picked Ricky White. Powell and Evans proceeded on the robbery/attempted murder case, gaining an arrest warrant and nabbing Ricky White, who was charged in the crimes.

I'll call one case "Martin meets Martin." Det. Dave Martin of the Denver robbery detail notified me that he had gotten information about White robbing a liquor store with an unknown white male.

They entered the store discharging their weapons and then robbed the clerk. I asked one of my informants about the robbery, and I learned that the robbers thought there was an armed guard inside and that is why they fired their guns.

White's accomplice was a gunman named Martin who looked like Yosemite Sam from Looney Toons. Our techs tried to make them on prints, but couldn't find anything conclusive. The perpetrators were wearing nylon masks and driving a stolen car. It was common knowledge that White was a master auto thief. However, they were not charged.

* * * *

Dave Martin was a funny guy. One day I went to the Stickup detail, and everyone was there. Martin pulled out a card and said, "Let's see here … Daril Cinquanta was

arrested in 1965 at the Galaxy 3.2 bar on West Alameda
Avenue trying to use a phony ID and jailed."

Yeah, that actually had happened. When I was 17 years
old, Denver P.D. transported me in the scout car, which
was the paddy wagon. They place me in a rectangular cell
with a trough of running water. The men seated around me
were puking into it. That image really made an impression
on me, and I didn't sleep at all that night. I was shocked
that Martin had that information from when I was 17 years
old, and that was hardly the last time girls made me do
crazy things.

* * * *

I loved the guys in the Stickup Detail because we got
along so well. I arrested countless stickups over the years,
and the officers in that unit appreciated it. The guys in the
unit were Dick Schaffer, Gene Shaw, Bob Partenheimer,
Dale Lawless, Dale Burkhardt, John Goodfellow, Chris
Erickson, Howard Dressel, Mike Ortiz, and Mike Rosales.

Big departments tend to have some dead wood, but all
of the men in the Stickup Unit were solid. They were really
good at clearing their cases. Experience pays, and a big
reason they could solve cases and make arrests was their
encyclopedic knowledge of the bad guys' M.O.'s and
physical descriptions.

* * * *

Cops never know when they will turn a radio call into
a big arrest. I answered a call to a car lot on Federal
Boulevard regarding damaged cars. I took the offense
report and began inquiring through the neighborhood if
there were any witnesses during the night.

I always tried to do as much as I could at a crime scene
to help the assigned detective. I would seize evidence and

call the crime lab if pictures or prints were needed. I was going door to door when I heard grinding and welding in a large garage. I knocked on the garage, and a male opened the door, came out, spun around to re-enter the garage, and locking the door. I called for backup and began knocking on the door again, suspecting I had just stumbled onto a chop shop.

Two guys inside unlocked the door, and I could see a cut-up truck. The backup officers and I got control of the garage, and the owner signed a consent form for searching the premises. He later confessed to the thefts. We found six stolen vehicles in various stages of being parted out. The victims were within one block and had no idea the thieves were a few doors down.

* * * *

One day I was in the Westwood Projects trying to find a suspect, and I rousted an old timer with joint tattoos. He copped an attitude, so I had to get his attention. He said, "You are just like that fucking Riggs." I took that as a compliment.

Paulie Riggs was a no-nonsense, tough cop who took no shit off of anyone. He would go toe to toe with a criminal at a drop of a disrespectful word. He had a prize fighter's nose; it had been punched and broke way too many times. He was old school, and a whole "Paulie Riggs Mythology" floated around the department.

I was very fond of him, and he invited me to group luncheons. He invited only the people he liked. He was very outspoken about cops, voicing his approval or disapproval, and was a kick to be around. He was part of the long lineage of legendary Denver policemen. There were some freaks of nature who could contend with, and sometimes dwarf, anything Hollywood could invent. Retired Sgt. Bill Yeros summarizes the saga of Roger Ramjet:

"In September of 1968, the Denver Police Department admitted Roger Allen Prince to the academy, with badge number 6854 pinned on his chest. Little did the department know what they were dealing with at the time. There has never been anything quite like him before and certainly nothing like him since.

Roger graduated from the academy after thirteen weeks and had already done more "real" police work before being assigned to District One than some officers did in a career. "Officer Prince"—working in the District One station house at 13th and Champa—is assigned a walking beat in lower downtown.

There were no Training officers in those days, and Roger was in the "sink or swim" system the department used as a filtering process at the time. You either cut the mustard, or you were cut from the department for "cause." There were no second chances back then or protection while you were on probation.

The "walking beat" was a tough assignment. Downtown was loaded with ethnic bars in low-rent places with low-life clients. Officers were baptized early in the dealing with "the people business." Certain avenues had Mexican bars, Indian bars, Negro bars and bars for every other form of lifestyle. In many parts of downtown, "Whitey" wasn't allowed, and the only Whites that ever ventured there were those who were members of the Denver Police Department.

Within the walls of these dens of inequity officers like Roger had to prove themselves immediately that they were the boss. Otherwise, they would have been chewed up and spit out on the sidewalk from which they came.

In 1968, the best place to work on the Denver Police Department was downtown, District One or Five Points in District Two. Roger cut his teeth fighting robbers, thieves, murderers and just bad people in an asphalt jungle surrounded by concrete and glass.

Officers were issued with a "nightstick" in those days, mace and stun guns didn't exist, and Roger became very proficient with this intimidating tool. The nightstick was used as a persuader, a come along if you will, and defense mechanism when needed. It was an officer's best friend, next to his partner and his revolver.

Many bad guys couldn't get their hat back on their head after an encounter with Roger. Roger and his night stick "Billy" may have de-escalated and prevented more resistance than any other police policy or verbal judo program the department had incorporated. Roger had a reputation, and many knew it, and when he grabbed "Billy" the stick, those in attendance wanted no part of that, and they either moved along or compiled leaving them the ability to go home wearing their hat comfortably. Deterrence, what a beautiful thing!

Roger is transferred to District Four and becomes "The Ram Jet." In today's world, Roger would be classified as ADHD or suffering with "Attention Deficit Hyperactivity Disorder." He would be evaluated by the company shrink as a risk, dangerous, and taken off the street and medicated with Ritalin. He would be assigned to work in the motor pool, handing out keys to detectives complaining they didn't get the car they wanted.

In Roger's world, he failed to realize there were other cops working besides himself. He had to be the first on the scene on every call. In 1970, District Four Officers Brian Deasy and Darrell Wagner couldn't believe their eyes when they first encountered Roger Prince.

Whenever a "hot call" came out requesting cover or dispatch calling "any car" to handle a code 10, it seemed that Roger was the first car on scene regardless of where he was in the District when the call came out. Deasy and Wagner thought Roger had a twin brother, how else could one guy show up so often beating the precinct car to the call?

One night, Roger showed up on one of their calls, arriving before they did, Deasy asked, "Do you have a ram jet in your cruiser"? That, my friend, stamped the legacy of "Roger Ram Jet." A more befitting name could not have been more accurate or more descriptive, and from that point forward everyone just called him, "Roger Ram Jet!"

Hardly a week went by where a story didn't surface, "Hey did ya hear what Roger Ram Jet did last night?" His antics were of such magnitude and so outrageous that they were the stuff you read about in superhero novels and comic books, all part of an ongoing series with each episode more exciting than the previous. Yes fans, "You ain't seen nothing yet!" Tune in next week and watch the Ram Jet save a damsel in distress and singlehandedly stop a riot in the Westwood Projects while out of service on a short seven!

Working solo, Ram Jet notices a rolling steal listed on the hot sheet he has thumbtacked to his dashboard. Roger pulls in behind the suspect vehicle where he calls in his location, and instantly the chase is on. Located near the

Lincoln Park Projects, the suspect—with several occupants aboard—takes Roger Ram Jet on a harrowing ride. Ram Jet has to call in the chase street by street and avenue by avenue while giving directions of travel, speed, location, description of vehicle and plate number.

Oh, and he has to use a foot-activated siren located next to the dimmer switch on the floorboard. If this weren't enough, he was using the driver's side spotlight to fill the rear windscreen of the fleeing vehicle. Roger has taken on the appearance of the toy monkey banging the brass cymbals, pounding the drum, blowing the horn and tipping his hat while exceeding speeds of 70 miles per hour.

Like a rat in a maze and looking for a way to get out, the suspect rolls the stolen vehicle at 10th and Mariposa with Ram Jet right on his rear bumper. The two-door coupe ends up lying on its side, with the driver's side door facing skyward. Instantly the car bursts into flames after rupturing the fuel cell.

In a panic to escape "Hell's kitchen", the suspects try to get out the only escape route by way of the driver's side door. Pushing with all their might to get the door to open it refuses to yield like there was an unknown force holding it shut.

Cover officers arrive on the scene and see the car engulfed in flames, and to their amazement, Roger Ram Jet is standing on top of the door using his body weight to contain the occupants inside. Screaming like an avid fan at a boxing smoker, Roger Ram Jet was advising the suspects they were under arrest and reading them the Miranda Warning.

Officers had to physically remove Roger from atop his perch as flames were licking at his feet. Officers assisted

Denver firefighters in extracting the suspects while hosing down the burning hulk. Realizing how close he had come to his own mortality, the Ram Jet hyperventilated and passed out.

While working Vice and Narcotics, Dets. Leroy Dominguez and Roger Ram Jet are working Five Points and decide to get a hot link and a listener at Zona's pig ear stand. After parking their undercover unit on the pad, the detective spots Willie Davis hanging out in front of the Capris Lounge. Davis is wanted on a warrant and wants nothing to do with Ram Jet or Dominguez.

Ram Jet calls out to Davis to come over, and he complies. As Ram Jet begins to question him, Davis pulls out a revolver and sticks the barrel into Roger's chest. Ram Jet grabs Davis' weapon by the barrel, and a struggle ensues between Davis and Ram Jet. Davis fires his weapon, striking Ram Jet in the thumb. Although wounded, Ram Jet is able to wrestle the weapon away from Davis, turn it on him and shooting him several times with his own weapon.

Davis retreats by running through the front door of the Capris Lounge with Ram Jet and Dominguez in hot pursuit. Severely wounded, Davis makes it out the back door of the bar and into the parking lot, where he expires. Detectives notified radio of a police shooting with an officer shot. When Homicide detectives arrived along with a DGH ambulance, they witness Roger Ram Jet and Dominguez standing over Davis' body, eating their hot links and listeners. Bon appetit!

One of the Denver Police Department's most spectacular shootings took place in November of 1978 at the McDonald's at East Colfax and Glencoe. Officers Bob Lyons and Bob Nice are dispatched on a robbery in progress call. Upon arrival, they discover the perp has the manager on his knees behind the counter with a gun at his head and 11 hostages frozen in fear sitting in the restaurant.

When the perp sees the cruiser pull up to the front of the restaurant and sees Officers Lyons and Nice get out of the car, he begins firing shots over the heads of the hostages toward the officers. In fear of striking one of the hostages, Officers Lyons and Nice do not return fire and summon backup as they seek cover.

In a matter of seconds it seems, Roger Ram Jet appears out of nowhere. Ram Jet had observed the situation through the front window of McDonald's as he skidded his cruiser into a four-wheel drift up to the front door. Exiting his cruiser and without hesitation, he grabs his 12-gauge shotgun, walks past Officers Lyons and Nice and enters the front door.

The suspect, still standing over the manager and holding his weapon on him, is in shock to see Officer Ram Jet walk right in and invade his comfort zone. Instantly the perp raises his weapon toward Ram Jet, an explosion of double-aught buck exits the muzzle and hits the suspect in the ten ring, lifting him off his feet and sending him in a trajectory backward about six feet.

The perp flies under a wash sink, taking all of the plumbing out with him, creating a small flood on the kitchen floor. A clanking sound fills the air and makes a continuous pinging noise which seems to last for minutes.

Glittering silver debris fills the air along with smoke and the acrid smell of gunpowder, and it is raining down on the Ram Jet and the store manager, who is now in the fetal position on the floor. To Ram Jet's surprise, it was hundreds of coins raining from the sky, flying about the restaurant sounding like a giant wind chime. When the suspect takes the shot to the chest, he is holding in his off hand a money bag filled with hundreds of cash coins he stole from the safe. The blast was so powerful that several coins were reportedly embedded into the skin of the suspect.

One of the most notorious crimes in Denver history involved Phillip Hutchinson, an escaped kidnapper from the Texas penal system. Hutchinson ends up in Denver where he holds up the Rocky Mountain Credit Union at 48th and Pecos. Radio sends out a "BOLO" on the suspect's vehicle, with District One Officers Rollins and Baldwin spotting the suspect car and giving chase.

Det. Bob Wallis and Sgt. Parisi are on Tennyson Street near Berkeley Park when they observe the suspect vehicle heading toward them, with Rollins and Baldwin in pursuit. Hutchinson is on a collision course with Wallis and Baldwin. Fearing a massive head-on crash, the two officers jump from their unit to run for safety. Det. Wallis is deliberately run down by Hutchinson and dies instantly on the scene.

Officer Roger Prince has been listening to the chatter on his District Four channel and heads over to cover and give back up to District One from his location at Evans and Sheridan. Ram Jet realizes the Channel 4 news helicopter is on scene following the suspect and airing his location to Denver Police Dispatch, which then is relaying information to officers.

Shortly after running down Det. Wallis Hutchinson, the suspect crashes his vehicle and sets out on foot. After a failed attempt at carjacking a woman at gunpoint while in her vehicle, Hutchinson fired shots at her and her baby as she sped off. Mike Silva, the pilot of the Channel 4 helicopter, is hovering over the suspect who now begins firing his weapon at the helicopter. Hutchinson is still on foot and runs through a trailer park at 53rd and Sheridan, where he hijacks an old man in a green pick-up truck at gunpoint.

By now, Ram Jet is on the scene and under the helicopter entering the trailer park. Holding a gun on the driver of the pick-up Hutchinson orders him to drive out of the trailer park. Silva, a Vietnam helicopter pilot, positions the chopper low and in front of the truck blocking its exit from the park.

Ram Jet, suddenly and without warning, rams the truck with his patrol car disabling the vehicle and ending any chance of escape. Roger immediately exits his damaged cruiser and runs up to the passenger side of the truck where Hutchinson is seated. Ram Jet fires his .357 revolver into the head of Phillip Hutchinson.

Secondary officers on scene following Ram Jet's lead began firing into the cab at Huchinson who's already mortally wounded. Inadvertently Ram Jet was shot in the forehead by pellets from a shotgun blast executed by another officer. Ram Jet stated, "I was so pumped at the time, I didn't even notice I had been shot".

Roger Allen Prince was the right officer at the right time on the right police department, a marriage made in heaven. The antics and unorthodox police work fostered by his demeanor, would hardly work in today's environment or be tolerated by the brass or the politicians who now run the job.

Long gone are the days when cover officers watched in amazement with eyes wide open and jaw dropping expressions as to what they just witnessed when in the presence of Roger Allen Prince.

If he were to be cast in a Hollywood production, he would be the good guy that women and children hid behind for protection. He would run the gunslinger out of town or shoot him down in the street like a dog he is. He would be the man other men would want to emulate. He would be "Dirty Harry" a pain in top brasses ass, but always doing the dirty work, no one else would.

Roger had a knack, an instinct for police work, he felt it in his bones, and it ran through his veins, it can't be taught or learned, you either have it, or you don't. Roger Prince was one of a kind, and there will never be another like him. Just about anyone can be a policeman, just look around, but only a rare few were called "Good Cops" the highest praise you could give an officer back in the day.

Roger Ram Jet was one of the best. It was a joy to watch a professional excel in his craft, whether it's sports, entertainment or police work. For over thirty-five years, I was fortunate enough to watch of the greatest shows the Denver Police Department ever produced, featuring Roger "The Ram Jet" Prince, uncensored, uncut, untamed. What a performance.

--Sgt. Bill Yeros (retired)
Denver Police Department

* * * *

I was just hitting my stride in District Four and got some solid information that career criminal Joyce Schillo, who I nicknamed "The Paper Lady," was counterfeiting driver's licenses to pass stolen checks and to forge IDs for wanted felons. I had been working on her for about two years, receiving information about her nefarious activities, but never having enough to hit her.

The information indicated that she was counterfeiting out of a motel on Colorado Boulevard. SCAT agreed to help and conducted a three-day surveillance as we collected the information needed for the search warrant. SCAT observed her exiting the room to use the sunlight to photograph the framed manufactured driver's license with a Polaroid SX 70 camera.

She used the same method as "Eskimo," the wheelchair-bound forger we had busted while he fabricated IDs from a hospital bed. We executed the search warrant and seized all of her counterfeiting paraphernalia, as well as federal checks from burglaries of U.S. Mail relay boxes.

It was a sophisticated operation. The counterfeit driver's licenses were made to match the names on the checks. We arrested and charged the five people in the motel room with forgery, possession of forgery devices and conspiracy. In one fell swoop, we nabbed Schillo's entire check ring.

I later heard from other women that when Schillo went to the female joint, she ran it. I was told that some girls would engage in lesbian activities when they were in and when they got out, they would resume relations with men. The men's prison was the same. Inmates were raped and forced to be someone's "bitch," and they complied to survive.

Chief Deputy D.A. Chuck Lepley wrote a commendation which read in part, "I want to specifically refer to the 'textbook' quality of the search warrant prepared by Daril to search vehicles and residences. The six-page affidavit could be used as a model for others to follow. It could certainly be the technical and thoroughness standard for others to seek to achieve."

People in all walks of life do great work every day, going above and beyond to be professionals. It was reaffirming to know that the countless hours I spent ensuring my affidavits were of high quality was recognized and appreciated by the District Attorney's Office.

* * * *

One day we got a call to the Anderson Motel at Federal and Alameda, which had been converted to one-bedroom apartments. We found the body of a man who had been beaten to death by fists. Witnesses told us that his brother had beaten him to death and headed westbound.

Officer Danny Cram started to take statements. Officers Hildi Lorandi, M. Boyd and I started looking for his brother in nearby bars, suspecting that alcohol had to be a contributing factor. We eventually checked the Aeroplane Club Bar and found him seated at the bar, dried blood crusted down his chest. He confirmed his identity, and we arrested him.

Some cops think they are accomplishing something by roughing up a suspect when they find him. I have always believed that a confession begins at the time of arrest, so I always tried to treat suspects with respect. In this case, my approach paid off. He was advised of his Miranda warnings, and he confessed to murdering his brother because he was mad at him. We made some homicide detective happy because he didn't have to chase him.

* * * *

Hildi was a good cop and liked to chase bad guys. When I joined the department, the Old Heads did not like policewomen and even refused to work with them. When a gal was assigned to work with him, the crusty veteran would run into the sergeant after the roll call and refuse to work with her. They claimed the women cops were inferior, dangerous and could not win a fight with a bad guy.

I did not mind working with a policewoman. I felt it was an opportunity to make them safer and better than they were. I also knew I might have to depend on a woman cop to save my life one day, so I wanted to teach her things I had learned or taught myself.

I noticed that, like some of their male counterparts, women cops didn't have an intuitive understanding of how to approach vehicles, or how to return to the Police car. They often turned their backs on the occupants of the stopped car, and consistently had a problem containing multiple occupants of a vehicle. I just tried to teach them the small techniques to help keep them and me alive.

I also shared my knowledge of dealing with the bad guys. It's about physics and geometry, executed in real time and real life. The strongest wrestler doesn't always win; often the grappler who understands leverage and pressure points takes the match. Of course, the women were not as physically strong as the men, but many of them would dive right into the middle of a skirmish, fighting alongside me to get control of the suspect to arrest him.

In District Four, I got to work with several female officers, and each of them was competent and enjoyable to work with. Bobette Hinds was a real go-getter. Debbie Clair was a smart, solid cop. Sue McDonald had a lot of natural potential as a crime fighter. Cindy Duncan was a fun partner who liked to find and arrest the crooks. Arla Buckley was a thorough and fun partner.

Eleanor Baem came on the job with me, and we dated during our time at the Police Academy. I always felt she was going to be a star. She ended up in narcotics but resigned from the job when she got married and moved with her husband to a job out of state. Carmen Sanchez was another go-getter who liked to catch criminals.

The gals who joined the Denver Police Department wanted acceptance from the guys. Everyone wants to be respected in their lives, at work and home, and these women didn't want to be considered an inconvenience or an afterthought. Women had an uphill battle to be treated as equals in a very virile, even macho, man's world. They had the brains, talent, and desire.

Some of the command took advantage of the young policewomen for assignments of cars or partners. I guess sometimes the supervisors were actually dating policewomen because they liked them, and other times they were misleading them with false promises of sex.

The best female street cop was Patty Jeung, whom we nicknamed "Lotus Flower" in The Police Academy. When she graduated, she was sent to the Crimes Against Persons Bureau. Under Chief Seaton, policewomen were not allowed to work the streets.

When Art Dill became chief, women were treated as full-fledged police officers. He said no officer, including a woman, can make detective or technician without working the street. Patty was assigned to the Detective Bureau for two years, going into the patrol division in 1974. Patty never made detective, but she was promoted to a Field Training Officer position.

Lotus Flower remained on the street for 31 years before retiring. It takes one tough gal—with guile, lots of smarts and a silver tongue—to survive the street for over three decades. I have my own personal Denver Police Hall of Fame in my mind and heart, and Patty Jeung is enshrined.

Gayle Reidel was a special detective who carved out her own niche in the department. She worked the Theft Bureau, handling shoplifters. She put out periodic bulletins listing all of the individuals arrested for "boosting." Most boosters were heroin, cocaine and amphetamine addicts.

Their lives were a succession of desperate moves— arrested on Saturday for theft, and on Monday they are pulling a burglary, followed up by a Thursday stickup. Then they were dealing every day of the week because what better way to support a drug habit than having drugs coming through their hands every few days.

The females would participate in property crimes and often engage in prostitution and drug dealing. Crime is a way of life. Some criminals change up their M.O.'s, thinking there is less likelihood they will be arrested; this is not true.

Gayle also coordinated the monthly meeting of various Denver Metro police departments. Officers met to exchange information such as identities of individuals arrested for theft. Officers attending these meetings also put the spotlight on suspects who had used weapons when a security officer attempted to arrest them. The assembled cops also swapped files on groups engaged in organized thefts on department stores.

And there was the glitzy element, with boutiques that sold jewelry and fur, as well as specialty stores with high-end items being highlighted. I got mug shots of every thief who appeared in one of her bulletins.

* * * *

In October of 1987, members of the Career Criminal Unit got onto a Mexican national serial rapist, about 5-8, 165, who had a history of sex offenses, robbery, and kidnapping. The Unit began following him, and we soon learned that he was erratic in his behavior and focus. At first, we found it difficult to determine how he was going to pick his next victim. His behavior seemed random.

One night we followed him to a southwest Denver neighborhood with no street lights. A lady had gotten off a city bus and was walking to her house. He parked and jumped from his vehicle and was moving along the houses across the street in the same direction as his target. He stayed close to the houses, lurking in the dark as he prepared to attack the unsuspecting woman.

Officers could barely see him in the shadows because he wore dark clothing. He crossed the street diagonally to attack her. She reached her door, opened it and made it inside, but he timed his attack precisely to burst inside to rape her. But she beat him inside, safely locking the door behind her. This was the first time I had ever witnessed a rapist stalk his prey/victim. He was a dangerous animal.

We figured out he was dogging the buses to find a victim he could follow on foot and attack. We contacted DPD Officer Kathy Davis, who agreed to be a decoy on the bus in an attempt to catch him in the act of attacking a victim. We ended up stationing her on several buses, hoping he would take the bait and pick her bus.

At West 32nd Avenue and Federal Blvd., he followed her bus. We had six patrol cars on the detail. She got off and was crossing the street walking north and then east on West 32nd Avenue, and he punched her as she crossed the intersection. He was trying to drag her into the shrubbery where he could rape her.

I think he compulsively needed to stalk women and rape them. He was a predator spinning farther and farther out of control. The middle of a busy intersection was an unusual place to make a move on his victim because it was out in the open and well lit. When we raced in, he bolted, but we found him hiding in a backyard in some bushes after a foot chase. Kathy and the unit did a phenomenal job of catching this rapist.

* * * *

By 1986, "The Ski Mask Rapist" had sexually assaulted and beaten 20 victims over a two-year period in one area of Denver. His M.O. was methodical and ensured there would be no evidence for Investigators to prove his crimes.

The predator stalked his target, using a glass cutter to create a hole in a window of her residence and pulling the phone line away from the wall so it would be easier to snip. Returning when his target was home, he cut the phone line and made a silent entry by reaching through the hole to open the window. That was a brazen move because he had to visit the crime scene multiple times.

The rapist placed a pillow over the face of the sleeping female victim. After the rapes, he made comments to the victims to convince them that he had been watching them. His goal was to frighten his victims with the threat that he might return.

Sgt. John Thompson was a hell of a cop and was investigating an attempted burglary in the Washington Park area when he found that a next-door ground level apartment, inhabited by a young single female, appeared to have been staged for The Ski Mask rapist's next attack. The female occupant was contacted and she agreed to let an undercover decoy assume her place in the apartment. She said she suspected she was being watched and believed someone had been in her apartment, moving around items in her underwear drawer.

Thompson recruited Det. Chris Bridges-Wallis to be the decoy. She jumped on the detail because she knew we could end the predator's string of rapes. Chris was not an ordinary policewoman. She was aggressive and liked to work undercover.

On the designated night, Chris drove up in a vehicle that matched that of the occupant of the rapist's suspected target and went into the dwelling. Chris and the target shared blonde hair and a similar physical stature.

Det. Dave Pontarelli was hiding in a closet, poised to ensure she was not harmed and to help execute the arrest. Sgt. Thompson and the backup team waited blocks away to avoid spooking the suspect. In the suspected target's apartment, Chris ate dinner, watched TV, turned off the lights and lay on the bed, pretending to have fallen asleep.

On the bed for an hour, staring at the window, she watched the suspect's gloved hand reach through his jagged hole to slowly unlatch the window. He inched open the window. Chris could see that he wore a thick wool ski mask and his hand bore a thin object she suspected was a knife.

When the window was open, he vaulted over the ledge and landed on all fours. Chris had her revolver in her hand under the blanket for the past three hours. The intruder got to the foot of the bed and was reaching for Chris when Dave and Chris pulled their guns and placed him under arrest. He pleaded, "Don't shoot me. Don't shoot me."

When they transported the intruder downtown to book him, they found out why he had been so elusive. Frank Vargas had never before been arrested, and his fingerprints were nowhere in the database. He was a married man with three children. His wife had no idea of her husband's obsession and extra-curricular activities.

Vargas pled guilty and was sentenced to 48 years in prison. Chris Bridges-Wallis had a distinguished career and passed after contracting Lou Gehrig's disease years later.

* * * *

For months when I was in the Westwood Projects I smelled a foul odor. It wasn't at all familiar to me, but I picked up on it every time I went to that neighborhood.

One day I got a call to one of the units on a disturbance. As I walked to the door, I got a strong whiff of the stench. I went inside, nearly gagging, and took the complaint from an Asian gal.

I looked into the kitchen to see four legs sticking out of a tall pot on the stove. She was boiling a dog in a cauldron of spices. I could not prove she had stolen the dog, and nobody else was home. No citations were issued.

* * * *

During my time in District Four, I received The Citizens Appreciation Award for saving the life of the man in the truck who was preparing to commit suicide with a hose from the exhaust pipe. That took some of the stings out of what I had endured with the suspension and demotion.

The only way I could endure the humiliation was to keep doing what I did best: developing cases and busting felons. I hit my stride again in District Four. It allowed me to cope and put a smile on my face to know that my detractors were reading about me in the *Rocky Mountain News* every time I scored a big arrest. I made it clear that they could not break me, no matter what they did to me.

The system created me and my defiance to succeed in spite of all of the criticism. I fought back by doing my job as well as it could be done. If they couldn't break me, I would win.

* * * *

I got a tip on an individual who had committed a murder in Nevada. I passed the information on to Nevada, not knowing if it was good or not. To my amazement, my tip was the break they needed to make their case and arrest the perp. They wrote a thank you letter to the chief.

During my career, I sent many tips to agencies all over the country regarding homicides, stickups, burglaries and thefts, and many of them resulted in arrests and successful prosecutions.

* * * *

One day my friend Joe Black and I got into a high-speed chase. Joe was pretty new to the force, and this may have been his first chase. I was glad I was driving because I trusted my experience.

The driver eventually pulled over the vehicle, and as we approached, he leaned over and was opening a gym bag on the passenger seat. We took him at gunpoint and saw marijuana in the bag, which also contained large quantities of psilocybin mushrooms and cocaine, two pounds of marijuana, narcotics trafficking paraphernalia and $1,800 in cash.

We received a commendation for the pinch. I was happy to see Joe's get his first commendation, and launch into a career filled with a lot of quality pinches. Joe was a smart guy and would retire as a captain.

* * * *

One day I attended proceedings in Jefferson County Courthouse in Golden. As I left, I saw two major career criminals, Donald Zorens and Elias "Groucho" Archuleta. Zorens was a cop killer, and both were stickups. Archuleta was known as Groucho because he always had a big stogie clenched between his teeth. They were convicted felons out on parole.

I went to my car to call the ID bureau to get their DOB's, and another radio call to NCIC and clear them. They were not wanted, but as I watched them a big, tall black guy in a three-piece suit walked up and started bullshitting with them. It was evident that they knew each other. In looking through my binoculars, the one thing that stood out was this black man's nose. I had never seen a nose like this on a black guy. It was quite distinctive.

I wrote down his plate number and ran it. He was George Benningfield, a career criminal with convictions for restaurant and bank robberies. He must have had 40 felony arrests on his rap sheet and four convictions. His record also indicated he was a drug user. I didn't have anything to act on that day, but I would not forget about George Benningfield.

During 1981, a black male began hitting Columbia Savings branches on Fridays. The robber was described a tall black man who wore a three-piece suit, glasses and a hat, and had curly hair described as "looking like pubic hair" on his face, mustache and eyebrows. His M.O. featured carrying a *Wall Street Journal* containing a revolver into the banks, walking up to the cashier and stating he wanted to make a withdrawal. Brian Jovick of the FBI came out with a surveillance photo of the gunman, and there was that nose. I asked Brian, "Isn't that George Benningfield?" He replied, "No way. Benningfield has a government job."

I showed the picture to several veteran detectives who said they had known George and believed it was not him. I began doubting myself, and then I came to my senses. Why do I care what their opinion is? Years earlier I had seen him at the Jefferson County Courthouse. Now I was looking at the picture, and I knew it was him.

I learned that when he was in Leavenworth Prison, Benningfield started a program called "Don't Follow Me" in which he and some fellow inmates gave lectures to students outside of the walls. I also learned that he was fired by Employex, an organization that helped ex-cons find jobs, for absenteeism.

All of the elements were adding up to me. Now all I had to do was find George Benningfield. I was having a difficult time locating him, so I began hitting bars frequented by ex-cons.

One night I dropped into McFann's on East 11th Avenue and went in to routine it. Seated at the bar was attorney Raymond Buckles. He had some problems with the American Bar Association, but I liked him. Buckles was an associate of many career criminals, and he opposed me as a defense attorney in a number of criminal cases over the years, but I respected him. He never attacked me or my credibility as a cop or a man in court and stuck to the facts of each case. In my eyes, he was a good, stand-up attorney.

I walked over and sat next to Raymond, and we began talking. I told him I was in The Classic Thunderbird Club, which hosted guest speakers, and claimed I was thinking about inviting George Benningfield to speak. I asked Raymond if he saw George to give him my business card. He gave me George's phone number, and I almost fainted. Raymond said George was living with a white gal who was an attorney. I finished my drink and went home, and I could hardly sleep knowing I was going to catch him.

The next day, before I was to report to District Four for my shift, I listed the phone number and it took me to a flat on East 17th Avenue. I was sitting on Benningfield's "cool pad" early in the morning, and he strolled out onto the front porch in a three-piece suit and adjusted his tie. Now I knew I was going to get him.

He walked over to a gold-colored vehicle and drove off. The car was a piece of the puzzle. Weeks before, a man described as the suspect in the string of robberies entered a Columbia Savings. He was in full disguise and got in line, carrying a folded Wall Street Journal. He got spooked when he saw an off-duty, uniformed policewoman walk in, broke the line and walked to a gold car and drove away.

Ken Hawkins was a fraud investigator with the D.A.'s office and was my friend. He helped convince Columbia Savings to put off-duty armed police officers in the branches that the bandit had not hit. Three weeks went by, and bank officers canceled the surveillance because he had not struck.

When he had time, Ken helped me keep track of George, because I was stuck in District Four during the day. One morning when I was off, I sat on George's flat and followed him to a Columbia Savings in Capitol Hill. He was not in disguise nor was he carrying anything as he went into the building. After he had left, I went in to find out what he had done. George had passed a forged check for $200, stealing the blank check from the back of his girlfriend's checkbook. He had passed several of her checks.

One technique used by check kiters is to steal checks from the back of personal and business checkbooks, hoping some time passes before the victim discovers the checks missing and can stop payment on them. Knowing that Benningfield was resorting to stealing from his girlfriend to feed his drug habit, I predicted he would hit a bank soon.

The following Friday, I was out of service in District Four when a bank robbery was aired at Columbia Savings on South Colorado Boulevard. I jumped in my police vehicle and headed red light and siren across town to George's "cool pad."

As I drove up East 17th Avenue, I turned off my emergency equipment. George was heading toward me and turned in front of me and pulled to the curb. I have no idea how he did not see me in my marked unit—or if he did why he didn't suspect I was going to pop him. I pulled up behind him and got out, gun in hand.

Benningfield came out of his car, cash falling from his suit jacket pockets. The bills sequential numbered "bait money." George started grabbing his crotch and jumping around and requested to go into the house and go to the bathroom. I denied his request and arrested him, then called for backup on police radio channel three.

On the front seat of the gold car were the curly haired disguise, glue, and glasses. The choicest bit of evidence was a list of all the Columbia Savings branches, with the ones he had robbed checked off. Under the driver's seat was a loaded revolver wrapped in a Wall Street Journal.

The gun was found to be registered to Raymond Buckles, which did not surprise me. Ray probably "rented" him the gun. In the ashtray were "doobies," partially smoked marijuana cigarettes.

When I finally got the guts to call dispatch, I said 414, to identify my precinct, and informed the dispatch operator I had the Columbia Savings bank robber at 2104 East 17th Avenue. After a pause, the dispatcher asked, "Where are you, 414?" Still, on the adrenalin rush from a thrilling bust, I knew I was going to be in big trouble for many rule violations. I was not wrong.

I heard that Capt. Mulnix was livid, and one sergeant wanted to file a score of internal charges against me. Sgt. Tony Iacovetta came to my rescue, claiming he had given me permission to go on the mission. Capt. Brannan had something to do with the sergeant covering my ass and piled on by adding I was going to get a commendation. Brannan always appreciated good police work, and he had my back.

I had Benningfield's gold car towed, and we took George downtown to Headquarters. I called Brian Jovick—the FBI agent who did not support my notion that it was Benningfield in the surveillance photos weeks earlier—and asked him to come down because I had arrested the Columbia Savings robber. This was Benningfield's sixth robbery. Jovick came down and could not believe I was right. I had bragging rights.

George said he needed to know how I caught him. I told him it was his nose and I showed him the picture from the bank surveillance camera. He said he was glad I got him, rather than some rookie.

The next day, the headline in the *Rocky Mountain News* read "S&L Robbery Unites 2 Police Celebrities." I smiled, imagining my detractors cringing that I was still out there catching the bad guys, and garnering headlines to boot. This was a big pinch.

George Benningfield pled guilty to the bank robberies and got 20 years. In 1983, a Federal judge cut his sentence to 5-1/2 years. The man robbed six banks at gunpoint, then received a huge reduction in his sentence. I never figured out how he accomplished this magic trick, but he wasn't our average criminal.

When George got out of the joint, we occasionally went to Furr's Cafeteria for lunch. He had great stories and told me a lot about how the big-time armed robbers cased their targets before robbing them. They had tricks like double-switching vehicles, donning disguises and layered clothing, equipping their getaway vehicles with radios that tuned to police frequencies. And seasoned bank robbers had proven strategies on how to take and maintain control of the robbery scene with their guns.

Years after his criminal exploits, George and I had gone to lunch a couple of times. One day I noticed that all of the condiments had disappeared from the table. I asked George, "Where are the salt and pepper shakers, sugar packets and other stuff that were on the table." He was matter of fact, without a hint of guilt. Crime was a way of life for George, and it never crossed his mind to do anything differently. "I gots them in my pockets so I can take them home." I told him to put them back on the table. I could just imagine the headlines, "Bank Robber and Super Cop Arrested for Theft of Condiments."

By the way, I did have George speak at my Little Bird Club meeting. He was fabulous, regaling the Thunderbird enthusiasts with stories about his life of crime. George said he started off stealing bicycles, but once he developed a drug habit, he escalated to committing armed robberies of restaurants and banks. He hedged his bets by traveling outside Colorado for most of his heists.

The club members were in awe. I have been in the club for over 25 years and have developed many friends. Cruising down the road listening to oldies while driving my "Little Bird" always made me happy. One time when I was defending myself in a department investigation, the club members stepped forward to defend me. True friendship and loyalty are rare, and I've never forgotten my real friends.

* * * *

When I was under Department probe, most of my "friends" would scatter. They did not want to stand near me, fearing the lightning would strike them. This hurt and made me sad. Throughout my career, I never testified against a fellow officer in a departmental hearing or a court of law.

I was "Old School" and would never give up a cop. We don't "eat our own." My loyalty limit would have been reached if a cop was dealing drugs or committing crimes such as rape, burglary, theft or robbery. They are not worthy of wearing the badge.

* * * *

I once had solid information that two cops were dealing marijuana, so I drafted a search warrant to kick in their house. I showed up at the office and told Sgt. Michaud that I was going to get a search warrant signed for two cops.

He made me wait while he talked it over with Capt. Mulnix, who told me I had to take my affidavit and search warrant to the Internal Affairs Bureau. A cop shop is a paramilitary organization, in structure and operation. Young cops are pounded with the policy that they must do everything they are ordered to do and to follow the chain of command. Unfortunately, that often leads to paralysis by analysis. Too much thinking and not enough action.

My mistake in the cop pot situation was if I had gotten a judge to sign it before I went to the office, the brass would have been forced to let me execute it. I heard many months later someone got the dope dealing cops after they had left the job.

I realized early on that not all of my fellow officers shared my enthusiasm for doing police work. They criticized me, saying I was an egomaniac and a grandstander. Some cops claimed I broke the law and violated people's rights. They never slammed me to my face; they didn't have the balls. In many cases, it was just professional jealousy, and I had rubbed their egos raw.

There was nothing stopping any other officer from becoming what I saw in myself—an effective pro-active cop who over a long period had developed skills and systems to catch bad guys. Many of my cohorts apparently were satisfied with their "business as usual" approach, but they enjoyed criticizing me.

I have always had respect for officers who work their patrol cars, answer their calls and strive to be the best cops they can be. I also respect detectives who work their cases and solve many of them.

Not every officer was cut out to do what I did. It required lots of dedication and time in working informants, verifying and corroborating information, surveillance, and research. The exposure I subjected myself to would be shared by few. They wouldn't put themselves in a vulnerable position.

Every day I matched wits with—and dealt with—dangerous characters who committed crimes as a way of life. Regular civilians go to work every day, taking on whatever tasks are necessary to do their job. Criminals have the same approach, except they operate from the perspective of a base opportunist, committing whatever crimes becomes available that might benefit them, or intentionally choosing and planning a criminal act.

A substantial percentage of bad guys and gals are supporting a drug habit. The bad guys were not safe from my knowledge of the criminal element, my network of informants and my ability to piece together complex information and investigations. Each day when I went to work, I was hoping to catch some of these criminals and separate them from society. I wanted to look them in the eye and tell them, "You can't hurt anyone today."

CHAPTER 15—
SPECIAL WEAPONS AND TACTICS (SWAT)—
7-83 to 9-84

In July of 1983, Capt. Jerry Kennedy was the commander of Special Weapons and Tactics (SWAT) Unit, which was part of The Metro Unit. He somehow got me transferred out of District Four to the SWAT unit. He and Capt. Brannan worked together in hopes of getting me back into position to be promoted to detective again.

Capt. Kennedy wanted me to develop information on cases that the SWAT Unit could turn into investigations and arrests. The Metro/SWAT guys were a cool team of highly trained professionals who conducted dangerous assignments, often confronting armed, desperate individuals. The SWAT was involved in its fair share of shootings and deserved the recognition it received.

SWAT was doing all the "entries" for the Denver Police Department, which removed a fun element from my police work. However, much work officers like me did in laying the groundwork for a case and gaining the search warrant, the SWAT got to kick in the door and secure the premises. Once the SWAT got into full swing, I had to retire "The Key"—which is what I called my 10-pound sledgehammer—that I had used for years for my entries.

After I joined the SWAT, our first arrests were two escapees from the Department of Corrections and two parole violators who were all holed up together in a home. I know some cops would have felt privileged and relieved to have their own entry team. But for me, it took the fun out of doing search warrants and apprehending wanted felons. Of course, I kept The Key, just in case.

The SWAT Unit got credit for correctly identifying and arresting two gunmen who robbed a Shop 'N' Go when I IDed them from a surveillance photo. The Unit supplied info to Nevada law enforcement that resulted in an arrest in an unsolved homicide.

Lakewood Dets. Powell and Evans obtained arrest warrants for two dangerous individuals from The Westwood Projects. The SWAT unit responded to the address I provided and found the suspects out in the open, in front of the tenement. They were arrested for multiple stabbings in Lakewood. Both were career criminals, and the SWAT captured a third man for possession of illegal drugs.

The SWAT Unit worked in harmony to locate and arrest Solomon Vigil, who had been molesting children of both genders for over 15 years. There was no crime too low for the career criminal and drug addict, who also committed burglaries, armed robberies, and forgeries. He proved slippery, and locating and arresting him required many attempts and misses. But at the end of the process, numerous cases were prosecuted against him.

The Metro Unit, along with Sgt. J. Lindsey and Officer Pat Powers, entered a residence seeking two men wanted for felony theft. We hooked the two suspects, stolen checks, altered IDs and a stolen car. They were running a forgery ring.

* * * *

We were making small arrests, which kept me busy, but I also was working on some big investigations. I developed information that a fugitive wanted out of Utah for a triple murder was laying up in a North Denver home. Officers Gary Hoffman and Dave Quinones and I set up surveillance of the house.

We observed four individuals leaving the house in a truck, which we followed and stopped. Our target was not with them, but they confirmed he was inside the house. Members of the Metro unit, led by Sgts. Vince DiManna and Tony DiPinto made entry and Ulibarri was arrested. He stated his name was Sonny Murillo, but we already had him pegged as Ulibarri based on the mug shots from Utah.

* * * *

Det. Dennis Cribari and I got onto a major check passer, Mauri McCance, who built a major racket by stealing numerous payroll checks from area businesses. In one year, she passed hundreds of those checks for about $450 each.

Her check ring members worked in various janitorial services just long enough to duplicate the building keys. They entered the buildings weeks later to steal the checks from the back of the checkbooks. They then passed them on weekends after 6 p.m. when the banks were closed, and none of the information could be verified.

We executed search warrants at a number of her homes, seizing 1,700 stolen checks and a cache of cocaine. McCance's ring included 10 check passers. She was the most wanted check passer in Colorado at the time and was ripping off business owners for hundreds of thousands of dollars. The Metro Unit hit three homes to put the forgery operation out of business after their year long run of "paper and ink" crimes.

* * * *

One of my top informants contacted me to tell me a couple of "ounce men" were traveling to Colorado Springs to cop multiple ounces of drugs from a Hispanic male who looks like a black man. I immediately thought of the fugitive Benny "Tar Baby" Maciel, who had been on the lam for a decade. He was the main "mule" for Jaime Quintana—the primary supplier of heroin to Colorado.

Benny got nabbed in 1974 coming across the Mexican border with 11-1/2 pounds of high-grade heroin, 19 ounces of cocaine and 38 ounces of marijuana. The destination for that huge supply of drugs was Jaime Quintana in Denver. Benny and David Maciel were part of a 13-member drug ring.

Benny had been a fugitive since pleading guilty and failing to show up for sentencing. "Tar Baby" had been on my hit parade for 10 years and this tip gave me hope I just may have found him. It made sense. Benny was able to travel to the source in Mexico, meaning he could go direct. I would have bet at the time he had to pay back some amount of money to the "connect" to get even. If he was now dealing only ounces, he had to be importing multi kilos, at 2.2 pounds per kilo, of heroin per month.

In further questioning, my CI described a 5'8" Hispanic male in his fifties who looked black but was definitely Hispanic. My CI said he had traveled with these "ounce men" on two occasions and had seen the dark-skinned man who had no name. I showed my CI an old picture, and he said it could be the same guy. I felt it had to be my fugitive.

I went to the Major Peddler Unit because I knew I would need help following the ounce man to the Springs. I met with Sgt. Dino DeNovellis, who was nicknamed "The Torpedo." He was tall and slim and was a seasoned narc. I proposed that he would run the deal while I ran the informant. He wanted both ends of the operation, and I said no.

I was not going to have my informant identified or burned in this deal. Besides, I did not have a good experience with him during the "Popeye" investigation. I was shocked he did not want a piece of the action, considering whom I believed the major player to be and with the prospect of seizing kilos of heroin.

So, I went right over to the DEA Task Force which was comprised of agents from the DEA, and officers from police departments along Denver's Front Range. My timing was perfect. The Task Force had nothing of note going, and I used my salesmanship to convince them it would be fun, with the potential of nabbing multiple kilos of smack.

The fugitive alone would have been a big pinch. My deal was explicit and clear: They would stay away from my CI, there was no documentation of my CI, and my CI would be paid a fair sum of money if we scored big. They agreed, and we organized the operation. I teamed with DEA Agents Lee Chamberlain and Rick Barrett.

They put the eye in the sky with DPD Det. Mike Patrick aboard and we followed the ounce man to The Bamboo Hut Bar on Larimer Street, where he switched vehicles and took off south through Denver. He got on southbound I -25, stopping for a "tail check" at a rest stop between Castle Rock and the Springs, then continuing southward.

We followed the ounce man to a restaurant in Colorado Springs, where he met a man who turned out to be David Maciel, Benny's brother. We tailed him to Benny Maciel's home where he linked up with Benny. They drove together to and entered a wooded area south of town, then returned to Benny's house.

The Drug Enforcement Agency airplane guided agents on the ground into the woods to the spot where the suspects had stopped. The ground team found a kilo of heroin buried in a modified Prestone antifreeze container.

The Maciel brothers were arrested at their home. Benny had four ounces of heroin in his pocket. I explained to him that I was going to serve a search warrant on his house and vehicles. He told me that there were six to seven pounds of heroin in his trunk and more in the house.

Neighbors called the gated house the "Fortress." I bristled when one of the DEA agents said we got "lucky." When a basketball player makes 90 percent of his free throws, it's not luck. When a goalie lunges from one post to the other to snatch the puck out of mid-air, it's not luck. Luck is when preparation meets opportunity. I had never stopped being vigilant about "Tar Baby" Maciel, and when I received the tip from my CI, I engineered a pursuit and arrest. There was no luck involved.

Benny was really interesting to talk with. He told me the story of how he rose to be the major supplier of heroin in Colorado. It all stemmed from him working for Jaime Quintana for many years and Jaime going on the run. Benny just kept the business going with the same supplier and ounce men. He did not have to fear reprisal from the supplier for the drugs that were seized, or ever have to pay him back because he paid for the large shipment of smack up front. Now that's cash flow.

At the time we brought down their operation, Benny and David Maciel were selling 12 pounds of heroin a month, netting in the neighborhood of $1.5 million dollars, depending on the strength of the batch. I estimate they were bringing in about $10 million dollars a year. The house and all of their vehicles were registered in false names. Benjamin had ID in the name Chris Martinez, David was using the name David Cortez, and both had government driver's licenses.

Colorado Springs P.D. seized the house, $43,000 cash, and all of the cars. The seizure was nine pounds of high-grade heroin. It's hard to get my mind around the money and heroin we did not seize. Over the decade Maciel was a fugitive, the ring didn't miss a beat.

The "Tar Baby" investigation constituted the largest heroin seizure in Colorado in a decade. The investigation team went out that night to celebrate, and they treated me to a lobster dinner. Next day's *Rocky Mountain News* headline: "Police Arrest Number One Heroin Dealer in State."

This was a whopper for The Tactical Support Bureau and Capt. Kennedy got bragging rights. He always appreciated good police work and would make his officers feel good about doing hard work.

I went to Headquarters the next day, and when I got off the elevator, Division Chief Mulnix jumped my ass in the hallway. He was livid that I did not give the case to the Major Peddler Unit. I explained that Dino "The Torpedo" demanded the deal plus my CI, and I said no. I further informed Division Chief Mulnix that he would not have given up his CI either. That stopped him dead in his tracks.

He thought about what I said and walked off after we had made a scene and screamed at me in front of my cohorts. Days later I received a commendation from Mulnix, praising me and the quality of the bust. I just shook my head. Sometimes the words have been said, and the damage is done.

One constant in the Denver Police Department for all of the years I worked there: Most of the brass were ready to fly into a rage over any perceived misdeed, but they were never willing to apologize for anything they did, no matter how wrong they were.

* * * *

Det. Larry Subia and I teamed up to pursue a female speed cook from Winter Haven, Florida who was reported to be a sophisticated chemist. My informant stated she would move her methamphetamine lab after every cook, but that she was moving around the Denver Metro area. This poses a lot of long-term problems because methamphetamine manufacture is a messy operation that spews toxins into its environment.

I initiated a joint investigation with the Major Peddler Unit and Det. Gary Salazar. She was reported to have professional glassware and chemicals. We had worked on her from September of 1983 to April of 1984, but always found ourselves one step behind her.

We received solid information that she was at the address. Our surveillance team consisted of Dets. Gary Salazar, Darrell Wisdom, Mike Martinez, Pat Fitzgibbons, Mike Fetro, George Fortunato, Jeff Reutz and Dennis Cribari. Surveillance observed the "cook," Nikki Carr, repeatedly moving items from the home reported to house her lab to a waiting vehicle. Our information was that she was moving her lab back to a storage locker.

Metro Unit Officers Harlan and Palermo made the stop, and a search warrant for the vehicle was executed. Nikki Carr had a "stand up" lab with all of the glassware, and the chemicals, including Phenyl 2 Propanol (P2P) and ether. Seized from the vehicle were chemicals, a written formula to make methamphetamine, glassware and liquid speed that had not yet been converted to powder.

Sgt. Tony Iacovetta led a SWAT team that made entry into the home. We seized chemicals, glassware, cash and a gun. A room was located in the basement which was still partially set up as a lab. All of the windows were blacked out, and water had been piped in.

The third search warrant was executed at a self-storage facility. Seized from the locker were chemicals including ether, glassware, chemistry books, a book on court testimony and several pounds of speed powder. The methamphetamine was of very high grade. Her product was selling for about $1,400 per ounce wholesale. Once she "stepped on" the synthesized amphetamine by cutting it with inert ingredients, it was worth many times that amount. Nikki Carr was truly a master "cook" and a major distributor of methamphetamine in the Denver Metro area.

* * * *

In 1984, Alan Berg was a nationally recognized radio show host and got through-the-roof ratings based on his bombastic and caustic style. He was one of the early shock jocks. A lot of it was schtick, but he was extremely bright and knowledgeable about a wide range of subjects.

Berg reveled in ticking people off, and in at least one instance it all went far too far. He had gone out to dinner with his ex-wife, Judith, and rolled up to his residence in his VW beetle. His voice was silenced there, in his driveway, in a hail of automatic gunfire.

Berg was passionate about a number of issues, including standing up against any form of hatred based on bigotry. Over the air, he had engaged in heated arguments with members of a white supremacist group called The

Order. One of their primary goals was annihilating Jews, and Alan Berg was quite clearly a Jew.

He had antagonized them openly, and when they couldn't win the war of words, they resorted to a war of bullets. Berg was educated, flamboyant in speech and dress, and billed himself as "The man you love to hate." But despite his broad intellect, he had no comprehension of the scope of hatred he would reap.

In 1987, the Feds arrested four members of The Order. David Lane was sentenced to 150 years and died in a Terre Haute, Indiana prison in 2007 of an epileptic seizure. Bruce Pierce received the same 150-year sentence, plus another century of incarceration for robberies he had committed to financially support The Order. Pierce was 56 years old and in year 23 of a 252-year sentence at the Allenwood Federal Correctional Complex in Pennsylvania when he died of "natural causes" in 2010.

Richard Scutari was the alleged lookout during Berg's murder and was sentenced to 60 years on federal racketeering charges. He has been at the Marion federal prison in Illinois—regarded as one of the nation's most brutal—since 2008. Jean Craig was charged, but acquitted, of helping The Order prepare for the murder by following Berg. However, she was convicted of other related charges.

Bob Mathews, co-founder of The Order, was believed to be a lookout during the assassination. Before he could be prosecuted, he died in a blaze of F.B.I. gunfire near his home on Whidbey Island off the coast of Washington.

No one was ever convicted of Alan Berg's murder, per se. However, the case is a testament to how law enforcement, working in concert and over time, can get its tentacles around even massive criminal organizations. It often starts with one case, carefully investigated by local cops. The Order investigation resulted in eight trials and convictions of more than 75 people on charges including conspiracy, racketeering, armored car robbery, counterfeiting, transporting stolen money, and violation of civil rights.

On a personal level, we as police feared that Alan could become a victim of violence, spurred by his rhetoric toward the white supremacists. One day not long before his murder, I shared that concern with him. Away from the microphone, out of the studio, Alan was generally a calm and even reserved man.

He was generous, and people liked him. Fellow Denver talk show giant Peter Boyle had worked at the same stations with Berg, and had competed with him for Nielson and Arbitron ratings, but was always his friend. Peter was devastated by Alan's murder.

* * * *

An informant gave up a bad guy, Benny Lovato, who was wanted out of Raton, New Mexico for aggravated assault of a police officer. Though he was wanted out of New Mexico, Lovato was a career criminal from Denver with a lengthy record.

Sgt. Tony Iacovetta led Metro SWAT officers Mark Lewis, Bruce Tow, and Kenny Overman, with assistance from District Four officers Pringle, Scott, and Escobedo. They set up surveillance on a "cool pad" on Lincoln Street.

Two suspects exited the apartment and entered the vehicle described by the informant. The car was stopped, and the driver produced a phony California driver's license bearing a fictitious name. The driver was Lovato. He had shaved off his mustache and dyed his white hair black in an attempt to avoid apprehension.

The passenger was also a career crook. We learned that they were visiting another long-time bad guy who we had targeted in 1977 and caught both of them burglarizing two homes. They were convicted and served time on the 1977 rap.

* * * *

I received information from an informant that four men were going to rob Tiffany Travel in Lakewood. I contacted Lakewood Officers Mike Powell and Steve Evans, who I had worked with on countless stickup cases and executing search warrants. They were great "old school" detectives and agreed to set up a stakeout.

Sgt. Burdell Burch was in charge of the stakeout and decided two undercover detectives would pose as travel agents inside Tiffany Travel. The rest of the team set up a perimeter. Surveillance was set up at 9 a.m., and two hours later a vehicle matching the description of the stickup vehicle pulled into the complex with three males inside.

They parked, and Henry "Cornyo" Alavarez and his son Ruben Alvarez exited the vehicle. They got to the door and pulled down their masks and attempted to enter, but the door was locked. They went to the other door and again pulled down their masks, guns in hand, and entered the agency.

The staged officers challenged the bandits, who escaped from the agency with detectives in pursuit. Ruben threw away a loaded and cocked Beretta semi-automatic pistol as he fled. Henry left his mask on as he ran away, tossing his loaded automatic weapon just before I caught and arrested him.

The getaway driver took off when he saw the foot chase and was not apprehended. Neither the senior nor junior Alvarez would give up the identity of the getaway driver. I suspected he was another relative since they were traveling on the "family plan." Henry is a career criminal with prior convictions for armed robbery. Both were sent to the pen for the armed robbery.

CHAPTER 16—
CRIMINAL INVESTIGATIONS DIVISION—
9-84 to 10-86

I was in SWAT for a year when Division Chief Mulnix went to Capt. Kennedy and told him he was taking me to the Detective Bureau because frankly he said, "I cannot take the competition of Cinquanta grabbing the headlines." I went to Chief Coogan to try to derail this train; I was happy where I was. My effort accomplished nothing; I was headed to the Detective Training Program.

I started in Auto Theft. Then I was moved to the Fugitive Detail with Jimmy Wessels, a smart, detailed detective also enjoyed chasing and capturing outlaws. He was a big guy, so I informed him he would enter first when we were kicking a door. He thought that was funny.

We nabbed a bunch of fugitives and were having fun. I got the feeling Sgt. Boydston did not like me very much. He kept an incident book on me, listing minor infractions. I didn't have to be a detective to sense he was building a case on me.

We returned late one night after an arrest, and as I passed his door, I checked the knob. It was unlocked, which was pretty sloppy for a sergeant. The next day we heard that someone had entered his office to steal items. It was being investigated.

* * * *

I was on the third floor of the downtown Police HQ when I saw a command officer studying in his office on the taxpayer's dime. He was not the first person to study for a promotional exam or a degree. Cops commonly brought stacks of 3"x5" cards to study on off-duty jobs. Exam results were posted.

A typical list showed that 30 people had passed the test, and they were ranked 1 to 30. Number 1 scored the highest, but funny business kicked in around number 9 with some wild cards such as someone was a friend of the brass or a "chosen one" designated for promotion before the test was taken.

The administration would dig all the way to number 9 to promote their guy, then promote everyone above him on the list. Then the list might die. I sometimes predicted how deep the brass would reach into the list to get their favored choice.

Rank and abuse of power were constant bedfellows on the Denver Police Department. I worked with boozers and wild horse riders. They would party, drink, chase women and have fun with the guys. Then one day they got rank and changed. They had taken a "pure pill" and were suddenly qualified and emboldened to pass judgment on their fellow officers and friends. They suddenly were part of The Brass in The Ivory Tower, and some would go out of their way to hand out discipline that sometimes resulted in suspensions or worse.

The best supervisors were those who would talk to the officer about what he may have done wrong rather than filing on him. Once an internal punishment was filed, it could cost an officer money with a suspension or even end his career.

Some sergeants who were exceptional supervisors and good people were Casey Simpson, Chuck Saterberg, Al Kinney, Fred Carter, Ralph Benfante, Tony Iacovetta, Mike

O'Neil, Doug Hildebrandt, Harold Oaks, Ed Hanson, Bob Cantwell, Fred Carter and John Thompson.

The command officers I worked under and respected were Chief Art Dill, Division Chief Paul Montoya, Capts. Larry Britton, John Hindes, Doug White, Don Brannan, Tom Lahey, Jerry Kennedy and Art Hutchinson, and Lts. Steve Metros and George Torsney.

I had great respect for John Simonet. He had integrity and could not be influenced by the Liberal Political Machine in Denver. He believed in the truth and had a sense of fair play. He came to my defense when he was Denver Manager of Safety over the Police, Fire and Sheriff Departments.

Simonet blocked Division Chief Mulnix from suspending me after a kid laid down his bicycle while I was stopped at a stop sign. I had nothing to do with him hitting the pavement. He refused my offer of aid, then rode off. Later the father complained, and the department made me buy him a new bike. It was unbelievable. At various points, Simonet was Director of Corrections and Denver Sheriff. They named the new jail after him.

* * * *

A criminal crew was targeting cigarette delivery trucks and robbing the drivers at gunpoint in Lakewood and Denver. I received a tip from an informant that Paul Quintana and Richard Mascarenas were pulling the hijackings, taking the driver at gunpoint, tying him up and putting him in the back of the truck. They drove off with the vans, unloaded the cases of cigarettes and left the drivers tied up in the rear of the vans.

Capt. Doug White gave me permission to gather some men to conduct an eight-day surveillance on the duo.

Lakewood P.D. pitched in, and we deployed Sgts. Tim Cuthrell and Doug Hildebrandt, Dets. Calvin Hemphill, Jim Wessels and Lt. Dave Michaud. Jim Negri piloted the helicopter.

We observed the suspects casing vending machine distributors. They seemed to key on one distributor, which loaned us a delivery van for use as bait. Det. Hemphill took the wheel while Sgt. Cuthrell hid among the cigarette cases in the back of the van.

Surveillance followed a trio of men from their home to the distributor that was working with us. Hemphill picked up cases of cigarettes at the distribution center and drove to the rear of King Soopers at West Alameda Avenue and Zuni Street. The trio was following the van. The secluded loading dock lured them into feeling comfortable in pulling another armed robbery.

Hemphill parked the van as the trio was advancing on him. He exited the van as the surveillance team closed in and made the arrest. Tim burst from the rear door of the van in Hollywood style, gun in hand. They were armed, but we nabbed them with no shots fired. Quintana, Mascarenas and their accomplice were convicted of aggravated robbery and kidnapping.

* * * *

Early one September morning in 1984, I was headed to work down Federal Boulevard when an armed robbery alert came out of the McDonald's restaurant on West 38th Avenue. An ambulance was called because someone had been shot.

I drove to the scene and found that a young female clerk had been shot with a shotgun by a lone masked gunman. Her name was Pauline Roybal. As I looked at this young woman. I knew that her parents and friends were going to be devastated. I also knew that I wanted to work on solving this tragic killing.

The gunman had walked in, shot a defenseless woman with a shotgun, forced the manager at gunpoint to open the safe, and taken the money from the safe while she lay on the floor bleeding. I drove directly to Headquarters and into the Robbery Unit to view all of the new surveillance photos they had recently gathered. One was of a suspect who had robbed a Farm Crest store a month earlier. In that robbery, the masked gunman used a sawed-off shotgun.

I figured out the gunman had committed a dozen armed robberies to date. While examining the photos, I noticed the eyebrow and head shape of the suspect resembled those of a bad guy I knew as Banner Molinar. I showed the picture to Bob Hollingshead, who had arrested Molinar in the past, and he agreed. He focused in on the suspect's beard line and wrists. My partner Jim Wessels also agreed.

Capt. White gave me permission to draw together a team to be led by Lt. Dave Michaud of the Homicide detail. Capt. White never denied me when I wanted men to conduct surveillance to catch a crook. The team consisted of members of the Assault detail—Dets. Ron Mayoral, James Wessels, and Don Gabel—along with Jefferson County D.A. Investigator Mike Russell.

We had to tail Molinar because even though we had internal consensus on his identity based on the surveillance photos, we did not have enough probable cause to execute a search warrant. The goal was to search his home to seize evidence such as the sawed-off shotgun, mask, and clothing to link him to Pauline's killing.

One of my informants indicated Molinar was pulling armed robberies and burglaries to support his out-of-control drug habit, which centered on mainlining heroin and using coke. We began around-the-clock surveillance of Molinar, who was living on Umatilla Street. One night we followed him on foot to a supermarket.

On his way back home, he stopped in a residential area and removed meat items from his pants that he had boosted. Our van was parked on the street, one house down from his home. One night Molinar walked across the street, smoking a joint, and stood in front of the van with his hands on his hips like he was daring whoever was inside to come out. The detective inside the van whispered into the radio that if Molinar broke into the van, he was going to blast him.

Twelve days after the killing at McDonald's, Molinar and accomplice Larry Garcia drove around for eight hours, chasing targets. They looked over restaurants, fast food spots, gas stations, and bars. Molinar finally got out of the car at a Pester gas station on South Wadsworth Boulevard in Lakewood. He crouched to put on a mask and armed himself with a handgun, then walked toward the station. Surveillance officers confronted him and repeatedly told him to drop his gun. Molinar moved between two fences and turned to point his gun at officers when Det. Mayoral shot him in the leg.

After his arrest, Molinar stated to me that the shotgun he had was faulty and would just go off. He told me to check out his leg. He stated he had put the rifle in his belt pointing downward when it just went off and strafed his leg. There was evidence that his leg had suffered trauma, with vertical wounds consistent with buckshot marks. I told him that was not a defense to murder. Molinar would not confess.

I served a search warrant on his house, and we recovered clothing—but no shotgun. He had kept all of the newspaper articles detailing his robberies, including Pauline's killing.

Following the arrest, I provided some of Molinar's drug connections to Sgt. B.J. Hays. Through his interviews, he developed Sandra Morehouse, who told him that her boyfriend Jim Knight was the driver of a borrowed car in commission of the McDonald's homicide and robbery. Sgt. Hays had just developed the most important piece of evidence to link Molinar to the murder.

Knight admitted to Sgt. Hays that he drove Molinar to and from the McDonald's because he owed Molinar $1,500 for cocaine. Knight said Molinar had told him after exiting the robbery scene that he had shot the female clerk in the shoulder. She was shot in the abdomen. Knight also admitted to burying the shotgun in a trash dumpster, which was hauled away the next day.

Molinar made jailhouse confessions to a number of inmates, but they sounded more like bragging than remorse. According to the inmates, Molinar said he did not like heroes and thought she was trying to be one, so he blew her head off. Banner Molinar was a vicious criminal with no conscience. His rap sheet showed convictions on 12 felonies, including murder, aggravated robbery, burglary, and theft. He was a habitual criminal and a menace to society.

Pauline was a young woman with a big dream of saving money from her job at McDonald's to buy a Corvette that she wanted to drive to a Bronco game. One day a slimeball stole a special young lady from the world. Her family was exceptional and loved her very much, with her Dad driving her the two blocks to work every day.

The trial was held before Judge Robert Fullerton. The prosecution was led by Bill Buckley, a seasoned prosecutor who had sent many murderers to the penitentiary. Steve Flavin was the attorney defending Molinar. We gave Buckley an airtight case, and he prosecuted it flawlessly.

At the end, the jury was out for two hours before entering their verdict of guilty to first-degree murder. Molinar received a life sentence, plus 30 years for the attempted robbery of the gas station. The court sentenced him to two additional life sentences for a pair of armed burglaries in Adams County.

In April of 1986, Banner Molinar was found dead in his prison cell. Authorities determined he overdosed on heroin and codeine and choked on his own vomit. He had recent needle marks on his arm and heroin in his system. The coroner ruled it an accidental overdose. The thing that doesn't add up: there was no syringe near the body. To me, this indicates that he got a "hot shot." I figure someone intentionally supplied him with a super-strong syringe full of smack or someone actually shot him up with heroin to kill him.

Drugs routinely are smuggled into correctional facilities, whether by visitors who transfer the drugs during a kiss, hide the drugs in a body cavity or on their children, or by corrupt corrections staff. A scattering of inmates deal drugs behind bars, and more than a few prison assaults and murders result from debts to drug suppliers.

The solving of the Roybal murder was one of the most fulfilling of my career. I know Molinar's death gave the

Roybal family a degree of closure for the loss of their daughter, but I also know some wounds never heal.

* * * *

In June of 1984, serial stickup Anthony Martinez was on a roll, having committed 17 armed robberies in Denver, Lakewood, Wheat Ridge, Aurora, Westminster, Thornton and Adams County. Officers from all of those jurisdictions were pursuing Martinez and his female accomplice.

Sgt. Paul Mueller, Det. Jim Wessels and I located a vehicle known to be used by Martinez on Hazel Court. The car was being driven by a career criminal one evening, and we followed it to the Mesa Motel on West Colfax Avenue in Lakewood.

We set up surveillance on the room, which was entered by the driver, a known heroin dealer and user. We observed Martinez looking out the window. However, we did not realize that Lakewood Agents Ken Perry, Greg Bramblett, and John Kuebler had been running the motels on Colfax to show Martinez' picture and had learned that he was in room 24.

Every jurisdiction and officer were doing their jobs, but this was not our most coordinated effort. We also did not know Dets. Larry Subia and Dennis Cribari were running intelligence on the motels and had gotten a hit from the manager and had set up surveillance from a room at the Mesa Motel. They were told that Lakewood agents were in another room, watching the activity surrounding room 24. I did not know the Lakewood agents, and they did not know us.

All of the officers were undercover, making for an unpredictable and possibly dangerous situation. The most dangerous situations sometimes involved undercover officers from different jurisdictions who were unaware of each other's presence on a stakeout.

So here we are on surveillance from the parking lot—gearing up to kick the door if the suspects don't come out soon—not realizing we are in a precarious situation that could result in a shootout and crossfire.

The bad guy and gal exited the room when seven detectives jumped them, cutting off access to their car. Lakewood cops seized the evidence and the suspect because it was in their jurisdiction. We ended the three-person crime spree by arresting Martinez, his female accomplice, and the driver—and recovered the gun used in the robberies.

* * * *

Lots of Americans live in the streets. Considering the policeman's job is keep people safe, the good cops spend lots of time in the streets. One night a wino informed me that I could find someone who had died next to a certain building. Sure enough, the body was there. Many cops made a habit of using their nightsticks to break the bottles of winos, leaving glass shards in brown paper bag. I never did that, because it wasn't my job to be sadistic. That's why the down-and-outer had bothered to tell me about the dead man.

One night I got a call from a homeless man whom I had befriended, occasionally handing him a few dollars. He was articulate and had come from a good family, but fell on bad times. He told me he lived in a "Hobo Jungle" at Santa Fe Drive and Mississippi Avenue. Neither I nor any of my fellow officers had ever heard of a "Hobo Jungle" anywhere in Denver. But it was there because we went to investigate.

The area was lined with culverts nearly large enough to stand in. The homeless men had made a dwelling in each culvert. Somewhere along the line, the hobos had stolen baseball bats out of a boxcar, and each pipe house was equipped with a shiny new baseball bat for self-defense. The homeless men had formed a community, with a code that no resident would steal from another.

However, in his call, the homeless man told me that he watched someone beat the Hobo Ruler to death with one of the bats, just to take over his house. As the Hobo Ruler, he lived in an abandoned boxcar. My partner and I turned the case over to the Homicide unit, and Baker-4, the crime lab, came to investigate the murder.

* * * *

I had been working on solving a number of capers that Dets. Subia and Cribari were scoring first. They were a very effective team, having developed a network of informants that they knew how to capitalize on. In one case, I had been looking for a crook, and here came Subia and Cribari out of a house I was going to hit.

They had the guy in chains, and Subia said, "You snooze, you lose." That got my attention. I knew I was going to have to work harder, smarter and quicker because they were on a mission. I could see they were really happy when they beat me to a pinch. But it was healthy competition because we were getting criminals off the street, and I was willing to prove I was up to the actual challenge.

* * * *

Wessels and I heard about a serial rapist who was targeting single women living in ground-floor apartments. He was hitting the area from Wolff to Ames Street in

Lakewood and from West 6th Avenue to West Colfax Avenue.

The violence of his sexual assaults was escalating, and he was using sharp objects to get his victims to cooperate. Twice he had cut the backs of his victims with a knife. It was only a matter of time until he killed his first victim.

Most of the women were single or divorced mothers, 23 to 34 years of age, with their child or children sleeping nearby. He made his entry through open windows and doors during the summer months, when it was the only means the women had to keep their apartments cool.

He was described as a thin Hispanic male, about 17 years old. We suspected he walked, rode a bicycle or took the bus, which would increase his visibility, contrasted to the relative anonymity of driving in a car. We believed he was chasing the victims to making sure they were alone before burglarizing their apartments and raping them.

I have always had a theory about budding juvenile rapists: they start out as "peepers" and burglars who steal female underwear, bras or lingerie.

We pulled ten "squawks"—complaints—in the geographic box that we suspected were connected to the serial rapist. He had been raping women for two years. Jimmy went to work on the computer looking for a young burglar in or near the "box" who pilfered female undergarments.

We had previously received information from an informant about a burglar and rapist named Toby who was active in Denver. Bingo! It all locked together when zeroed in on Toby Zapata, who lived at 658 Perry St., which was close to the target area.

We grabbed the fingerprint files from an offense in Denver and one in Lakewood. We pulled Zapata's print card, mug shot and criminal record and went to the crime lab to have them compared. We got positive comparisons in Denver and Lakewood. Jimmy and I went to the Sex Detail and notified Sgt. Curt Williams and Det. Darrold Hudley of our investigation.

We had dubbed this predator "The Walking Rapist." Williams and Hudley obtained a probable-cause warrant for Zapata's arrest. We went to his house in the early morning and arrested him in his bed.

He denied being a rapist. We told Toby he was right, he was not a rapist but was a burglar, and while he was ripping off a home, the female occupants wanted him sexually. He nodded yes, but would not talk about each offense that we suspected him of committing.

Toby Zapata ultimately admitted to nine rapes but was suspected by the Sex Detail of committing 30 sexual assaults over a two-year span. He went on trial in Denver. The D.A.'s ace prosecutors were Bob Mullan and Lamar Simms. Mullan was the most outspoken D.A. I ever met, and he brought lots of jury appeal to the courtroom.

Mullan described Zapata as a predator that should be caged, and as a threat to society. In one Denver case, he raped a victim twice in one year while her children were nearby. In the second rape, the woman's two-year-old son woke up as she was being raped. Both were raped at knifepoint.

Zapata's attorney, David Joyce, told the judge and jury that Zapata was sorry for what he had done. Zapata didn't exactly back up any remorse claims, testifying he had no idea why it happened and that he had raped the women because "they were there."

Toby stated he needed help, but told Judge Lynne Hufnagel he didn't think raping a woman seemed so serious. An outraged Judge Hufnagel heard that statement and threw out Zapata's plea bargain. He was forced to stand during the trial and received a 112-year sentence on six counts of rape and burglary. In the Jefferson County rape trial, Judge Connie Peterson added another 40 years in prison to bring his sentence to a total of 152 years. I liked both of those judges.

Solving the Zapata case resulted from old-fashioned police work. Wessels and I were really proud of our investigation. We stopped another predator that would have continued adding victims to his ever-growing list. He had ruined the lives of a long list of females and children who witnessed the attacks and would spend the rest of his days in the cage the prosecutor had designated for him.

Toby Zapata is now 51 years old and lives in Sterling Correctional Facility on Colorado's desolate eastern plains. If he lives long enough to make his first parole hearing in 2036, he would be 71 years old.

* * * *

In May of 1986, I was moved to the Crimes against Persons/Assault Detail. I immediately went into shock when I realized I was receiving up to ten "squawks" a day. I handled the administrative aspects of police work because they were a necessary evil. I knew my arrest and search warrant affidavits had to be thorough and complete, so I painstakingly put in as much effort as I had to complete the paperwork.

But this was different. This was dealing with complaints such as "jail cases," in which I had to interview suspects already arrested, and "hospital cases" in which I had to interview a victim of violence in the hospital.

I immediately set out to find a way to handle this enormous case load so I could hit the streets to work on my "projects." First, I secured some secretaries who would type my handwritten cases. I typed two fingered, so this would save me time and brain damage.

Second, I came in at least an hour and a half early to assign my own cases from the stacks of squawks. In the interest of fairness, I took an equal amount of jail and hospital cases, but I made sure I was taking my share of the "who done its" out of the pile. I researched my jail suspects by pulling their records in the ID Bureau, their cards of contacts and letters submitted about them by the Intelligence Bureau, and their juvenile and family histories from the Juvenile Bureau.

Then I went up to the Denver City Jail to interview them. It usually started with small talk designed to establish rapport. My research usually provided some common ground before I began interviewing each suspect. Eventually, I got around to asking them for their side of the story. I would advise them of their rights in a low-key way and get them to sign the acknowledgment form, then take their statement.

During my time in Assaults, there was only one person, Eugene Alvarez, who did not give me a statement or confession; I had sent his family to prison for armed robbery. Every morning I called each of my victims and talked to them about their assault. Everything an officer does as a case detective is noted in the case file in chronological order in the supplementary report.

The cops in the unit were first-class case detectives. They were talented and solved many of their cases. There were some characters in the Unit. One large detective reportedly found a chair that he fit into at the Denver City & County Building and "borrowed" it. He pushed it across the street to the Police Building and thereafter sat in it as he worked. He also pulled out his beads and chanted when he had a hospital case.

Every cop deals with an identity that other officers assign, a reputation he earns, and a persona he creates. On my desk was a voodoo doll, complete with pins. I found it stashed in one of my drawers, pretty much every day. To rattle the brass, I also placed on my desk pictures of two of my two greatest heroes—Pappy Boyington and Gen. George Patton. I wanted no doubts about my personality and who I looked up to as role models.

Det. Doug Jones looked exactly like Radar O'Reilly in M.A.S.H. All he needed to win costume contests were wire-rim glasses and a camouflage hat. Rick Polak was a thorough detective who solved a lot of his cases. I enjoyed working with all of the detectives in the unit. I'd have a breaking caper and never had a problem getting lots of volunteers to join in the pursuit.

* * * *

In April of 1985, an informant shared information that Richard Ball was pulling burglaries while in possession of a gun. Det. Larry Subia and I teamed up to locate and follow him. Attempts were made to set up surveillance to follow him but Ball did not go. In September of 1985, a burglary and homicide occurred on Marina Drive in

Aurora. A man and his wife returned home to find they had been burglarized. He went to the lobby of the apartment building to find the suspect loading their belongings into a vehicle. The homeowner confronted the thief at the car, got into a struggle, and was shot to death.

Det. Callahan of the Aurora Police Department was contacted and indicated several armed burglaries had been committed by a male/female tag team based on Aurora P.D. information. He obtained an arrest warrant for them for one of the burglaries.

We could not locate Ball for a short period of time, but an informant one day told us the couple was driving a gray Datsun and staying in an unknown motel on West Colfax Avenue. The plates on the vehicle had been stolen in Fort Collins.

We found the Datsun at The Four Winds Motel on West Colfax, but they were not in their room. When they returned, we jumped him in the elevator and had a hell of a fight with him. After he was cuffed, we took a loaded handgun, foil packets of heroin and one balloon of heroin off of his person.

We executed a search warrant for their motel room and car, recovering a large quantity of burglary loot, including the proceeds of two recent burglaries. Ball was jailed for armed robbery, possession of a firearm by a previous offender, possession of a controlled substance and burglary.

He was placed on hold for the U.S. Marshal Service, and his companion was jailed for suspicion of burglary. They were suspected in 20 burglaries. According to the Colorado Department of Corrections, Richard Ball is 76 years old and was paroled somewhere in the state's Northeast Region. Being on parole means he still must report to his parole officers and can be immediately returned to the penitentiary if he commits any violation of his parole agreement.

The FBI had circulated a bank surveillance photo of a guy who had done some bank robberies in Denver. Subia, Joe Black and I identified the gunman as John Sandy Chavez. We knew Chavez had moved to Portland, Oregon. New place, new life? Nah, just about never for career criminals. The FBI made him on seven Portland bank robberies and two Denver robberies. It's just too bad that we could not have made the pinch.

One day I got a great idea. I was going to have some Denver Police Department business cards printed up that would read "Detective Daril Cinquanta" on the top line and "Crime Fighter" on the second line. I was not handing these out to the public. They went only to friends and CIs.

Shortly after my trip to the printers, Division Chief Mulnix ordered me into his office "NOW!" I knew this was not going to be good and was going to turn to shit. But my mind was racing as to what I could have done this time. He launched into a tirade about my cards and asked to see one.

He took one look at it, and his lip started to quiver, and he lost it. He ranted at me for several minutes, calling me arrogant, egotistical and on and on. He ordered me to not give them out anymore and told me to leave.

I looked back over my shoulder and asked, "Would you like for me to autograph the back, Chief?'' His only response was "Out. He obviously did not share my sense of humor, but I didn't take it personally because he seemed to approach everything in life without humor.

CHAPTER 17—
CAREER CRIMINAL UNIT—
11-86 to 8-89

In September of 1987, I was transferred to the newly formed Career Criminal Unit. Our mission was to target the 733 menaces to society who had made the list. A career criminal has been convicted of at least two felonies. We believed that 10 percent of the bad guys committed 80 percent of the crimes.

I found that most of the degenerate criminals were stealing or dealing to support their drug habits. The Unit would be proactive—not reactive. We planned to target, follow and apprehend them in the act of committing a crime. The Career Criminal Unit was a perfect fit for me.

The detectives were handpicked because of our knowledge of the streets and the bad actors. The original seven officers all were aggressive and shared the mission of the unit: Steve Carter, Jim Lebedoff, Bobby Miller, Larry Subia, Sgt. John Thompson and Lt. Dave Michaud.

Officers including Rex Freeburg, Steve Barnhill, and Don Rask later joined the unit. Our secretary was Rosalie Estrada, and she should have been a cop. She was one of us, and we really enjoyed working with her. She also worked Crime Stoppers with Jim Hess in the same office.

The unit detectives designed a unit patch that showed a crossed sword and a thunderbolt. The sword signified justice and the thunderbolt referred to the unit's effectiveness in making arrests. The crossed sword and thunderbolt created four quadrants representing Denver's four police districts. The skyline of Denver was the backdrop, and the seven red stars represented the seven original members of the unit. The logo was encircled by the words "Career Criminal Unit" and "Denver Police Department."

* * * *

In October of 1986, Michael Martinez and John Gutierrez were found murdered in the basement of the Sunshine Inn on Larimer Street. The owners were blown away with a shotgun, execution style to the back of their heads, and the cash drawers were left open and empty. It was later learned that $400 and a jar of silver coins were missing.

The Homicide Unit identified Robert "Horse" Baca as one of the shooters. He had prior convictions for rape, burglary, and robbery. An arrest warrant was put out for first-degree murder and aggravated robbery. In 1975, Baca robbed the same bar and threatened to blow the head off of the owner, Martinez. Baca could not be located and was thought to have fled the state. At the time, he was called "the most dangerous person in the city of Denver" by DPD.

I developed information from an informant that Baca and Debbie Nolasco had fled Colorado together and were in the Orange County, California Jail under unknown, assumed names. Michaud and I worked closely with officers at the Orange County (California) Jail as they began sorting through the 1,400 inmates in an attempt to identify the duo by fingerprints, tattoos, and physical characteristics.

They were identified as Lambert and Debbie Miera, who were booked as man and wife. Baca and Nolasco were extradited back to Colorado where he was tried and convicted of first-degree murder and aggravated robbery.

* * * *

The Career Criminal Unit targeted Jerry Joe Ortega after I received a tip that he was pulling burglaries daily to support his heroin habit. He was a loner and worked alone. We targeted him and followed him to Oneida Street and East Girard Avenue, where he eluded us.

It took a lot of self-discipline, but we preferred to lose a target rather than "burn" the surveillance, effectively terminating the operation. We found two burglaries had been committed in separate apartments, resulting in theft of $7,000 worth of goods.

Days later we got back on Ortega and followed him to a construction site, where he sold a video recorder. We tailed him to an apartment complex on West 2nd Avenue in Lakewood and watched him enter one of the buildings. We found a unit that had been broken into and the goods were stacked by the door, staged for loading into his car. Ortega took off on foot, and we chased him down and arrested him.

Two months earlier he had been arrested for burglary and menacing but was out on bond. Jerry Joe Ortega was a prime suspect for the Career Criminal Unit, with his long two-decade rap sheet filled with felonies.

* * * *

During my career, I endured the deaths of eight fellow officers. Patrolman William Wirtz died in a motorcycle accident. Gunfire claimed Patrolmen Merle Nading, William Smith and James Weir and Patrolwoman Kathy Garcia, as well as Det. Donald DeBruno and Officer Pat Pollock. Det. Robert Wallis died from vehicular homicide. They were all good cops.

Joe and Fred Moreno were bail bondsmen in Denver for years. They became my friends and other detectives, and I helped them find and arrest bond skips. They were self-insured, so if a $50,000 bond skipped bail, they either nabbed the elusive defendant or had to pay it out of their pockets.

The Moreno brothers were sharp and experienced, so they usually secured bonds by tying up houses. We made a lot of good arrests with the Morenos over the years, and they were good company. One night we went to a steakhouse, and Joe pulled jalapeno peppers out of his sports coat, then diced them over their steaks.

* * * *

The Super Bowl Sting was a fantastic work of deception on the part of the Career Criminal Unit. We sent out notifications to the known addresses of wanted felons to notify them they had won two Super Bowl tickets. We invited them to Currigan Hall on a specific date and asked them to bring a picture ID to claim their tickets. All of the undercover policemen and women were dressed to the nines in tuxedos.

It was really a successful operation that required minimal resources, was a ton of fun for the cops, and netted about 50 felony arrests. Lt. Dave Michaud, Sgts. John Mulligan, John Thompson, and Art Hutchison, Dets. Milt Gras, Jim Lebedoff, Steve Carter, Diane Montoya, Terri Hayes, Chris Bridges, Yuda Pringle, Carolyn Priest, Larry Subia and Daril Cinquanta comprised the undercover team.

"Super Bowl Ticket Giveaway" was posted on the marquee, which added to the credibility of the sting. As our "winners" arrived, they were escorted by our undercover "babes" to a back room where their IDs were verified, and they were arrested. Many of them asked, "Do I still get my Super Bowl tickets?"

* * * *

In May of 1988, we received a tip that the Walgreen's at East Colfax and Race Street was going to be robbed. The informant indicated that a black male named Roy Tyler was going to stick it up and might be accompanied by George Benningfield. Sgt. John Thompson, and Dets. Jim Lebedoff and Bobby Miller assisted in the surveillance of the drug store.

We set up in strategic locations to prevent them from making it inside where we could rapidly lose control of the robbery, and they could take hostages. Snow was coming down heavily. Suddenly it was going down, too. A vehicle pulled up to the curb, and two black males exited. Det. Lebedoff could not read the plate or see if it was a male or female driver.

The duo pulled their nylon masks down from under their hats and approached the front door. One was carrying a sawed-off shotgun in a garbage bag, and the other held a briefcase. We confronted them before they could get into the store and arrested them without a shootout. The getaway driver drove off and was not located.

At Headquarters, suspect Dale Robinson consented to talk to us after his Miranda warnings were read to him. He indicated that George Benningfield drove them to Walgreens. He stated he was carrying the empty briefcase to carry envelopes he was going to buy for Benningfield.

Robinson denied knowing that Roy had a sawed-off shotgun or that he was going to rob the store. When asked about the nylon mask, he stated he had just gotten up and wears one because it helps to keep his hair soft and manageable. He would not write a statement or testify against Tyler or Benningfield.

Days later, Benningfield was contacted through his wife and agreed to come in to talk with us. We advised him of his Miranda rights. He denied any knowledge or involvement in the robbery. He did acknowledge knowing both of the suspects but denied being the getaway driver. Lacking eyewitness testimony or a confession, we could not charge Benningfield. However, the arrest—and my careful documentation—eventually became very important.

All of the facts were placed in an Interdepartmental Correspondence letter detailing the arrest and interview with Benningfield on 5-3-88. Every arrest I ever made was documented in an Interdepartmental letter. As far as I was concerned, if it wasn't documented, it never happened—or at least I could never prove it had happened, which was what counted in the eyes of the department and the courts.

* * * *

We developed information that two men and a woman were engaged in a nine-day armed robbery spree. All three had long felony records and were heroin users.

We joined forces with the Narcotics and Robbery details and arrested two of the suspects at a motel. The third was arrested after a North Denver convenience store robbery. The trio was suspected in 13 bar and convenience store robberies. Five of the armed robberies occurred in one day.

One victim, the manager of a Larimer Street bar, was shot in the chest and abdomen when he refused to turn over the money. He survived.

The robberies were similar in the description of the suspects and their M.O. in casing targets before they committed the robberies. They were caught bare-faced on some of the surveillance cameras. In some of the robberies, they wore masks. All three were convicted of armed robbery.

* * * *

An informant indicated that a member of the Bueno crime family was pulling dock burglaries. We got the Career Criminal Unit together and began surveillance on him. The team consisted of Sgt. Don Rask, Dets. Lebedoff, Subia, Gene Guigli, Dave Haley and Rex "Vic" Freburg. We followed Bueno and an unknown female to The Viking Freight Docks where he was observed and photographed by Det. Lebedoff removing a large box from the dock area and placing it in the trunk of his vehicle. We surrounded and arrested him and his female accomplice.

* * * *

In June of 1988, we targeted a long time wrongdoer and his female accomplice. The Unit followed them from area to area, where they knocked on corner houses with vacant areas across from the houses, only to find that the owners were home. They found one house where no one answered the door. The female stood outside and acted as a "lookout" while the man broke in, and they entered the residence.

The Surveillance team, Sgt. John Thompson and Don Rask, Dets. Larry Subia, James Lebedoff, Rex Freeburg and Gene Guigli closed in and surrounded the house. The woman tried to run out the back door but changed her mind when she saw waiting police. She and her accomplice ran out the front door where they were arrested.

The Channel 7 TV news crew led by Scott Sobel apparently was monitoring the police channel and showed up to film the bust. DPD did not call them. Once inside, the suspects had removed a case from a pillow and placed jewelry in it. Both suspects admitted being strung out on heroin. The driver said he was Waldy Muniz, but we knew that was a fictitious name. The arrest appeared to be a routine burglary, but it later took on great importance.

* * * *

Det. Vic Freburg developed information that Roland Moran was going to stick up the Western Sizzlin' Steakhouse at 4095 South Santa Fe Drive in Sheridan. We teamed with the Sheridan Police Department and began surveillance.

The Denver Police Department contingent consisted of Sgts. Don Rask and John Thompson, Dets. J. Lebedoff, R. Miller, G. Guigli and L. Weant. The Sheridan Officers were Capts. Michael Chick and Michael Anthony, and Dets. Dave Bell and Mike Grenwell.

We observed Moran on three occasions. He and his accomplices were targeting the manager's van, apparently knowing he would make a run to the bank with the deposit. The suspect and the surveillance team followed the manager to his bank at South University Boulevard and Arapahoe Road.

The manager entered the bank, made the deposit and left. The suspects left the scene when he entered the bank. We figured the subject's activity were a dry run for the bandits to dial in the manager's daily pattern.

On July 5, 1988, a different vehicle—an extended cab pickup—showed up at the Western Sizzlin' Steakhouse containing two individuals. The suspect was observed in the rear seat, and a 10-speed bicycle was laying down in the bed of the truck. The truck was observed cruising the area like a shark circling its next victim. On one pass, there was

only one in the truck, and the bike was gone. The suspect
was observed riding the bicycle.

We instructed the manager to exit the steakhouse with
the money bags and enter his van, in which Det. Subia was
hiding. I had hidden behind a door in the southwest corner
of the restaurant, about 10 feet from the driver's side of the
van. The other members of the surveillance team were
strategically positioned around the area to cut off all
possible escape routes.

The manager exited with the bank bags and entered his
van. Moran cruised up on his bicycle to the driver's side
and confronted the manager at gunpoint, stating, "Open the
door." Once the door was open, the suspect said, "Hi there,
guess what this is?"

At that point I stepped from behind the door to
challenge him at gunpoint, ordering him to drop his gun. At
the same instant, Det. Subia lunged over the seat to also put
him in his gunsights. The suspect dropped the gun,
shouting, "It's not loaded."

His accomplice was arrested in the vehicle. Both
confessed to the armed robbery, and six additional
robberies were cleared. Some officers received Police
Service Crosses for this dangerous arrest.

Lt. Michaud and I liked to "run" the bars, looking for
wanted felons and informants and rousting the bad actors,
which often netted a cheap pinch. One day we were in an
alley on Larimer Street and saw a known ex-convict go up
some stairs to the second floor.

We followed him and opened a curtain on another
level of illicit activity along Larimer Street. We found a
room where junkies were shooting up and rooms where

prostitutes were turning tricks. We made a couple of arrests of wanted felons.

As much time as we had spent rubbing elbows with the criminal element, and despite the fact everyone in the Metro Denver area knew Larimer Street was the epicenter of drug and alcohol abuse and other manners of illegal behavior, it was a shock to Michaud and me, that there was a second level to the crime there.

Lower Downtown was instantly revitalized and gentrified with the construction of Coors Field, home of the Colorado Rockies baseball team. Brewpubs, restaurants, and upscale apartments filled abandoned warehouses, and the skyline was filled with cranes to build new skyscrapers.

But one day when it was still one rough neighborhood, we were starting back down the steps when two thugs came up the steps. We identified ourselves and confiscated a pistol from each of them. Both were convicted felons, and they bounced back to jail.

* * * *

In another incident, Michaud and I went into the Mexico City bar, and I saw a guy who looked like a "character" sitting at the bar. I did not know him, but I wanted to know who he was so I went up to ID him. He was a belligerent asshole, and I took him outside and cuffed him and threw him in the car.

I was going to take him downtown for "habeas maybeas" and to determine who he was. We got in the car, and as we are driving off, Michaud says, "You just arrested Det. Ralph Gonzales, who is probably undercover." Ralph was laughing in the back seat and confirmed that he was in the bar to buy heroin.

Well… we did bolster Gonzales' street credibility in the skids of Lower Downtown. Us taking him out was commonplace with us, and the criminals knew it. Michaud knew Gonzales and laughed his ass off. So did Gonzales, who still ribs me about it to this day. Unbeknownst to me, Michaud was chuckling under his breath, and he busted out laughing when we got Gonzales to the patrol car.

* * * *

Philip "Lepa" Espinoza escaped from prison in 1970. He was a member of the "Society Burglars," a band of thieves who targeted the homes of the wealthy residents in and around the upscale Polo Grounds neighborhood. His M.O. included making a nighttime telephone call to the target home, and if he got no answer, breaking in.

When he was taken into custody, he was carrying a "who's who" list of Denver socialites who had been targeted with a burglary or attempted break-in. Espinoza's roster included rich jewelers, doctors, and realtors.

We executed a search warrant on a motel room he had been occupying and recovered some loot from his residential burglaries, as well as an array of burglary tools. Espinoza had only recently hit the streets and was ramping up his campaign of burglaries.

The South Metro Task Force, which included officers from the Denver Police Department, teamed with the Arapahoe County Sheriff's Office and Sgt. Bob Glen of the Bureau of Alcohol, Tobacco & Firearms to execute a search warrant in Arapahoe County. My informant had told me that the resident of the house possessed cocaine, methamphetamine, and marijuana.

In addition to the drugs he had tipped me to, we seized a handful of firearms, including an AR-15 assault rifle that had been converted to fully automatic and a sawed-off shotgun. The suspect was Larry Kaneczny, a felon convicted of a conspiracy charge who was awaiting sentencing on a drug charge when we nabbed him.

The Career Criminal Unit developed information that two men and a woman were on a nine-day armed robbery spree. Their extensive felony records were largely fueled by their heroin habits. The CCU joined forces with the Narcotics and Robbery details to arrest two of the suspects at a motel.

The third suspect was nabbed just after he had robbed a convenience store in north Denver. The trio was suspected of committing 13 robberies at convenience stores and bars. They were serious junkies and did five of the armed robberies in one day.

The manager of a Larimer Street bar refused to hand over the cash and was shot in the chest and abdomen. He survived. We combined our intelligence to find the suspects matched descriptions given in many of the string of recent robberies, and their M.O. while casing their targets was consistent. Better yet, though they sometimes wore masks, they got sloppy, and several surveillance cameras captured them bare-faced. All three were convicted of armed robbery.

* * * *

The Career Criminal Unit engaged in a four-day rolling "cat and mouse" surveillance of two burglars, Williams and Archibeque. They were suspected of committing at least 50 daylight burglaries per month to support their cocaine and speed habits.

We followed them to residential neighborhoods where they would cruise looking for a target. We had lost the pair a couple of times and figured they might have suspected a tail even though we were rotating five cars. They were experienced burglars.

The next day we followed them to a complex on East Florida Avenue. They entered an apartment and exited with a TV, stereo, record turntable and a vacuum cleaner. After Williams and Archibeque loaded up and entered the car, the six-man surveillance team surrounded them and made the pinch, recovering the stolen jewelry.

They were a real challenge to follow because they were good at "tail checking"— but not *that* good. Our Unit was adept at tailing bad guys, and we had an evolved, practiced system of rotating the "eye" and their backup.

Williams was an ex-con who had served time for a burglary offense and was wanted for parole violation. He and Archibeque were convicted of several burglary offenses. Williams received a 75-year sentence after confessing to a number of burglaries, and also admitted he would have resorted to violence against police to avoid returning to prison. He stated that the day before his arrest, he felt he was being followed and was armed with a handgun that he would have used in a shootout if police had stopped him.

* * * *

In December of 1988, the media gave partial credit to the Career Criminal Unit for a 17 percent reduction in the crime rate in Denver. We had arrested about 200 bad guys up to that point. Because they were career criminals, they had lifestyles based on committing acts, often to support their drug habit, in which they victimized individuals and society in general. In other words, our team's ability to make 200 arrests resulted in prevention of thousands of crimes.

I had the privilege of working with some great cops from other jurisdictions throughout my career, and the success of many of our operations depended on a cooperative spirit among various departments. These officers were my go-to guys when I had a deal that was going down in their back yards:

Dave Allen, Boulder P.D.
Frank Spotke, Northglenn P.D.
Willie Newman, Adams County S.O.
Jim Farrell, Aurora P.D.
Mike Powell and Steve Evans, Lakewood P.D.
"Little" Pete Peterson, Adams County S.O.
John Koncilja, Pueblo P.D.
Del Wedge, Colorado Springs P.D.
Lou Martinelli, Jefferson County S.O.
Dante Carbone, Thornton P.D.
Kenny Brown, Colorado Bureau of Investigation
Jim Horton, Arvada P.D.
Dave Taketa, U.S. Drug Enforcement Agency

* * * *

Based on informant information, we entered into a three-month investigation dubbed operation "Koo Koo." Which targeted a major cocaine dealer. This was a joint operation in conjunction with the FBI, Immigration & Customs Enforcement, and Lakewood and Westminster Police Departments.

Information indicated a kingpin nicknamed Koo Koo was trafficking ounces of cocaine to his dealers, who in turn sold to street dealers. Koo Koo stowed his kilos in storage lockers, and we followed the leads to a west Denver storage facility.

We secured a search warrant and seized a kilo of cocaine with an estimated street value of $250,000. The team secured a warrant for his safety deposit box which contained $95,000 in cash, which was tainted with drug residue. Koo Koo was not getting back that cash.

Officers set up surveillance on the storage locker and arrested Koo Koo when he entered to retrieve his kilo of cocaine. The team then worked down the web of the drug network, executing a series of search warrants throughout the Denver Metro area to seize drugs and cash from his dealers and place them under arrest for trafficking illegal narcotics.

* * * *

One day I got a call from a friend in Arapahoe County as to a "secret investigation" leveled at me in connection with the John Lefebre and Martha Ball burglary case. My source told me that they believed I had set up the burglary for the media.

Subia and I confronted the DPD command, who gave us a cold shoulder and acted as though nothing was wrong. Days later they admitted an investigation was in progress, and we were to do no police work.

We set up a meeting with Police Chief Ari Zavaras, which I secretly taped. We told them there was nothing wrong with the case, and that it most assuredly was not a publicity stunt. Zavaras' told us his big concern for some time had been to avert a Civilian Police Review Board.

Zavaras did not want any incidents to ripple the waters and to tip the scales in favor of the City installing a police review board that had been proposed and discussed. He said he was taking a preemptive strike by doing something to signal the powers that we were policing our own.

The police department brass thought the Lefebre-Ball case was mine, so we shocked them when we informed them Larry had initiated it. The story broke in the newspapers and on television, blaring allegations that the accused burglars were set up by me with the intention that the media would be on hand to cover the bust.

Our Investigators were in for a big surprise. First, television newsman Scott Sobel corroborated our version of events, telling them we did not invite them to shoot this bust. He said they were following standard operating procedure in most newsrooms by monitoring the police channel on their scanner, and they were merely following that lead as it came in. Sobel had a lot of experience covering cops, and he issued the opinion the arrest was not staged.

Then we dropped the bombshell on the interrogators, informing them it was not my deal. It was Larry's case and his informant. It was my belief they were on a witch hunt for me, and suddenly had to acknowledge I wasn't a witch, and there wasn't a witch anywhere within the village they were investigating. Now they did not know what to do because the whole investigation was predicated on getting me.

We next learned that they were investigating our last 100 follow jobs. As our Investigators, they assigned Tom Sanchez, with whom Larry had an unfavorable history; and Byron Haze, whom I had numerous disagreements with over the years. There was no love among any of us, other than Larry and me. We objected they had assigned an investigation to two men with vendettas against us, but Sanchez and Haze were left in place.

Internal Affairs called us in to provide statements and failed to give us our Garrity advisement or Miranda warnings, which was legally necessary if they anticipated charging us with criminal offenses. Subia and I both declined to give them a statement and were suspended with pay. They took our badges and guns.

Anticipating the worst, I surreptitiously tape-recorded every interaction with our accusers. Arapahoe County released Lefebre and Ball, dropping a valid burglary case. The brass brought in Special Prosecutors John Suthers and Bob Brown, out of Colorado Springs. Suthers has held about every public office known to man, spent some time pimping the Patriot Act, and went on to become mayor of Colorado Springs.

Larry and I interviewed Larry's informant, who denied entrapping the burglars or participating in the burglary. I knew the informant, but never had worked with him. He was later brought in by the investigative team, and flip-flopped on his statement.

He admitted to Larry and me that he had to tell the interrogators what they wanted to hear and he blamed everything on me. He further stated to Larry and me that he was a "junkie," and would say anything that saved him from going through heroin withdrawal in jail.

It got deeper and deeper as he said he would not testify in court because that was essentially signing his death warrant with criminals he had ratted out over the years. The District Attorney's Office gave him money, a plane ticket, and consideration on a case against his brother for his cooperation against us. Isn't that what Larry and I do with informants?

I knew a jury was going to enjoy hearing what the state was willing to do to convince him to "flip." And this was just the beginning of the Denver Police Department's effort to hand-cut the pieces to fit the puzzle.

I don't think Zavaras had any idea how big a can of worms he was opening. By trying to scapegoat me for his convenience to sidestep creation of a police review panel, he had allowed the media to declare open season on virtually everything the police do and how they do it.

The media immediately became obsessed with "entrapment" and asked how many convicted felons had been entrapped. The brass had inadvertently created the "criminal defense of the '80s"—with prosecutors and cops having to prepare for allegations of entrapment in case after case.

There was nothing thoughtful or judicious about The Investigation, which for all the world felt like an inquisition. They next alleged we had entrapped the perpetrators, Tyler and Robinson, who were arrested as they initiated the stickup of the Walgreen's store.

My informant had implicated George Benningfield in the upcoming robbery. In my Inter-Departmental Correspondence dated 5-3-88, I outlined the information from the Confidential Informant implicating Benningfield. When I received this information, I wasn't surprised that George was double dealing me—a huge percentage of informants eventually or habitually do.

If he had shown up at the scene of the robbery, I was going to be able to put a "hook" into him again and have him on the line to provide me with more leads on criminals.

In the past, Benningfield had given me wanted felons and information on two career criminals who were going to pull a stickup on a business that handled large amounts of cash. In that case, the bad guys showed up in a stolen vehicle and cruised their target and left. I figured they would return, but they never did. He also turned a couple of dope dealers.

George was good for a lot more criminal information, but he had to be motivated. He had a coke burner going for the past 40 years that he could not extinguish, and I knew that meant he would never be far from the criminal element.

The night of the Walgreen's robbery it was snowing heavily. The informant said they waited for the stormy weather to pull the heist. It is not unusual for bad guys to be staged to pull off a crime, then go forward when they get nasty weather. The surveillance team consisted of Sgt. John Thompson and Dets. Cinquanta, Subia, Miller and Lebedoff. I would trust my life with any of these great officers.

I was surprised that the robbers followed through with the Walgreen's caper because I had not heard from my informant in days. Scott Sobel from Channel 7 News was there and had filmed the bust for his "Super Cops" series.

We had confiscated the sawed-off shotgun in the garbage bag and the empty briefcase, which would have been a handy place to stash some stolen cash. At Headquarters, they were advised of their Miranda rights and Robinson made a statement that Benningfield had driven them to the Walgreen's to buy envelopes which needed to fit in the briefcase.

Robinson claimed he did not know that Tyler was going to rob the store with a sawed off loaded shotgun.

However, Robinson was wearing a nylon mask over his face as he approached the Walgreen's entrance. The arrested stickup men made no outcry that they had been set up. Why? Because they hadn't been set up. George was not the CI.

On 3-2-88, we called Benningfield and asked him to come into the station. On the phone, he denied driving or being involved in the robbery. I taped his denial. When he came in, we advised him of his Miranda rights, and he again denied being the driver. He admitted owning a gold Oldsmobile, knowing both men we had arrested in the robbery, and being with Robinson earlier in the day.

Benningfield would not confess, so we could not charge him unless we were willing to go to trial on Robinson's testimony. Did I think he was a participant? Hell, yes. But I did not really care. Like every other day for every other drug addict, Benningfield was doing what he felt necessary to feed his habit.

I don't believe in rehabilitation—only recidivism. Also, I never got confused as to whether I was a police officer or a social worker. It wasn't my job to try to get someone to stop using drugs. It always comes down to the choices that people make during their lives. Some are good; some are bad.

I had two taped statements from Benningfield and one written statement that he dictated to me at Headquarters. He had reviewed it for accuracy and signed it.

The Investigation continued with another case in which they picked an informant who really surprised me. He was not really happy with me for letting him go to jail after he had worked for me. The Investigators ground on him, but he told the truth, testifying I had not asked him to set up individuals by entrapping anyone. He had given me the following job, and we stopped two burglaries in progress.

The interrogators tried hard to get him to incriminate me, but he held his ground in stating that the burglars had tried to convince him to join them on thefts. He remained steadfast that I had never asked him to set up anybody, and had only asked him to tell me who was pulling stickups and burglaries. I knew if the truth prevailed, I was safe because I had always been honest in my dealings with CIs.

The CI admitted to me that he had stolen plates on his car, which I told him to bring to me. He kept hedging and would not give them to me, so I put them on NCIC as wanted because they had been used in commission of a crime.

The Investigators claimed I had told him to get rid of the stolen plates. They also made an issue out of the description of the suspect in my report, stating it did not match the CI. They claimed I was trying to conceal the identity of the informant. No one can tell you what you had seen or not seen. Their interpretation was ridiculous.

During the preliminary hearing, the same CI admitted he was shooting eight bags of heroin a day, which means he was supporting a $500-a-day habit. He testified that we lied to each other all the time when in reality we constantly argued about him disappearing, and I would have to find him in the middle of an investigation.

Even though he was injecting immense volumes of heroin, he said his memory was perfect. He was committing crimes to support his huge habit behind my back. He also admitted he was a "con man," which I knew was the case with him and about every other CI in my network.

We were working some stickups that he insisted did not carry guns, which I found hard to believe considering what I knew about them. He could have been leading me on to buy time to continue committing crimes. I told him to keep checking with the stickups and let me know when they got a "piece."

He testified that I told him to get them a gun, which is ridiculous, and never happened. If we were part of a conspiracy that supplied robbers with a gun and they killed someone, we were accomplices to murder. The informant and I got crosswise over two continuances I got him to find the cash to pay a $750 fine. I also told him if he turned a big case I would pay the fine for him.

He ended up doing 60 days and claims that was when he found The Lord. Hallelujah! The Investigation pored through hundreds of complex cases involving society's most dangerous criminals, and the best ammo they could come up with to shoot at me was the claim I had told a CI to get rid of a stolen license plate.

During the Investigation, I was notified that Sanchez and Haze were trying to interview informants who ended up in the joint, and the informants stonewalled them. First of all, they did not want to die behind the walls when someone they had been instrumental in sending to prison was able to get to them, and second, they respected me based on professional relationships built over the years and knew I did not ask them to entrap anyone. The bush league Investigators were not going to get to first base with them.

During the Investigation, I was contacted by a female acquaintance I hadn't heard from in some time. I had never dated her, and she was somewhere between an acquaintance and a borderline friend. We got together, and

I became suspicious that the Department had run her into me to see what I would tell her. So, I fed her a line of crap and was talking about how we could make her "one" of the informants and we could coach her.

She was planted to somehow convince me to admit wrongdoing. This was never going to happen because I hadn't done anything. I boxed her in so tightly that she wanted to run. I later found a report in their case that she had contacted me and was very uncomfortable as to my rhetoric about the Investigation. This girl had never smoked weed or even stolen a pack of gum in her life.

There is no doubt in my mind that she was directed to get next to me. I had dealt with the most cunning and manipulative con men in Colorado. It was ridiculous for the Investigators to think that I would divulge anything to their unsophisticated plant.

The Investigators interviewed 40-year career criminal George Benningfield no fewer than five times. After enough coercion, he finally broke down and stated that he had tipped me off before the robbery—which was not true. He eventually told them what they wanted to hear.

Not only did I name him as a probable accomplice in the upcoming Walgreen's robbery in my letter dated 5-3-88, but I also told the D.A.'s Office that Benningfield was not the CI. I taped him on the phone the day after the robbery, at Headquarters and then investigator John Foster interviewed him.

In three separate interviews, he denied driving the suspects to the Walgreen's or giving me the information on the robbery. Now, well after that crime, they leaned on him hard enough that he changed his story. I can only guess what went down when they were pressuring him to implicate me.

George confirmed my suspicion, telling me they threatened to file conspiracy charges on him and throw his ass in jail based on Robinson's statement that Benningfield had engineered the robbery and was the driver. They did not threaten him on tape.

He called me after he gave them the statement they so desperately wanted and told me how it had gone down. He also stated he "owed me one," but added he would not testify at my trial and then he hung up on me. I didn't feel I needed his testimony because I believed I had this case beat. What they all did not know was that I had a complete, detailed tape recording of the actual CI giving me the information on the robbery which I knew the jury was going to love to hear.

It raised a huge question: If the D.A.'s Office was on a mission of justice, why did they not charge Benningfield when he confessed to being a co-conspirator to the armed robbery? I would have charged him if he had admitted it to me. They didn't charge him because he had just become their star witness against me. My guess is they granted him immunity.

There was another twist that put the stench of culpability on my Investigators. Ron Tyler got arrested before the robbery trial for possession of narcotics. They said they could not prove the drugs belonged to him even though they were in his pocket when he was arrested, and he confessed the drugs were his.

I guess from their perspective, "The end justifies the means." They apparently figured it was okay if the Investigators and the D.A.'s Office conspire to preserve the "integrity" of their witnesses by allowing them a "pass" on a felony arrest if they can win a case against a scapegoat cop.

Then Pete Lopez, the alleged CI on the Lefebre-Ball investigation, was arrested in Los Angeles for auto theft, but they claimed the victim would not cooperate in the prosecution. Was he supremely lucky or did he get some help from a "guardian angel" with high-level credentials in Denver?

Lefebre and Ball, while out on their "get out of jail free" card, caught a felony theft rap for shoplifting. I could not find any record of the legal resolution in that case. It apparently was sprinkled with legal magic dust and … poof!... It disappeared.

There was a taint on each of their star witnesses, and the prosecution was proceeding in a case that hinged on their words against ours. Unbelievable. George Benningfield was arrested again for bank robbery some years later.

George was a case study of my "way of life" theory with drug addicts. They never stop doing crimes when they are continually driven by the need for drugs. And they are never going to stop doing drugs.

I recently worked with Rich Vaccaro, whom I learned was Benningfield's federal parole officer after his last bank robbery. Vaccaro did a home visit with Benningfield, finding him in a dank basement. Vaccaro was so disturbed by the squalid conditions that he spent his own money on a TV for Benningfield. A few months later George died alone, on drugs, bringing to an end a lifetime of crime.

During the Investigation and before the trial, Investigator Randy Gordanier received information that

Lefebre and Ball were planning to cause death or injury to numerous criminal justice officials as a result of the pending burglary and conspiracy charges. Lefebre was soliciting outside help to shoot some of his targets. He also wanted to throw acid in the face of the deputy district attorney during the trial.

Lefebre had bragged that his co-conspirators had already followed some of the targets to their homes. The Lefebre-Ball hit list included District Attorney John Hower, Det. Daril Cinquanta, Det. Larry Subia, Channel 7 News reporter Scott Sobel, Judge Jack Smith, Sheriff's Deputy Richard Martinez and Pete Lopez.

Lefebre had his cohorts case out the courthouse to outline security measures and determine which entrances and exits the D.A.'s staff utilized on a daily basis. They determined Scott Sobel would be easy to attack. Lefebre was considering stabbing a sharp pencil in John Hower's eye.

Ball indicated Lefebre's goons were trying to find Pete Lopez to give him a "hot shot"—a lethal dose of drugs. She also stated that if Lefebre got a "bad" deal she may come to the courthouse with a gun. The attacks never happened because they were forewarned. These two sterling individuals were the star witnesses in the Arapahoe case. But again, the prosecutors were taking their word over ours.

They made a big deal out of the fact that Benningfield had received money from Crime Stoppers for information regarding the robbery. I learned after the robbery that Benningfield had called Crime Stoppers prior to the robbery, unbeknownst to anyone. I had told my CI, George Vigil, that he could make a few dollars by calling in the

Crime Stoppers tip, so I at first thought Vigil had made the call.

We let Benningfield collect the $750 Crime Stoppers reward, which I then documented. Benningfield's statement to the Investigators indicated that Larry and never told him to call Crime Stoppers, which was true. Benningfield collected the additional $400 for reporting the case in which the suspects drove up to the robbery target, but left and never returned.

That same crew was now planning an armored car heist in which they would intercept the courier between the business and the armored car to rob two bags of money. The stickups were career criminals, and one of them had killed a cop. My accusers never could figure out the source of the extra $400 that I gave Benningfield. I will keep them guessing on that point.

We had found a loophole in the system through which our informants called Crime Stoppers with tips. There was no law or rule against it. I sometimes fed information to our informants, which they then called in to collect some money. This was a means we had devised because our meager informant fund thought $50 or $100 was adequate payment for information leading to high-level arrests or seizures. It was embarrassing to present an informant with an offer that low.

Many of my informants were working off a case and were not entitled to any money. Occasionally, one informant gave me a good deal of information, some of which I provided to another informant to be called into Crime Stoppers.

The authorizations were issued by Michaud or me, and Dave knew exactly what I was doing. He also knew that

Benningfield was not the CI because I told him so when the attempted Walgreen's heist went down. And the Crime Stoppers payment angle was used by other bureaus in the Denver Police Department to adequately compensate informants for valuable information.

I felt more security knowing I had my "Bankers" as backup sources of funding but used them only in special cases. Nobody else knew that I had these individuals bankrolling me when I needed big money. I kept them under wraps because I feared the brass would tell me I could not use them as a resource. They did not know about the Bankers, and they were my ace in the hole.

I leaned on them only about five times, but they were crucial to some huge busts. None of my important informants were ever revealed to my co-workers, and I kept the key informants out of making claims on Crime Stoppers.

The CIs who gave routine information were sometimes seen by other detectives, but I seldom confirmed they were "the" informant on a particular case. This confidentiality and secrecy policy extended to partners. It wasn't based on lack of trust; it was more about simplicity and clarity.

Larry and I never talked about our informants, to each other or anyone else, and never divulged who gave us what deal. This also protected us. The less we knew about someone else's case, the better, in case something turned to shit. However, I had told Larry that Benningfield was not the informant in the Walgreen's case, and when he testified he was telling the truth, not committing perjury.

I was saddened that the Investigators were interrogating my friends Bobby Miller, James Lebedoff, and John Thompson. They were all great cops who would never be dishonest. None of them knew the intricacies of the case—or really any of my cases—except that a robbery was planned by two black males and George Benningfield might be the driver. I felt really bad that they got caught up in a real mess. They knew nothing that would help the Investigation, or hurt me.

One thing I learned being a cop: There is no such thing as a safe conspiracy. They dinged Miller for submitting the authorization form that I drafted. I could not figure out what they claimed he knowingly did. My only conclusion was that they did it to set up another violation for any upcoming departmental hearing on me.

Michaud and I filled out and submitted numerous authorization forms granting our informants Crime Stopper payments for supplying information. Well, if it's suddenly a violation, then why did they not charge Michaud? I knew a jury might zero in on the stack of the same forms submitted by Michaud.

Robinson claimed Benningfield talked them into pulling the robbery. I had no idea if he did or not, but it was immaterial because he was not the CI. Benningfield was trying to make money to support his cocaine habit, and Robinson was stringing together a bogus entrapment defense. They were all guilty and should have gone to the joint.

The entire affair spun farther and farther out of orbit, going from absurd to ludicrous. The Denver D.A.'s Office issued a statement that they were going to scrutinize our last 700 investigations. Seven hundred cases, thrown open for review.

Not to be beaten in the race to lunacy, the Denver Police Department issued a statement that they were going to pull and review our last 100 follow jobs to see if we entrapped anyone. So, the guys I thought were part of our team are now picky referees, looking over 800 of our cases.

I never saw a media release as to their findings—whether we had entrapped anyone or not. That is because they could not find one bad case. In terms of perspective and context, if any of our suspects had screamed entrapment at the time of their arrest, my partners and I would not have filed on them and would have kicked our informant's ass for entrapping them.

So, after this monumental failure to prove a pattern of entrapment, the attention shrunk back to the two cases in which they originally alleged wrongdoing. My source in the District Attorney's office told me they had found nothing. I knew the only threat was our accusers convincing a CI to lie about us. The Department's inquiry also netted no bad cases. If they took us to trial, they would have to admit they had nothing.

The bad guys they let loose in their effort to make us look guilty were guilty as hell and should never have been released. Lakewood, Jefferson County, and Boulder had the balls to stand by our information in cases they had filed. Their efforts to nail us to a wall ended up looking like mad desperation.

The Investigators also attempted to get the Parole department to throw us under the bus. One parole officer, Max Winkler, said he had no problem that I followed his parolee for four days and arrested him during a burglary in progress. The D.A.'s office also tried to convince Winkler to say we knew the parolee was wanted on a parole violation when we were following him, and we should have halted the surveillance and arrested him. That did not fly either, because we did not have the knowledge nor would it have mattered to Parole, Department of Corrections or us.

I heard the D.A.'s Office had additional problems with outside jurisdictions that I had given many tips to that resulted in arrests always for felonies. The Investigation was trying to get them to scrutinize our follow jobs, which already had been cleared. It seemed Denver and Arapahoe County, which was handling Larry's case with Lefebre and Ball, wanted nothing more than to stick it to us. I believed Arapahoe County wanted to get even over the Grand Jury fiasco in which their officer had made claims against me.

It's important to note that the cases they were looking at were "filed" as opposed to "not filed" cases. The D.A. and judges never saw our bad cases because we would not file them. They were "catch and release." Many were bad search cases that we then used as leverage against our informants and potential informants, threatening to file them if they did not produce.

Another illuminating point: I estimate at least one-third of my cases involved a past or present informant I was arresting in the commission of a new crime. Double dealing was central to their M.O., and we knew it.

When we made a new case on a CIs, that meant hitting the reset button on the relationship, and at that moment the CI would usually give up some other lawbreaker. I always tried to climb up the ladder from the crime they were arrested for. When I arrested a gal in possession of five balloons of heroin, I'd expect her to turn me someone who was dealing ounces, or someone pulling stickups or burglaries. They needed to hand me something bigger to work off their case.

The secret to success in informant cases was to "verify and corroborate" everything, to protect myself and to build a bulletproof case. This applied to affidavit/search warrant cases, as well as follow jobs. The only problems I had winning affidavit/search warrant cases came from the defense. They attacked every shred of evidence, alleging I was lying or had made up the CI, the CI was eyes and ears to the crime, the CI was never in the house, or any other story they could fabricate that a jury might believe.

If an affidavit wasn't rock solid, I did not submit it. By the time they came around with the Investigation, I had done hundreds of search warrants. To the best of my knowledge, every fact claimed in the affidavits was true, and that didn't change regardless how much they tried to spin reality.

By sheer volume over 20 years of constantly attacking my credibility, defense lawyers influenced judges and D.A.'s to question my veracity in just about any case. Our own leadership had been complicit in undermining our perception by the public and the courts. They were not able to find or prove any pattern of wrongdoing, or even a string of sloppy cases or an example of lousy police work.

All they succeeded in was embarrassing and humiliating us and portraying us as "bad cops." Nothing they claimed about us was true. We were tried, convicted and sentenced in the media. Dealing with the bad guys was easy. It was my dealings with the administration that were tough.

During our ordeal, a friend, Tony Troilo, stood up to defend us. He owned a Phillips 66 station at Zuni Street and West 44 Avenue for many years. He was an old-fashioned gas station owner who pumped your fuel, washed your windows, checked your oil and even checked your tire pressure. Nobody did that anymore. He had a big following and was more than reasonable in his repair charges. I don't know how he made any money. Then again, he was a small-time bookmaker, so he had another income source.

The old ladies loved Tony and brought him pies, cakes, fruit, and cigars. We always found the gifts in his office and would cut a slice of pie or take some fruit—and always a cigar. Sometimes he would be working on a car in the garage and never see us indulging in his treats. Tony was a great guy and friend to many, and we appreciated his friendship.

One day, about the time we thought the storm had blown over, Special Prosecutor Bob Brown told Larry and me that they were not going to charge us. He made it clear this was not the type of case they wanted to file. We thought it was over and then a couple of days later there was a laundry list of charges against us, printed in the newspaper.

I immediately tried to figure out who the hell had nixed the decision to not file on us. It could have been Mayor Federico Pena, a carpetbagger like so many successful Colorado politicians, who had no love for me because I was instrumental in bringing down Juan Haro and the Crusade for Justice, and by extension, Corky Gonzales. I was figuring this might be payback time for me exposing the Crusade Justice as a terrorist organization.

But the whole thing could have been stirred up again within the Denver Police Department. I heard a word that Capt. Jim "Round and Red" Fitzpatrick was walking the halls with the case file under his arm, "downing" us and blowing in the Chief's ear. Envy is a powerful force, and plenty of fellow officers were delighting in our problems because they had not enjoyed our success over the years. Many had never turned a lick in terms of doing meaningful police work.

Amid this cesspool of animosity, vengeance, and jealousy, there was still plenty of powerful loyalty. The hits just kept coming, and Capt. Kennedy was standing strong, defending us daily. He was so active in his inquiries as to the state of the Investigation that the prosecutors warned him that they would charge him for interfering in the case if he did not stop.

Sgt. Cribari was in Internal Affairs, and he also was warned not to interfere with the case or contact us. The Investigators knew Cribari and Larry were long-time partners and we all were friends. If we called Cribari for any reason, he was required to report it.

Years later, we heard from a source in the D.A.'s Office that Suthers had overruled Brown to set the gears back in motion to file the case. If that was true, the question is who influenced Suthers to push forward with the charges. Suthers is an ultimate Dudley Doright, a black-and-white thinker in a world made up of 50,000 shades of gray. Plus, of all of his characteristics, ambition was probably John Suthers' most refined skill, so it could have been just another chance for him to pump up his resume for a run at public office.

Before the Investigation ran its course, several individuals would sell their souls to the Devil in an attempt to make a case against us. Once they decided to try to hang us, there were virtually no limits on what they were willing to do. One district attorney left office to go into private practice because he couldn't abide by what the special prosecutors were doing to us and how they were misrepresenting the evidence.

The pre-trial publicity in our case became a runaway train. There was no way our defense attorneys could seat an impartial jury. I felt the courts would never have allowed that much negative publicity in a case against a criminal. The press and TV news media were relentless in their daily attacks on the Denver Police Department and us. I received little to no support within the department. Most officers were distancing themselves from Larry and me, doing everything possible to stay clear of the lightning storm.

I reviewed the 10 Denver charges against me and concluded I could probably win at trial if our attorneys could succeed in the selection of an intelligent jury. I sensed it would take reasonably astute people to understand some of the nuances of what they were purporting.

Most of the charges were perjury and attempt to influence a public servant—the D.A.'s office—in the Tyler-Robinson case. I felt that we could drive them off a cliff on those charges because that entire accusation was based on Benningfield being the CI, and there was no evidence he was because he did not provide the tip about the impending armed robbery.

They were hinging the Arapahoe County case on the testimony of seven-time convicted felon Pete Lopez. Most critically, I believed any charges against me would fall like a house of cards because of what I did and did not know. It was Larry's case, and in this instance ignorance IS the best defense. I had no knowledge of how the deal came together with Larry's CI.

Eventually, they finished filing a litany of charges, which is a time-worn overkill strategy designed to scare the defendant into taking a plea bargain. I made sure they knew I was gearing up to stand trial. I was already making my "war book." One of my techniques during the trial would be to educate the jury about how the Denver Police Department conducts "business." Everyone in the courtroom—and the public, because the proceedings would be covered relentlessly in the media—would learn the down-and-dirty details of how officers handle investigations, informants, and surveillance.

The jury would gain a clear understanding of the loophole that officers from just about every bureau routinely used to get money for informants from Crime Stoppers. All of these facts would be admissible in my trial, and it was going to be a long one because I had a lot to say when I took the stand. I also let it be known that I was taking my trusted friend and long-time partner Dave Michaud along on the entire bumpy ride.

When I joined the force, cops sometimes took uncooperative bad guys for a ride in the cruiser trunk over rough railroad tracks. If I was going to be "railroaded," Michaud was riding in the trunk with me. When the dust started gathering around the case, Michaud apparently took the "pure pill." Not only were the prosecutors ignoring his misdeeds, but he turned on Larry and me.

Loyalty and betrayal are two sides of a coin, and that's what makes disloyalty so potent. At one time—and that time lasted for years—I would have taken a bullet for Dave Michaud. I had the cassette tape of the actual informant made before he died, and my defense team believed we could get it admitted as evidence.

That maneuver alone would be devastating to the prosecution, but I also was trying to figure out how I could appear at trial wearing my uniform shirt and pants, including all of my medals and decorations. I paid for every part of my uniform, including my badge, which I ordered when I got the detective/technician badges approved for the department. They were made from the Sachs-Lawlor dies for the old style badge that had all smooth edges, unlike the ones today. It was all my personal property, and I planned on wearing my uniform on the stand.

As had been my ethic and my standard and my oath throughout my career, I had protected the informant in the Tyler-Robinson case. To keep snoops off of his trail, I leaked out different names as my possible informant in the case. I did not want them to bring my true informant into the cop shop to and lean on him.

Before the Investigation really ramped up, I had told a number of people from the D.A.'s Office that the informant had died and that George Benningfield was not the CI. All of that was true. I did not identify the CI to my attorneys until just before the preliminary hearing because I feared they might disclose his name at an inopportune time.

George Vigil was my CI in the Walgreen's robbery arrest. The attempted robbery happened on May 1, 1988, and Vigil committed suicide shortly after that. The instant we introduced this information, the prosecution had a real kink in their case. They had to try to hurdle beyond a reasonable doubt. If we went to trial, they would then stumble into an even bigger obstacle when I presented the audio tape of George Vigil, and my defense team rolled out Vigil's friend, whom I had busted for possession of illegal narcotics.

Knowing that I was saying that George Vigil gave me the information, we got Mario Luchetta worked up to the point that he wrote a letter to the special prosecutor in an attempt to cut off my defense. Luchetta really had to dislike me to do this and put the Department on notice that he could not be trusted. He indicated that Vigil would never inform because he could not get him to flip. That did not surprise me. He said that George was opposed to ever being an informant.

Apparently, Luchetta did not know that Vigil was rolled up by the FBI for several hand-to-hand sales of illegal narcotics. He then turned around and testified against two individuals. I got him to talk to me because I had busted his friend for possession of heroin and he was trying to keep his friend out of the joint. Vigil was a pretty good informant. He knew a lot of bad actors and his information was accurate.

The Investigators talked to George Vigil's girlfriend after his death, and she told them Vigil would never be an informer. She said she had been present when we tried to get Vigil to become a snitch. I knew her story was bogus because we are smart enough to only try to flip a person one-on-one. It was obvious that she did not know of the incident involving Vigil's friend or that someone had coerced her to fabricate the story. I never knew Vigil had a girlfriend.

The prosecution thought they had some real ammunition with Vigil's alleged girlfriend, but I was unimpressed. Her testimony would be a pebble on the beach when I rolled out my evidence at trial. The alleged girlfriend, whose name they did not reveal, surfaced for the first time in the Pre-sentence Report, which seemed to be staged to influence Judge Martin. The report also claimed I had lied and deceived prosecutors.

I believe the prosecutors were hoping the judge would put me in jail leading up to the trial. This was the prosecution's day to say, "See? We were right. He is pleading to a misdemeanor." The two counts were vague and did not state with any specificity what informant I had protected. Going on a "fishing" trip sometimes works with inexperienced or scared defendants, but I was neither.

Any good detective can attest that on any given day the most hardened criminal may become a snitch. It all depends on the level of motivation, which can range from needing a hit of dope for an addict on the threshold of withdrawal to the thought of heading back to a cell for a year or a decade.

Another point of leverage is arresting someone dear to the intended informant. I sent one old-time career criminal to the joint for drug possession. He got out, started shooting heroin again and resumed his life of crime to pay for his habit. This guy was over 70 years old, and there are not a lot of 70-year-old junkies. I got information that he had pulled a supermarket robbery. I showed a photo lineup to witnesses, but they could not ID him.

So, I cornered him and told him that I knew he had done the armed robbery and I was going to send him back to prison. For the first time in his long and crime-filled life, he became an informant, and I got my three deals out of him. That bluff worked more than once in my career.

I knew the Special Prosecutors would be looking to make a deal with me after the preliminary hearing. He may have gone into chambers thinking it was an open-and-shut case, but Suthers quickly saw that the defense could drive an 18-wheeler through the holes in his case. His carefully crafted case was falling apart because of his "hit parade" of felon witnesses.

My head was swimming. Do I throw the dice on a jury deciding my fate? How does any possible course and outcome affect my possible intention to stay on the Denver Police Department? Would my decision affect Larry's chances of staying on the job?

There were too many uncertainties to get my mind around, but I would make my decision very soon, based on a shocking bit of inside news. Chief Ari Zavaras, whom many considered a "political whore," was told by someone in a position of power when the whole debacle was unfolding that he could save only one of us, and he had picked Larry. My mind raced through the dozens of possibilities as to the identity of that person.

I was happy for Larry. The Zavaras revelation meant I would have to fight if I decided to stay on the force. Larry had a long golfing history with Chief Zavaras, Jerry Kennedy, Mark Pautler, Stan Schaub and Dave Michaud. They even took golfing vacations together in Mexico. Damn! I always suspected I should have kept playing "pasture pool," but I guess I was too busy chasing bad guys and having fun.

I had also learned the brass was compiling a separate case detailing the Department rules and regulations I allegedly had violated, just in case I won my case or took a plea deal and decided to stay on. Among the ironclad standards: No "Departmental Embarrassment" goes unpunished. I again would have to feed the Monster. This was a world in which people never admit they are wrong, much less apologize for anything. The administration would claim the scoreboard was wrong after I beat them on the Benningfield case, an outcome my attorneys and I anticipated.

Internal Affairs Capt. Art Hutchison knew that the Arapahoe County D.A.'s Office was conducting a criminal investigation on Larry and me in regards to the Lefebre-Ball case, but he would not call us in for a statement in the Robinson-Tyler investigation. They would not confirm the criminal investigation or advise us under Garrity or give us our Miranda warnings if there was a criminal investigation.

Larry and I refused to provide a statement unless it was for a Departmental investigation. We were protected under Garrity provisions. We were suspended, and they took our guns and badges. Days later they realized they violated the Police Officers Bill of Rights and failed in their duty to advise us of the criminal investigation, so they belatedly gave us the proper warnings. They then reinstated us with pay. They would eventually suspend us without pay after we were charged.

Special Prosecutor Bob Brown tipped his hand when he opened negotiations for a plea bargain for me. His offer: I plead guilty to two misdemeanors and all of the other charges in Denver, and Arapahoe County would be dropped. Let's see here … that would mean dropping nine felony charges and four misdemeanors while pleading guilty to influencing a public official. Tempting.

Law enforcement was my life. I lived it and studied it every day, but I had never heard of anyone ever getting a deal like this one. I asked if Larry was included in the deal. Brown said no. As for my plea deal, my attorney and I wanted a Class 2 misdemeanor, and they wanted a Class 1 for my plea.

The public probably would not get what this meant, but I did. He did not want to try this case against me for many reasons. The preliminary hearing transcript was nothing but trouble for the special prosecutor and the D.A.'s Office, and they couldn't seem to keep their intended witnesses out of jail.

Brown stood a substantial chance of losing the cases. The public would become privy to the inner workings of the Denver Police Department. Everyone would see what the prosecutors had done to us—on the word of felons.

District attorneys also have egos to feed—just like cops. They get teased by their peers when they lose cases or get their asses handed to them by some defense attorney or some judge in a suppression hearing. Occasionally they just make a mistake, and it affects the outcome of a trial, and they draw heat from their peers and firms.

That's the personal side, but there is a darker, bigger motivating force that results in denial of justice. Recent high-profile cases have illustrated that far too many district attorneys are as concerned with their batting averages and scorecards as they are with justice.

Bottom line in my case: Brown could not overcome the reasonable doubt that the evidence would introduce to a jury. He would be required to prove his case "beyond" a reasonable doubt. He was not offering me a deal because he was a fan and wanted my autograph. Nor did he like Larry or me. After putting in immense time and effort to set up Larry and me for a trip through a meat grinder, he was reduced to scrambling for damage control.

At this point in the negotiations, I was dealing with Bob Brown and John Suthers. Brown wanted something resembling a win, and hoped to convince me to plead to anything, however minor, so they could walk away from the courthouse claiming victory. Brown never felt good about pursuing the prosecution, and he told me as much later.

When an officer is suspended and awaiting trial, the rest of the force passes the hat and chips in on a payroll deduction to help their fellow officer. In our case, the contributions were not indicative of full support from the department. I was really deflated, in light of all of the good police work I had done over the years. Over the years I had contributed to every officer who needed financial assistance—for any reason.

When the ice gets thin or even breaks, it's surprising who comes through with loyalty and courage. Stew Jackson owned Denver Burglar Alarm, and I considered him a friend. I guess I never before knew how much of a friend he was. Stew Jackson came forward, unsolicited by anyone, and gave me money to keep my head above water. I will never forget his friendship during the darkest period in my life. My "bankers"—the people who had supplied money to pay informants—also surprised me with some monetary help down the road.

I had to make a decision, and this is the way I looked at it: I could fight the case and put my fate in the hands of a jury even though I knew my case was a winner. I could take a plea and remain on the job, with the uncertainty of the departmental charges that sources inside the department told me would be filed, based on the case they were busy preparing. If I took the plea and clung to my job, I anticipated they would bust me down from detective again. I spent 20 years with them busting rungs out from under my feet, and I was worn out from trying to climb their broken ladder.

There also was the possibility the administration would suspend or fire me, prolonging this legal struggle, with me then battling to get back on the job. I'd already trudged through several unpleasant job assignments at the Denver Police Department, and I knew they could bust my rank and bury me at the Car Pound or worse. My final option was to take the plea and retire on a medical disability.

The more I visualized going back into uniform, the more I realized they already had taken the fun—and the satisfaction—out of the job. I started with a passion for investigating, finding and arresting lawbreakers. That daily challenge, that chase, that endeavor meant everything to me. It was disheartening to know my commanders did not back two damned fine cops and were willing to stand in a court of law behind the words of career criminal dope addicts.

I had always figured if I lived long enough I would stay with the Denver Police Department another ten years, every morning pinning on my badge, fighting crime and carting bad men and women off to jail. Betrayal is one of the hardest things for loyal people to get our minds around.

My own administration was trying to put me in prison for things I did not do. They were willing to use Larry and me as an example, but really only scapegoat us, for their own cynical intentions. They had stooped to indescribable levels of unethical behavior to destroy two men's careers. Did I really want to stay on the job with these cutthroats?

I talked with my family, friends, and attorneys and decided to take a medical retirement. I accepted the plea and turned in my papers to retire based on having Lupus. My sources within the walls of D.P.D HQ informed me the brass flippantly claimed that I did not have Lupus, and was trying to con the department.

They found no mention of Lupus in my personnel file. That's because I nor any of my physicians ever notified the DPD of my affliction. I loved the job so much that I kept my Lupus secret for 14 years. That, in and of itself, was often harrowing. The Denver Police Department sent me to three separate doctors who all affirmed that I had active Systemic Lupus (SLE).

Those doctors were amazed I had continued working all these years. The doctors also confirmed that I would have received a medical retirement back in 1976 if the department had known of my debilitating condition. No one would ever know what I went through on a daily basis to continue working, and the sacrifices I had made.

Dealing with daily fatigue, complications with disease attacking your body, indiscriminately and almost randomly going after a part of the body, in my case kidneys. Rheumatoid arthritis. Some people get ill and die. I feel fortunate.

I went before Judge Edward Simons to accept my plea deal. I liked him through the years because he had a sense of humor. He had toy soldiers up on the bench, and during trials, he would move them around. I always wondered if in his mind one group represented the prosecution and the other the defense, and he was keeping score based on the positioning of the soldiers. Based on the plea deal, I was put on probation for one year, required to do 50 hours of community service and fined $2,000.

Judge Simons asked if I could pay the fine that day and I said no. He removed a dollar bill from his wallet and said, "Let me help you." He then tore the bill in half and handed half to me. I framed my paper 50-cent piece as a reminder of a terrible chapter in my life.

I figured many of the people in the courtroom were eagerly anticipating me being cuffed and carted off to jail, hoping for their chance to applaud. The judge sent a subtle but very concrete message to me with his sentencing decision. His good-natured gesture and the recognition of the reality of the case will always offer some consolation to me.

The two counts that I pled to did not indicate I lied about my informant, but rather that I concealed the identity and the informant's degree of participation. Neither count named my informant. I did my community service by talking to ex-cons and addicts at Pier One, a diversion program at Ft. Logan. They treated me with respect, and I reciprocated. We had a lot of common ground and rather than being a punishment, it was a healing experience.

CHAPTER 18—
"THERE IS LIFE AFTER THE DEPARTMENT."

I left the Denver Police Department with $1,100, the balance of my final pay period, and received no deferred compensation or drop money. Only a handful of police friends openly stood by me during the Investigation. No one thought enough of me to organize a retirement party.

I felt alone during the ordeal, and I felt more alone after it. But I got my gun and badge back, just as I said I would. Now I could carry my badge, ID, and gun, and I still do today. I walked away with my police pension, which is considerable in the contemporary marketplace—and a lot of great memories.

I never went through the motions or settled for doing a mundane job or mediocre work. I had the satisfaction of a job well done, and the willingness and ability to perform for two decades to my high standards.

While my departure from the department was as flat as yesterday's stein of beer, I was amazed by all of the cards and letters I received from police officers, citizens, and most surprisingly inmates, criminals, and informants. For months, I called into Crime Stoppers to report information on cases I had been working on, and they paid me. It was a small way of making myself feel better, and I laughed all the way to the bank. There was no way to prevent anyone from calling and collecting money on legitimate tips, and Crime Stoppers was and should be designed to stop crimes.

I gave a number of my informants to other cops I liked, mainly narcs. A lot of my special informants refused to be handed off to another officer because once I left the department, no other cops knew the informants existed.

These were men and women who provided me with tips on big cases, and they didn't want to get burned working for other detectives. I had worked with one informant for 12 years.

I have always said my informants made me famous, and my partners made me look good. My knowledge helped me figure out complex "who done it" cases and turn them into big arrests, and that knowledge depended on the information I accumulated over the years.

I drove the administration of the Denver Police Department crazy for 20 years, always bouncing back with a "big one" every time they tried to break me. I am not ashamed of anything I did during my career. I caught lawbreakers fair and square, never entrapping anyone. Every one of them went to prison for the crime he or she committed.

My conscience was clear. It's a testament to my sense of fair play and ethics that I received bon voyage letters from people at every level of the system, including the criminal element I was sworn to bring to justice.

The Denver Police Department said during the Investigation that they believed I had arrested thousands of individuals and had put a thousand plus in penitentiaries across the United States. I concurred because I had proof. I saved all of my arrest letters, jail slips, commendations and news clippings.

My records show I solved more than 400 "who done it's" nationwide and arrested more than 100 escapees from correctional institutions around the country. I had drafted and executed more than 200 search warrants and taken hundreds of guns off of bad guys. Based on everything that went down in all of those pursuits and arrests, I have no explanation for how I avoided shooting anyone. I had many close calls, and I survived my career without getting killed.

I accomplished all of this by working almost every day and many nights for two decades. I was available 24 hours a day, 7 days a week to run on informant information the instant I received it. The sacrifices were many, and it leaves a bitter taste to realize it did not matter to anyone beyond the victims and me. That said, I know my police work made Colorado a better place to live, at least a bit safer, and a lot safer for the people who would have been victimized by the predators I put behind bars.

From the day the whole thing came tumbling down, I have missed the chase and the camaraderie I shared with all of the special cops I worked with. We shared many laughs, and sometimes I laughed so hard I would now have to take off my bulletproof vest. Years earlier I had painted the front of that vest with "Bad Guys" and "Admin" on the back. Perhaps I saw the downfall coming, even though the brass did shoot me in the back.

Not for an instant have I ever missed the politics of the Denver Police Department. I don't miss the administration that provided little to no backing. I don't miss the constant attacks on my credibility, with the defense attorneys constantly accusing me of lying, fabricating search warrants, planting evidence, mishandling informants, and lying in court.

I could not have accomplished hundreds of arrests and convictions if I had cheated in my investigations. Pretty much from the time I left the police academy and hit the ground running, I had to deal with the egos and petty jealousies of my fellow officers. They dished out hearsay, rumor, conjecture, innuendo and flat-out lies about my police work and my character. Shame on them.

After the smoke had cleared from the Investigation, I was concerned about my partner, Larry Subia, who had logged 14 years and was still on the job. During his career, Larry was assigned to the Narcotics Bureau for eight years and the Career Criminal Unit for three years. Larry stacked up letters of commendation from the DPD and outside agencies. Larry had received The Distinguished Service Cross, Medal of Valor and three Police Merit Awards for outstanding arrests. In 1980, he was Narcotics Detective of the Year and Optimist Policeman of the Year.

The Optimist Club had honored Larry five times for outstanding investigations and arrests. He was involved in several shootings, including an incident in which he shot and killed a man who was lunging at him with scissors.

He was the target of a criminal assassination attempt because of his effectiveness as a detective. He was the affiant on a lengthy wiretap investigation into the Herrera drug organization, which resulted in the arrest of 17 individuals and the seizure of narcotics.

Larry Subia made hundreds of arrests and was a great investigator. He had superior "street sense" and had amassed an army of informants. He was a great partner, and we had a lot of fun when we were chasing criminals, and when we were being friends. He survived our ordeal and was promoted to sergeant and retired to a golf course close to his home. I considered it an honor to have worked with him.

I was recognized for my performance throughout my career, earning the following medals, awards, and commendations:

- 10-3-71—Police Purple Heart Medal, for gunshot wounds while on duty in the case in which I was wounded by gunfire.
- 11-17-71—Veterans of Foreign Wars Law Enforcement Award.
- 2-21-72—National Law Enforcement Citation, Military Order of The Purple Heart.
- 5-12-72—Police Medal of Honor for not returning fire on an assailant to protect innocent bystanders after being shot by an escapee from Soledad Prison.
- 1-31-74—Optimist Club Policeman of the year Law Enforcement Award.
- 1-12-76—Metropolitan Law Enforcement Association Award.
- 2-10-76—Glendale Community Club Public Service Award.
- 3-28-77—Distinguished Police Service Cross for investigation and arrests in the Crusade for Justice bomb plot case.
- 2-25-8—Optimist Club Policeman of the Year Law Enforcement Award.
- 3-8-84—Award of Honor, Denver Citizens Appreciation Police Award for saving a life.
- 5-4-88—Optimist Club Policeman of the Year Law Enforcement Award.
- 7-11-88—Police Service Cross for arresting suspects in stickup in progress.
- 1970-1989—160 Official Commendations from Denver Police Department and outside agencies.
- 1975-1989—Six Police Merit Awards for Outstanding Investigations and Arrests.

The first thing I did after retiring was set up my private investigation company through the Secretary of State's office. Then I obtained insurance, business cards, and stationery. My private investigation firm would be called Professional Investigators, Inc. My attorney and friend Danny Schendzielos helped me set up everything.

I had no idea how I would establish a client base, so I sent out letters to all of the defense attorneys I had battled, as well as a bunch I did not know. I have never been afraid to shake things up, and I figured the conversation among defense attorneys alone might generate some business.

It's classic guy stuff, where we compete as though our life depends on it, but when the horn sounds, we smile, shake hands, and say, "Good game!" I figured some of those lawyers would have at least a grudging respect for my work ethic and attention to detail. Plus, they knew I got results because they were the ones scrambling to keep their clients out of jail, and generally failing.

Every year the Denver Police Department conducts a police memorial service in front of the Department Headquarters. Among the festivities are a bagpipe corps, a 21-gun salute, the reading of the names of our fallen officers and several speakers. Lt. Kenny Chavez, a colonel in the U.S. Army Reserve Special Operations Forces that currently focuses on fighting Terrorism Abroad serves as the emcee M.C. He has been deployed many times since being in the Department. I have always felt he would have made an excellent Chief of Police. He has always been one of my heroes.

After the ceremony, they have a luncheon for the retired cops. It's always a good time seeing those who you have served with.

331

Fallen Officers
"When duty called, there was no thought but answer;
No question, but the task that must be done.
Though Death their final payment for the victory,
For honor was the battle fought, and won,
No monument stands higher than their valor;
No words replace the loss of heroes, slain.
But if their names, remembered, give us courage,
Their sacrifice shall not have been in vain."
—Julian R. Lewis

My next step was to call P.I.s whom I suspected had been in the business for a long time to ask their advice. I was the new kid on the block, and they were not very receptive, pretty much across the board stating that I would not make it in their industry. They implied that all of the niches were taken. They obviously did not know me very well. I am very persistent.

Up until 2014, there was no licensing, and anyone could become a P.I. An organization Professional Private Investigators Association of Colorado (PPIAC) never had much use for me. They wanted licensing, and a lot of us did not welcome the government intrusion. Through the years I was one of the many P.I.'s who testified at the Colorado State Capitol in opposition of licensing.

My argument was that licensing would intrude in our business, giving the government the power to investigate complaints and issue suspensions or even terminate licenses. I didn't figure it was in our best interests to suffer a loss of income or have our licenses taken. I foresaw complaints being leveled at us to get out of monies owed.

Besides, we already were subject to all of the federal, state and local laws with which every other citizen had to comply. Over the years, the PPIAC made several attempts and finally got voluntary licensing. In one hearing I offered to buy all of the members of the PPIAC badges if that would satisfy their need to show they were P.I.'s. As of 2014, there are fees for a P.I. License, and requirements of a bond and liability insurance.

There will come a day when one a licensed P.I. will have to defend a complaint, which might wake them up as to the mistake they made. There was no need for licensing. The public was protected by criminal statute if there was an unethical P.I. There has been few in the past.

The first year in business was all about learning the ropes, but I developed a few clients. I think private practitioners in all walks of life, whether they are opening a restaurant or starting a junkyard, who think that once they open the doors, the customers will flock in. I knew I would have to capitalize on every lead that came my way to developing new clients and make a living.

Right out of the chute, I linked up with information brokers who were crucial to my success. I had no idea how to get the banking information or offshore investment data I would need to conduct asset searches. I figured out there was a person who could get me telephone info. There were people all over the USA, Canada, and Europe who, for a price, could get whatever information I needed.

Veda would be my loyal secretary for 26 years. We not only worked together, but we became friends and family. Veda always had my back and was on top of my business dealings. I was very fortunate to have her in my business, and in my life.

I subscribed to several databases over the years, particularly those that could provide Social Security numbers and dates of birth, because everything of note in the USA revolves around both. If you have the DOB and SSN, you own the individual. I had always been good at finding people, but once I became a P.I., I learned I could even be better "with a little help from my friends."

As a policeman, it was all about subpoenas. As a P.I., it is all about who you know. As time went on, I was turned on to higher-level info brokers across the country. Eventually, I had connections around the world.

After a few years, I developed my own niche, which was interviewing witnesses, defendants and victims. I had always been good on the phone with people as a cop, so I did my interviewing by phone, recording the interviews. Veda and I would transcribe the interview to be court ready. Business got really good, but I would learn it was a roller coaster ride.

Having a straight job for decades, I got used to having a regular paycheck. When I started freelancing, I quickly realized that a big month could be followed by a lean month or two. I often went from being extremely busy, with my schedule packed with several big cases, to not so busy. And that's how it has been for 26 years.

I got into protection duty while I was in the Denver Police Department and it carried over through my decades as a P.I. We guarded some extremely high-profile people— some powerful, some talented, but all famous. I have been part of crews that protected Henry Kissinger, one of the most influential Americans of the past century; Frank Sinatra, who got angry when a reporter sneaked into a cocktail party. I thought Sinatra was going to punch him. I helped guard Diane Sawyer, who is a real lady; Charlie Gibson, who has a mind of his own; Priscilla Presley, who is a class act; and John Denver, who always yodeled to warm up his voice before a concert. John Denver and I talked about flying airplanes, and an experimental aircraft eventually claimed his life. I thought he was a guy's guy and I liked his music.

Other famous people included Catherine Oxenberg was both beautiful and smart; Kenny Rogers, who was a cool guy; George Stephanopoulos, who was very intelligent and personable. Some lesser-known personalities we protected included the Sie family, who were very gracious and down to earth; and the Merage family; who were very classy and long-time friends.

We protected cliques of Asians, and I didn't understand at the time what was going on. They paid us to show up at a suite in a hotel at a certain time, then sit outside the door and let no one in. We finally learned why they had hired us. They were attracted to American women, and they were "entertaining" them in the hotel suites, and did not want anyone coming in and robbing or hurting them.

Television newsman Peter Jennings was my favorite celebrity I got to know in all of my years protecting famous people. We first met at the airport, and he had no idea the network had hired me to protect him. He told me to go home. I told him I had a limo at the airplane, and he replied that he preferred to walk.

We were walking down the concourse to baggage, and a lady asked him, "Are you Peter Jennings"? That initiated a 15-minute chat between them, and it was a two-way conversation in which he learned where details such as what she did for a living and where her family came from. He was an important man, but he always had time for people, and he had a knack at making each individual feel special.

Peter Jennings was from Canada, and many Americans had the misperception he did not like America. He told me that he loved Americans and America. I escorted him to the Brown Palace Hotel the night before his book signing the next morning at the Tattered Book Cover bookstore.

I arrived at the Brown Palace Hotel early, suspecting he would try to dodge me. He came down early, and I told him I had the limo out in front. He again said he preferred to walk. We began our hike to Larimer Street and along the way he engaged two separate people who recognized him in lengthy talks.

We got to the book signing, and he didn't do anything to diminish my admiration for him. He asked each purchaser who they would like their copy of the book to be signed to, and what the purchaser's relationship was to the recipient. He made every signature personal and special. A young gal came up and asked if she could have a picture taken with him, and he rose from his seat and said, "I would be honored." He put his arm around her and smiled.

When I protected him several months later, he mellowed out quite a bit. He told me about some of his harrowing reporting assignments in foreign countries. He liked to smoke cigarettes, and they eventually got the best of him when he died of throat cancer. I was saddened to learn of his death. Peter Jennings was one gracious individual. He taught me a thing or two about how to treat people. I ran into some who were downright arrogant and nasty. He was not only polite but was genuinely kind.

Muhammad Ali had an exhibition boxing match with Lyle Alzado, an all-pro defensive lineman for the Denver Broncos. "The Greatest" spent some time in the locker room with us at Mile High Stadium. He seemed to like cops and signed programs for the officers on his guard detail.

* * * *

After retiring, I visited Headquarters and went up to the Internal Affairs Bureau. I asked them if I could put up a small sign stating, "If you are suspended or fired, call Daril Cinquanta for employment." They did not share my sense of humor and asked me to leave. It made my day. For years after I would give work to suspended and fired police officers who were struggling to survive. I had been in that predicament and understood what they were dealing with.

Early on in my new career, I realized I had a lot to learn about being a P.I., especially the civil end of the business. I had always focused on the criminal part of the law-enforcement spectrum, directing my energies toward finding and arresting felons. I had no training in cases involving child custody, divorce, infidelity, personal injury claims, pre-employment, asset checks, worker's compensation and employment termination.

I knew criminal, auto accident and DUI investigation inside and out. I worked for defense attorneys, which stirred up reservations for a lot of active and former cops. It really did not bother me a lot. My response to the naysayers was that I would retire tomorrow if they would pay my bills; otherwise, I worked for the people who signed my checks.

* * * *

I had the privilege of riding with the Sons of Italy motorcycling group, led by Kenny and Larry Dardano. It was great fun riding with the club, which had about 40 members. We had to be voted in, and wore colors, without a rocker, because we were not a motorcycle club (M.C.).

We were sanctioned by the Colorado Federation of Clubs, which meant we could wear our colors without the fear of reprisal from clubs like the Hell's Angels or Banditos. The rides sometimes ended at a restaurant for Italian food or drinks. We conducted many charity rides for Laradon Hall, Toys for Tots and the Ronald McDonald House.

* * * *

In 1992, my uncle Joe returned to Colorado with his wife Kathy and daughter Leana. It had been many years since they abruptly pulled up stakes one morning and headed to California to start a new life. They decided to reunite with the Cinquanta clan, and we were glad to have them back among the family. We took Joe to the hangar, and he flew with me on several flights. He made me a safer pilot by correcting a few of my techniques. I smiled when he told me I was smooth on the controls, like my Dad.

Uncle Joe had forgotten more than I knew about flying. After our flights together, he signed my logbook. He did not like how the Cub handled, so he rigged it to his liking. Uncle Joe spent a lot of time with Frank and the rest of the family.

When they were going to return to the Midwest, I talked him into taking the biplane that he designed and had never finished. That was a happy day for me because I knew it would give him something to do that he loved. I had most of the parts to complete "The Hornet" so I felt he would complete it. I also gave him a van that I had because I thought he needed more than I did.

Only a few months down the road, Joe was diagnosed with cancer and wasn't able to beat it. Uncle Joe was a big part of my life. I had missed him when they moved out of Colorado but felt a sense of gratitude for having more time in his company near the end of his life. Then I would miss him again.

Izzy Rosenblum owned some bars in town and began hosting invitational luncheons for the cops. Jerry Kennedy was usually the master of ceremonies. He was an excellent policeman, but he could have been a comedian, with a full bunch of very funny off-color jokes. Kennedy was very connected and popular, and was always in demand to compete in foursomes because he was a great golfer.

The luncheons grew to about 200 people, including cops, lawyers, businessmen and city officials. Bill Coors and Stew Jackson sometimes served as the host. Bo Cottrell, a long-time Denver entertainer and a comedian in his own right, would attend and entertain us. He was a Jefferson County sheriff's deputy, and a member of the legendary band, "The Lawmen," which played at Taylor's Supper Club. The '70s and '80s were fun times when the cops had a lot of support from the business community.

Ken Danneberg and his wife Carol were great friends. Ken loved to run with the cops. Though he would not talk in any detail, we believe he had been a U.S. Navy pilot and served in Naval Intelligence. He was a close friend of Jerry Kennedy and was in with all of the big players including the special agents of the Federal Bureau of Investigation, the Central Intelligence Agency, the Bureau of Alcohol, Tobacco & Firearms, the U.S. Drug Enforcement Agency,

Colorado Bureau of Investigation, and probably pretty much every other law enforcement and military agency of note.

Danneberg was an oil man, and he and Carol had great sons. He, along with Cort Dietler and others from the 100 Club, often invited select cops to private luncheons at the Petroleum Club and Cherry Hills Country Club. One of the most enjoyable elements of these "league of extraordinary gentlemen" assemblies was the opportunity for us to regale the room with stories of our exploits.

Ken sponsored me for induction into the 100 Club, which is an organization that steps in anytime a member of the Denver Police Department, Colorado State Patrol or Denver Fire Department is killed in the line of duty. They came across in a big way with financial assistance to the families. The 100 Club has an annual dinner at which they honor one individual from each organization for heroism. Each honoree receives a plaque and a watch.

A lot of heavy hitters from the government and industry members. This connection proved to be not only an affirmation of the police work I had done for years but also a source of P.I. work after I retired from the DPD.

Ken and I somehow began having lunch with a group of female friends: Kitty Hook, Sam Phillips, Wendy Bergen, Susan Reed, Sherry Girard, and Mary Rae that lasted for years. The get-togethers at various restaurants were uproarious, with conversation topics running the gamut, from sexual preferences such as the concept of dating much younger men to politics and religion. It was always a journey into some surprise subject. Our roster of "mystery guests" also was a source of wonder and amusement.

* * * *

In 1994 my Dad was diagnosed with prostate cancer, and it rapidly spread throughout his body. Dad's body was wracked by a very aggressive form, and there was no way he was going to overcome it. My Dad was the most important person in my life.

He was my best friend, mentor, confidant, and the one person who had always believed in me and defended me through all of my battles in my life. I had always looked up to him, valued his advice and loved him openly. I always hugged and kissed him when I saw him; it's an Italian thing.

Dad's death was the darkest day in my life. I was truly devastated, as was the whole family. No longer would I be able to share special private conversations or other times with my father. Our Sunday family dinners were so special. We had spaghetti, meatballs, sausage, a great salad, pizza frittatas and homemade rolls which were all my grandmother's recipes.

I remember my Dad cooking the pizza fritz in a small frying pan one at a time in olive oil. Sometimes we had my Dad's favorite, crown roast. These Sunday dinners brought the entire family together...he was the glue, the peacemaker, the pillar that held us together.

My Dad loved his entire family and raised all of his kids by example. After his death, it was never the same. Blood makes you relatives, loyalty makes you family. I can always see him swinging a driver like a pro. He had a beautiful swing, and he loved to golf. He played in the Italian Open one year and had the best time. He dazzled them with his drives and flawless swing. I know It was one of the highlights of his life.

I was dating a gal, Margaret, who was very special. She was not only beautiful but was exceptional inside also. It was easy to be with her, and I was happy when I was with her. She had an Arabian horse, and we would ride together at the Horse Rescue. I had a quarter horse when I was young named Tornado that I enjoyed riding.

Margaret had a deep love for animals, and we had a lot in common. We had a lot of fun together, and I believe we loved each other than one day she was going back to Ohio with her son, dogs and her horse. She was gone, and what could have been was now a wish and I have a saying about wishes. "If wishes were horses, we would all ride."

* * * *

I received an unusual call one day from a man who said, "My name is Rod Clark, and I have been told that I need you." Rod was a Denver Police officer who had worked at Denver International Airport. He had been accused of sexual assault of a female Transportation Safety Administration employee in an area of a parking structure with no cameras.

Clark had been suspended and charged criminally. He explained that he would pay me personally because the PPA had not authorized an investigator. I inquired as to who was representing him, and he indicated he had hired Bruno & Bruno law firm but added they had not provided an investigator to attack the prosecution's case. I thought that was particularly odd. I read his discovery and knew that I was going to re-interview some people involved with his case.

I soon realized that the Denver Police sergeant who had investigated Rod's case was inept and had plainly botched the job. The first obligation of any detective is to clear the innocent. That sergeant failed. I contacted the outcry witness, the first person contacted by the alleged victim, and got a statement from her detailing what the alleged victim had told her. Right away I realized there was a discrepancy between the alleged victim's stories to the outcry witness and the police.

Seeing as my goal was to clear the cop, who I believed was falsely accused, finding this discrepancy in her statements was a good thing. It appeared to me that she might have fabricated the sexual assault accusation. I then learned that Clark had given a statement to Internal Affairs incidental to advisement of his Miranda rights warning—on his attorneys' advice. I was shocked that a defense attorney would allow his client to give that statement.

I would later learn that these sorts of unwise statements had been provided to the police by the accused in several cases. When an accused individual gives a statement after being advised, he immediately limits the scope of his defense to that statement. In my days on the force, the moment they advised you of your Miranda Warnings, you were wise to provide no further information. There is no upside to giving a statement because if you ever want to modify your defense, you are hamstrung by what you already stated.

When the trial date arrived, my client had to decide whether he would take a plea or go to trial. He was going to trial. He had steadfastly denied the charges and I believed him. During her testimony in court, the alleged victim changed her story again. Now she had laid out three renditions of what had occurred.

The jury saw through her lies and acquitted Rod. There were other contributing factors that led the jury to their decision, one of which was the location of the alleged assault, which was not private or secluded. We could not have been happier until Manager of Safety Al LaCabe turned around and fired Clark.

I was in shock because I could not figure what he McCabe was hanging his hat on. Rod had not departed from the truth, but something was not right. Rod's attorney was going to appeal the firing, but the outcome would be iffy.

One night I was out working on a case, and I took a break to drive over to Lechuga's to get a bag of Mini Hots, dough-wrapped Italian sausage with strips of green chile. I couldn't believe my eyes because there was Al LaCabe standing in front of the restaurant. I jumped out of my car and walked up, and I asked, "How did you justify firing Rod Clark?"

LaCabe rattled off some answers that were bullshit, and I replied, "How do you account for the victim changing her story three times between the police report, outcry witness account and her testimony in court?" He paused and said he had never read her various statements. I said I could prove her story was a clear-cut moving target, and he told me if I brought the information to him he would reopen the case. LaCabe followed through on his promise and put Rod Clark back to work.

Here's how the whole sordid mess went down: Internal Affairs submitted to the Manager of Safety a synopsis of the case, and he made his decision from that document. Yes, he had access to the entire file, but I assure you that no Manager of Safety is going to read the whole case. Higher ups often have way too much going on to delve into operational details, so they rely on their subordinates to provide recommendations.

LaCabe was relying on that report to contain all of the information that he would need to make an informed decision. He had been duped, and he knew it. There's sloppy work at all levels of government and industry, but it's inexcusable when someone loses his livelihood based on someone else's willingness to not do his job. Prosecutors sometimes put their ambitions, and winning a case, ahead of fairness and inclusion of possible exculpatory evidence.

In my estimation, Al LaCabe had risen to the pinnacle of honesty, fairness, and impartiality by doing the right thing in reinstating Rod and putting him back on the force. In my two decades as a Denver policeman, I had never seen anyone in the chain of command at the City of Denver and Denver Police Department say they were wrong, or say they were sorry. Al LaCabe admitted a mistake and righted a wrong. He had integrity.

I immediately went to Mike Mosco, president of the Police Protective Association and told him what just happened in the Rod Clark case. This was the PPA's chance to go after the Denver Police Department for what they probably did too many officers before Rod. In one fell swoop, they could open the floodgates and put hundreds of cases under scrutiny—or at least revisit a few injustices and set things right with those officers.

Based on the Clark case, officers would appeal their suspensions and firings. We would have the D.P.D tied up for years. I wondered how they would like an outside body crawling up their ass. I knew I had them cornered if the PPA would pursue some of the sketchy cases. Nothing happened, so I went to Brian Maas of Channel 4 and gave the story to him. His producers did not let him run with the story, which amazed me because I had set him up with Al LaCabe, who was not going to lie about what they had done.

I learned later from Nick Rogers of the Police Protective Association that Mosco had never alerted the PPA board of directors about the Clark case and its implications. I learned early in my career that many fellow officers just went through the motions, never rising to a challenge or take their responsibilities seriously. It was the same lax crap here, just more department politics as usual. Mosco wasn't going to make waves, apparently deciding he was going to let sleeping dogs lie. Oh, well, the PPA made a deal with their conscience, covering my bill. In turn, I returned the fees Rod had paid me.

But I wasn't letting go. I met with the PPA board to tell them that I would like them to consider using me as an investigator to work on select police officer cases. I offered to do the cases at a reduced rate because I really wanted to help the officers beat the questionable cases that the department had filed against them. This was a spectacular confluence of experience and need. No one would have fought harder than I, nor was there a person who understood the politics of the Denver Police Department better than I did. They never called me.

* * * *

The Father's Day Massacre

On Father's Day, June 16, 1991, a robbery was committed at the United Bank Tower in Denver. The perpetrator(s) killed four guards and took about $200,000 from six tellers in the vault. Denver Police Department and the FBI developed a suspect: retired Denver Police Sgt. James King.

Investigators immediately determined that the robber had knowledge of the operation, and had made an entry via a freight elevator. He took the guard hostage and transported him down to the basement, where he executed him. The assailant used the guard's electric pass card to get into the vault area. He then forced two guards into a secluded room and shot them to death. The intruder encountered a fourth guard and summarily shot and killed him as well. In all, the perpetrator fired 18 rounds.

The six tellers who were processing cash deliveries were ordered to cover their eyes and lie on the floor. At that point, the intruder got a vault manager to fill a large bag with cash. He made everyone crawl into a room known as a man trap, a locking area between the vaults and the less secure part of the bank.

The gunman retrieved all of the spent shell casings and wiped surfaces for any of his stray fingerprints. He removed bank keys, a two-way radio, ten video surveillance tapes and the guard log book, along with the money.

Then he made his escape. The only forensic evidence he didn't try to take or wipe away were the bullets inside of his victims. I never figured out exactly how the tellers used a spoon to free themselves about twenty minutes after he departed.

Investigators developed King as a suspect after interviewing employees and past guards. King had been a guard at the bank and was familiar with the layout and security systems. He once owned a .38 Colt Trooper matching the weapon used in the killings. When he was interviewed as a suspect, King stated he had broken the pistol and had dismantled it and thrown it away.

In the days following the robbery, King purchased a large safety deposit box and shaved off his mustache. Five of the tellers identified King as the perpetrator, even though he wore a hat and glasses. The robber had a mustache. James King was an accomplished chess player and claimed he had been downtown the morning of the robbery, looking for a chess match.

The bullets retrieved from the victims were an unusual mix of brands. At the police range, the department provides a range of bullet brands of bullets for the officers to use when they qualify monthly as marksmen. They would get mixed up over time and officers would sometimes grab a handful to take home.

In the civilian population, people generally load their guns from a box of 50 matching shells. Denver Police Investigators filed a case that was largely circumstantial and were bound for trial.

The prosecution team consisted of Bill Buckley and Lamar Simms who had tried many murder cases. The defense consisted of Walter Gerash, a flamboyant high-profile attorney whose theatrics in front of a jury were legendary. Scott Robinson who was another effective, creative attorney groomed by Gerash, the investigator was Tony DiVirgilio. The judge was Dick Spriggs, who had been an extremely competent assistant district attorney when I was a Denver Police detective.

The defense created a plastic overlay of the suspect showing a man wearing a hat, glasses and sporting a mustache. None of the jurors could identify the man. As you peeled the plastic layers back, the person behind the glasses, hat and mustache was Harrison Ford. It was a very effective technique to show the jury the uncertainty of eye-witness testimony.

There also was a question of a possible accomplice. During the robbery, an alarm was set off in a storage room. It was turned off by somebody in the guard room who would have to know who was in the storage room. His accomplice? Another possibility is that a guard inside the vault had assumed it was a false alarm and thoughtlessly switched it off.

The head of bank security testified that security changes instituted after King no longer worked at the bank would have captured the gunman in the "man trap" as he exited the bank unless he had inside information about the security change—or an accomplice.

I believe King had an inside accomplice, and he shot and killed him during the robbery. I also suggested that detectives not confront King, but plant a phony news story that a suspect had been developed in another state and authorities were attempting to arrest and question him. The FBI, having the resources, should follow King for an extended time to see if he would go to gather the money. Instead, they sent officers to his door to ask for his gun.

The jury found King not guilty. It would now take a corroborated confession to clear the heinous crime, and it appeared the "Father's Day Massacre" would go unsolved. Jim King lived a solitary life after the trial and died in 2009 with advancing dementia, taking any secrets he may have had to the grave with him.

* * * *

Dr. John McDonald was a special kind of guy and a long-time friend of the Denver Police Department. He was a forensic psychiatrist and dove headlong into the minds of some of Colorado's most dangerous criminals.

Dr. McDonald put his practical knowledge and theoretical expertise into a score of books, including "The Murder and the Victim," "Bombers and Firesetters," "The Armed Robber," "Criminal Investigations of Drug Offenses," "Criminal Interrogation," "Psychiatry and the Criminal," "Criminal Investigation," "Arson Investigation," "Burglary and Theft," and "Rape." These were not only fascinating reading but also were textbooks for anyone trying to solve and prosecute violent crimes.

One of his most high-profile cases was John Gilbert Graham, who in 1955 packed his mother's suitcase with dynamite and blew up a plane flying out of Denver. Not shockingly, Dr. McDonald stamped Graham's chart with "psychopath" after interviewing him.

Dr. McDonald interviewed serial killer Ted Bundy after his arrest. Virtually everyone in America knew of Bundy's murder spree, with his admissions and Investigators efforts tabulating at least 30 women at all compass points across the United States.

What people don't know is that Bundy's death toll could be several times higher, and that he also was a rapist, kidnapper, burglar and necrophile. Killers like Bundy tend to be the hardest to catch because they often operate with "no known address."

Dr. McDonald was one of the pioneers in psychological profiling and practiced the science before it had a name. He did the groundwork for understanding as fully as possible what goes on in the minds of the criminally insane.

He took notes in a tiny tablet that he carried in his vest pocket as he rode along with Denver Police detectives during stakeouts, execution of search warrants, and participated in interviews and interrogations. One interview went horribly awry when an inmate took him hostage and nearly bit off his ear.

But the Doc was not some disconnected academic. He drank with the cops and had a sense of humor. He made huge contributions to local and national law enforcement, and I was honored to contribute to sections of several of his books. Months before he died in 2007, a party was thrown in his honor, and Dr. John McDonald was named an honorary Denver District Attorney.

* * * *

One day I got a call from Ann Carnahan, a former *Rocky Mountain News* reporter. She was working the police beat when I first met her, and she had written a few articles about me. Every once in a while a reporter likes the work and covers the police beat for years or even decades, but more often it's an assignment for rookie reporters. It allows them to prove their mettle and hone their skills because it's often fast-paced and in your face.

I generated a lot of ink in my two decades on the force, and I didn't always have the sense from many of her stories that she was pro-police. Then again, the job of the media is not to pimp the cops. A lot of journalists take their job as watchdogs as seriously as I took my job of arresting felons.

I used to tell Ann she had great legs and she fired back sarcastic replies. She said she was calling me in regards to a series called, "Where Are They Now?" She wanted to do a story about me.

I had zero interest in helping her write an article rehashing all of the past criticisms of me. We set some ground rules, and I gave her an interview. The original story was much longer than the printed one, but both versions were fair and well-presented.

She had always been a great writer and had been commended several times for journalistic excellence. I liked her more after the "Where Are They Now?" piece. The title of the article was "Super cop Daril Cinquanta still chasing the bad guys." She took some heat on writing the story, and some people accused her of writing a "puff piece."

A friend, David Richardson, and I were running together in pursuit of "Miss Right." He was a classy, good-looking, fun guy who was in the oil business and had an office in one of the worst parts of town. The interior was a totally different story. It was set up as a lavish apartment/office, with a sunken jetted hot tub.

He eventually moved to downtown Denver and decorated his office with Harley Davidson motorcycles. He loved to collect motorcycles and even had them displayed in his home. This was the era of "Bump & Run" approach to women.

I was riding a Triumph at the time, and he had a Harley in his collection that matched the red-and-cream paint scheme of my airplane. I asked him if he would sell it to me and he declined. One day he called to tell me he was willing to sell me a red-and-black Harley Heritage Softail with very few miles. He told me to go to his house and take it for a spin to see if I liked it. He had souped it up a bit, and it was fun to ride.

About six months later David called and asked, "Do you have my Harley?" I replied, "Yes." He said, "Bring it back." I reminded him that he had said that he would sell it to me. He gave me a great deal on that cycle. I immediately removed all of the Harley garbage, such as turn signals, back rest and small flourishes that made it look cheesy. I went for a nostalgic look, and it looked great with white walls.

Whenever I ride my Harley or fly my Piper Cub, I realize that every day is a gift. Hell, I should have been dead years ago, but am lucky to have a life, and toys to make it more pleasurable. I have always lived for the moment, tried to be happy and shared the good times with my family and friends.

In 1993, Dave Michaud made Chief of Police. I wanted to be happy for him, but it wasn't possible. It's uncanny that a man can display unflinching courage in the literal line of fire, but then knuckle under in the face of social and job pressure. Then again, I guess it usually takes some sort of cultured personality to rise to the top.

When the ground starts to shake, some guys figure they have to be a politician above being a friend. I sometimes wonder if he ever tossed and turned in his bed, restless in the knowledge he had turned his back and betrayed Larry and me.

I could not help wondering if what he accomplished with Larry Subia and me were in Michaud's resume when he applied to become Denver Police Chief? In looking back, I think he had been calculating his ambition to be Denver Police chief for years. I can't recall any missteps as he picked his assignments and his political connections.

Michaud married a great gal who had a black son, and that couldn't hurt in ingratiating himself to everyone in a politically correct environment. It worked for him. During those thousands of hours in the cruiser and in the streets, I didn't suspect he lacked a conscience or any sense of loyalty to anyone beyond himself.

* * * *

Michaud followed Jim Collier. I liked Jim and worked a number of off-duty jobs with him. He had a great sense of humor, and we shared a love for aviation. He was a great pilot, and I had the opportunity to fly with him in his beautiful Cessna 180. Jim was taught to fly by Kenny Wells, who was a legend. We both belonged to "The Quiet Birdmen," a social organization of pilots.

For the past twenty years, I have been president of The Jeffco Aviation Association at Rocky Mountain Metro Airport in Broomfield. It was formed by Mark Johnson, a fellow pilot, and friend, based on concerns of corruption involving the airport administration and the Jefferson County Commissioners office.

At issue was the T-Hangar waiting list. People were waiting to use a hangar, and the airport manager would not release the list, so nobody knew where they were in the waiting order. We believed he was leveraging his power base by controlling who got hangars. We also had concerns about hangars at the airport that were being used for storage of things other than aircraft. The association fought to replace several airport managers who were not tenant-friendly.

There was one who stood out as the worst of the lot. He made all the T-Hangar tenants remove everything from their hangars. The association's stance was we rented the

T-Hangar by the square foot and should have been able to utilize that area as we saw fit. We had to go to war with that individual. I spoke to Jim Congrove, a long-time friend who had served in Colorado House of Representatives and Senate.

Congrove also had been a cop and had worked undercover in the Metropolitan Enforcement Group. As a pilot, he exercised an intriguing parenting strategy. Congrove made his two daughters take flying lessons and solo before they got permission to get their driver's licenses. His theory was that flying would teach them to pay closer attention.

Based largely on the mess at the airport, Congrove agreed to run for County Commissioner. He said the system was corrupt. He certainly had the vote of the airport tenants, because none of us were happy with the airport management. Plus, Jim wanted to address other issues in Jefferson County. Jim won the County Commissioner seat, and things were about to change at the airport. I asked him to fire the Airport Manager, and he agreed.

Congrove had the new airport administration revise the T-Hangar rental agreements, with the association's input. We were allowed to store cars, motorcycles, boats, desks, couches and refrigerators in our spaces, as long as we had an airplane in the hangar. We could again enjoy our hobby at our hangars.

The Jefferson county commissioners and the county attorney hired me to duplicate an investigative file that had been stolen. The file detailed an individual who routinely sued the county and attacked many individuals on his radio show. I conducted a background investigation and surveillance. I submitted my report to the commissioners for a pending court action against the county.

The man started making various accusations, including that he was not allowed to attend a commissioners meeting. Then he verbally assailed them for hiring me to investigate him. He alleged that I was hired to follow employees and citizens, which was not true. A very loud and squeaky wheel, he succeeded in convincing some oversight group to inquire and subpoena files.

Then the Colorado Bureau of Investigation appears, and they are investigating me. They attempted to acquire my report and found that it had been stolen from the Jefferson County attorney's office. This was the second time the files were stolen. I knew I had done nothing wrong, so I provided a copy to the C.B.I.

Then the guy who started the whole chaotic mess convinced his girlfriend to file a suit looking for free money. She alleged that Jim and I went to Malone's Restaurant where her daughter worked and harassed her daughter until she went to the back of the restaurant, curled up and sobbed. None of it happened because it was a complete fabrication by her boyfriend. The daughter later stated that it never occurred. His girlfriend also did not back all the information in her lawsuit and acknowledged she did not author it. The newspapers trashed us.

The boyfriend filed a lawsuit against Jefferson County, Jim Congrove and me. I turned in a request for legal representation on my insurance liability policy. They denied me, and I went crazy. I secured a law firm, which said the insurance company would not represent me and I would have to foot the bill.

Next, I went to the insurance commission and lodged a complaint that the company I was paying my premiums to every month was trying to avoid its responsibility to represent me in accordance with the policy. I provided a copy of the policy to the Colorado Insurance Commission, and pretty much immediately receive a phone call from a prestigious law firm that indicated they would represent me.

Turns out insurance companies collect premiums from their customers every month, but when it comes to those customers filing claims, the standard practice is to initially deny just about every claim. And a lot of those customers just roll over and say, "Oh, well, I guess they denied my claim. Sigh." Not me.

Next came a deposition. I despised their client, and they were in store for a rough ride. They attempted to get me to answer questions that I had no intention of answering. I frustrated them so badly they threatened to call the judge, which I encouraged them to do. Any question that was not relative to the case was nothing more than a fishing expedition, and I was not willing to participate.

I was cut out of the lawsuit at some point after he received a settlement from my insurance company—which I opposed. They took Jim to trial, and the jury was not impressed and awarded the plaintiff around $2,000. Some people are only about themselves and are capable of causing unbelievable levels of chaos, with little or no gain to anyone. I guess it could be argued the attorneys won in the whole brouhaha, but lawyers almost never come out on the short end of the financial stick.

Jim Congrove had heart problems and passed away after a long illness. I was saddened that I had lost a close friend I had spent a lot of time with. The Congrove family were also my long-time friends, and they were devastated when Jim passed.

The Jeffco Aviation Association recently celebrated its 20-year anniversary. We host an annual Fly at which we treat pilots from across the country with a pancake Italian sausage breakfast. They compete for trophies in various classes of aircraft, including home- and kit-built plans, classic tube-and-fabric, metal, contemporary, warbird trainers and warbirds, antique, sport pilot and special interest.

Every year, pilots call to ask if we still serve Italian sausage. No sense messing with successful traditions; Paisanos make the breakfast links for us for our Fly Ins.

For more than 15 years I have gone to breakfast at Rocky Mountain Metro Airport, formerly Jefferson County airport, with a group of pilots for the Saturday Morning Flyers Breakfast"—Steve Beach, Wayne Fry, Tom Powers, Jim Wood, Larry Johnston, John Capone, Tommy Ramsey, Jim Horton, Jeff Martin, Ricky Domenico, Ted Lemen, Jeff Adler, Carl Gilberg, Mark Johnson, Carlo Gains, Ed Gann, Cliff Goldstein and Dave Colwell. They have helped keep me sane over all of these years.

Three of my pilot friends have flown west—pilot terminology for passed away—over the years: Dean Cochran, Dave Ebershoff, and Ron Denight. They make it clear to me that it's crucial for cops to have acquaintances and friends other than fellow police officers.

* * * *

A missing person case came to Denver from the Middle East. A student, whom we will call "Ali," attended community college and had just flown back to Denver from

Saudi Arabia. He was picked up at Denver International Airport by a friend, his girlfriend and an acquaintance. They stopped by a residence in Aurora then dropped him off at his apartment in Denver. The trio had planned to meet for dinner, but Ali was not heard from again.

His friends frantically searched for him for two days. They forcibly entered his apartment but found nothing to indicate there had been a struggle. Expensive chocolates that Ali was going to give to his girlfriend had jumbled in their box, as though someone was looking for something.

His friends claimed that while in the apartment they found a note that may have been left on his windshield. It read, "Do you always drive like an asshole? You are now my project. Watch out. Black boys don't lie."

Ali's friends looked for his Volkswagen, but could not find it. They checked with the dealership where he bought the car a few months earlier. The dealership said a person they believed was Ali and one other person sold the car back to the dealership for $10,000. They were denied a request to view the videotape. Ali's friends then filed a report with the Denver Police Missing Persons Bureau.

Members of Ali's family soon arrived in Denver from Saudi Arabia to help search for Ali. The American Embassy/Saudi Arabian Consulate in New York recommended an attorney to the family. The lawyer contacted Tony DiVirgilio of Investigative Resources, who in turn contacted me to assist in the investigation.

We met with the family, who briefed us on what they had discovered so far. They identified the other party in the car the day they picked up Ali and said that man, another individual and a brother of one of Ali's friends lived together in Aurora. I went with the family to view the interior of Ali's apartment and to contact the manager to view the surveillance tape of the front area of the building.

I could not gain entry, but I did get a copy of the security tape. I asked the family to view the tape to determine if Ali had left with someone they recognized. The poor-quality tapes had to be professionally enhanced.

I was able to access the apartment the next day with Ali's family. I obtained Ali's banking information and telephone bills, documenting all of the numbers he had called and his recorded messages. A lot technician at the car dealership stated that as he drove them to US Bank, they spoke in Farsi and English in discussing a suitcase containing drugs and the police hassling them.

Investigator DiVirgilio requested a record of transactions on Ali's bank account that occurred after his disappearance. With a power of attorney from Ali's father, we learned of withdrawals of $10,000 and $9,900. One deposit represented the $10,080 check from the car dealership for the sell-back of the Volkswagen. Investigator DiVirgilio also requested copies of the checks so he could examine the signatures, and passed on the information to Denver Police Case Det. Gene Guigli.

The videotape footage was secured from the bank branch where the $9,900 had been withdrawn. Detective Guigli provided photos from the video to us. We took the photos of the two individuals making the withdrawal and the pictures of the people who took Ali's car back to the dealership to the family for identification.

Suddenly we had suspects, because Ali was not one of the individuals in the photos or video. Ali's family was unable to identify anyone in the photos. Ali's friends identified both parties in the footage and photos. One of the men was Ali's brother. However, the family did not reveal that they recognized him when they were shown the picture and footage.

At this point they revealed that after I had shown the images of the suspects to them, they went to the Aurora residence to confront them and to look for Ali. No one was home, so they entered through a broken window. Ali was not there, but they found and took his bank card.

Aurora Police were brought up to speed on the missing person case, the forgery and the suspects who had been developed. At this point, we had identified all three individuals who lived in the Aurora address, two of whom participated in the forgeries. They indicated they would obtain warrants for the suspects.

We met with the family, friends, and detectives of the Denver Police Department and briefed them on all of the evidence we had gathered. We received information that one of the suspects had returned to Saudi Arabia or Kuwait and a second suspect was attempting to leave the country. The brother of Ali's friend had met with one of the suspects, and he admitted to acquiring funds from Ali's bank account but denied any knowledge of his disappearance. The brother indicated that Ali had rented a car and was going to Florida. At this point, we knew that was a lie and something terrible had happened to Ali.

We began an intense inquiry to locate the rental car agency that the brother used to secure a vehicle with. We found that the other two suspects rented a car and drove 1,900 miles before returning it to the rental agency. This information was passed on to the Denver Police detectives.

We learned from Saudi authorities that they had one of the suspects in custody in their country. He admitted that he committed the forgeries to obtain money from Ali's account and that the brother of Ali's friend had strangled Ali and dumped his body in Nevada.

We caught a break when Denver Police detectives were notified that the brother was pulled over while speeding at 90 mph. However, the police in that Arizona jurisdiction could not hold him because the warrant had not been issued.

Denver Police Department was then notified that the brother was involved in a single-car rollover accident in New Mexico, but they were unable to hold him because no warrant had been entered into NCIC. However, they kept him under surveillance.

We secured two handwriting experts—one private and one from the C.B.I.—who confirmed that the signatures at the bank were not Ali's, but rather were forgeries. Retired D.A. Norm Early entered the investigation, representing attorney Bobby Horton of Aramco Services in Houston. He would participate in all meetings and investigative steps in this case. Early also helped to expedite issuance of the arrest warrant.

We again contacted New Mexico authorities and learned that the suspect was talking about taking a bus back to Denver. He had $400 on his person when they contacted him after the rollover crash. DiVirgilio contacted a retired New Mexico State Trooper, Gave Valdez, who went to the bus depot to make sure the suspect got on the bus.

Valdez handed off the surveillance duties to private investigator Peso Chavez and his partner Gave and continued the surveillance which will end in Walsenburg, in southern Colorado. They rode the bus to Walsenburg, and I got on at Walsenburg.

Bob Hollingshead and I drove to Walsenburg where I got on the bus to ensure he made it to Denver. I boarded the bus and observed the suspect. Hollingshead followed us northbound in his car. We were delayed for an hour by a snowstorm on Raton Pass. The bus stopped in Colorado Springs, and the suspect got off but returned for the home stretch to Denver.

We pulled into the Denver bus depot and DiVirgilio and I arrested and cuffed the suspect. When we notified him he was being arrested for forgery and the murder of Ali, the suspect blurted, "No. No. The family has forgiven me." I looked him in the eye and replied, "Well, I don't forgive you."

Dets. Gene Guigli and Ron Cramer took custody of the suspect. They transported him the handful of blocks from the bus station to HQ, advised him of his rights and videotaped his statement. The suspect explained exactly how he and his two friends had formulated a plan to kidnap, rob and kill Ali when he returned from Saudi Arabia. Before his arrival, they purchased tape and rope.

He said they had picked up Ali at the airport and dropped him off at his apartment. The suspect then went back on his own and took Ali back to the Aurora address, where they overpowered him, and duct-taped him to a chair in the basement. Ali begged for his release, offering them $1,000 that he had at his apartment.

The suspect described how they had put the rope around Ali's neck and strangled him. The suspect said he knew Ali was dead because he was cold and blue. They took his checkbooks and ID, keys and car.

The trio, now part of a murder conspiracy, drove to Ali's apartment where they found the $1,000 and returned to the Aurora address. They removed the rope and tape from Ali's body and put it in a black plastic garbage bag. They placed his body in the back seat of the rental car, then drove to an apartment complex in Littleton and dumped his body in a trash dumpster.

The next day they drove to the Volkswagen dealership, where they posed as Ali to sell back his car. The murderers then deposited the check in Ali's bank account and made withdrawals in excess of the check.

The suspect took detectives to the trash dumpster where they had dumped Ali's body. The trash from that dumpster had been picked up days before and taken to The Denver Regional Landfill in Erie, north of Denver in Weld County. Landfills have come a long way since they were known as "dumps." The waste-management companies chart activity and know within a high degree of certainty on the grid where a particular dumpster was unloaded. That narrowed the search area.

Some days later the landfill search produced a man's body that was identified through dental records as Ali. The suspect was charged with murder, along with forgery, conspiracy, kidnapping, and robbery. Denver D. A. Bill Ritter was undecided as to whether to file for extradition of the other two suspects.

A media conference was called, and the family answered questions. I had been through all sorts of investigations over the decades, and this one really set me back in my seat. Ali was a decent kid who was setting out to become an engineer—like his father. He called his family daily in Saudi Arabia, and he and his friends had dinner almost every night. It was a tragic loss of a good human being.

No other cases have rivaled this one in my 26 years as a private investigator. I have worked some cases with Tony, a top-notch P.I. in Denver who specializes in complex cases, including those centered on wiretaps.

* * * *

Over the years, I have hired a number of retired cops to work on private investigations. Still part of my crew are Gary Salazar, Darrell Wisdom, Gerry Fitzgibbons, Alane Mahuna, Darrell Wagner, Gary Lauricella, Jim Horton, and Mike Staskin. I need them, and they are still at the top of their game. It's been beneficial to have some talented, loyal P.I.'s in the game with me, such as Scott Smith and Tim Deasy. All of them are licensed P.I.'s.

My wife and I went to Debbie and Mike Dunafon's wedding at their castle on Bear Creek near Idledale, a tiny berg between Morrison and Kittredge in Jefferson County. They live in a stone castle built in 1941. The pristine grounds feature small lakes, a water wheel that generates electrical power and beautiful gardens. They are a wonderful couple and long-time friends.

The Dunafons did their wedding ceremony their way. They are extremely creative people and even brought a flair to the food truck business by providing varied menus with delicious food and beverages. Again, it was great stretching out a bit and enriching my life with even more people not involved in law enforcement.

Peter Boyles is a nationally recognized radio talk show host, and a friend of mine. He is one of the most well-read and smart people I know. He's kind and welcoming to his callers unless they are idiots, and then he squares them away in short order. Peter is a guy's guy, and we have ridden our Harleys up and down the canyons west of Denver.

He's still at it after all of these years, and his morning call-in and interview show on KNUS is entertaining. There were other high-profile Coloradans there, including talk show host duo Julie Hayden and Chuck Bonniwell. They have a style all their own and the chemistry that can only come from a married couple.

Also at the wedding were Harvey Steinberg and Jeff Springer, two of Colorado's pre-eminent defense attorneys and litigators. I've had the satisfaction of investigating cases for them, and it's always gratifying to work with professionals.

I had the same barber for years. Like mechanics and doctors, when you get one who does good work, you don't let them go. She was business partners with Denise in her successful family hair salon. She was exceptionally good looking, and I liked our conversations and the whole feeling of going to get my hair cut by her. She was family oriented.

Over the years, we talked about just about everything—family, mutual friends our histories, and common interests such as travel, and machines that move fast—and I learned that she was raised by her maternal grandmother Helen, her Aunt June and Uncle Sonny because her mother Shirley had health issues.

Chris' mother loved her and was very proud of her accomplishments. Chris loved animals. She had been all over the world and had interesting stories. She put up with me eating all of her candy and talking on my phone. She would have to spend an hour with me because I had phone interruptions and refused to leave the shop. Down the road, she told me she thought I was cheap because I didn't exactly set the record for tipping. My thinking was that I did not want to own her.

She was dating a guy who eventually left her high and broke. She believed she owned several real estate properties with him, but came to find out she did not. The shyster had given her an engagement/promise ring, but she found out it was not a diamond, but rather was a cubic zirconium.

It so happened that when Chris was suddenly no longer attached, and neither was I. I jumped in to ask her out. We dated for a couple of years, and we just kept doing it because we were having a lot of fun. Chris looked damned fine riding on the back of my Harley, and I never got tired of looking over to see her, and hear her voice, when we were cruising along in the Piper Cub.

Chris was a good sport, taking summer trips with me in the T-Bird which had air vents, but no air conditioning. It was cooler in all regards when we removed the hard top.

I think she thought my house was a little strange. I had a pool table in the living room. Framed prints of aircraft highlighted a probably overwhelming array of art on the walls. It was truly a bachelor's pad. I had a roommate, Joe Lazzara, who was introduced to me by my brother. Joe was trying to join the FBI or the DEA.

The story was that he had scored the highest written exam score ever recorded by the FBI I figured he was too smart a dude to stay on either of those paths, so I tried to help him change his mind. Instead, he aced the bar exam and became a lawyer. He was a great roommate who on occasion was influenced by my brother into various acts of chicanery. Living with Lazzara was a non-stop stream of practical jokes.

When Chris visited, she saw that my Christmas tree was still set up with ornaments and lights in the corner of the living room … in July. I loved Christmas since I was a child, and collected ornaments from around the world. I felt it was a hassle to take down the whole display every year, so there it stood.

I also hauled my own trash to protect sensitive and private information about my clients and myself. It was a novel date, the day she went along with me on a trash run. I wonder if that is when she fell for me.

I was remodeling my house, which had been built in 1968 and was dated in some areas. Her biggest jolt probably came when she descended into the basement to experience my offices, which are more like a museum featuring all of my Denver Police Department memorabilia covering every available space on the walls.

But the more time went on, and the more time we spent together, the more we realized we were a good fit for each other and had a lot in common. I upped my game from the trash run and proposed to her at the Flagstaff House sitting among the Flatirons overlooking Boulder. Then we moved in together. It's funny how love can just happen between two people who are not looking for it.

Chris and I have a lot of fun together, with constant laughing and smiling. And there's no substitute for the natural ease of being with the right person when it's comfortable just to be yourself. We dated for a couple of years, fell in love gradually, and got married as a foregone conclusion because some good things just need to happen and continue happening.

Chris later told me one of the things that she loved about me was how affectionate I was with my Dad when I brought him in for a haircut. I had no idea. We cruised the Caribbean on our honeymoon. It was my first cruise, and I hadn't imagined it was possible to eat spectacular food every waking moment and drink great wine. Cruise ships are floating pleasure cities, and feature amenities like spas and gyms. Also on our cruise were the Tetis, Ron Malpiede, and Jolene and John Stay.

It was gratifying to have friends to share our joy. We got remarried on Barbados in an old church with Father Malpiedo performing the spoof ceremony. As we videotaped the "ritual," tourists and parishioners walked in and immediately excused themselves, thinking they had interrupted an actual wedding. While on the island, we sought the cream from the "Braciole Bush," which we did not find after hours of searching.

I had a full family life as a child, and I've had a full, new family life as a man. I have grown to love Chris' daughter and son. Eileen got a degree in communications but was a natural in restaurant management. She excelled as a sales rep for a large liquor company and earned a string of sales achievement awards. She became a sommelier and relished her knowledge of the world of wines. She met a great guy from Michigan who grew up on a farm.

He was an executive chef at Morton's steakhouse and now manages a restaurant that he hopes to have part ownership in one day. If work ethics and values are the keys, he's in. Eileen and Patrick spend a lot of time raising their boys Nicholas and Blake. The boys are just getting involved in sports, and Nick appears to be a natural golfer, just like his grandmother, who recently scored a hole in one.

I have groomed Chris' son Rick into an outstanding licensed private investigator. He excels at locating people and is a wizard at tracking down people and developing information through social media. He has the persistence to stay on the scent until he eventually finds people. Attorneys call us and request that he track down individuals whom no one else can serve.

Rick's surveillance skills surpass those of many detectives I worked with as a Denver Police detective. One sign of talent is that someone continues to improve over time. Rick has a great sense of humor and keeps his co-workers and us laughing all of the time. Sometimes I have flashbacks to the days of my brother and Lazzara because Rick is constantly playing practical jokes.

Chris's family—Aunt June and Uncle Sonny, her siblings and their spouses Gina, Rob, Denise and Ed and their children, Sydney, Zach, Lauren and Dano have accepted me into the family, and we have shared many good times over the years. I am thankful for finding and having Chris, but I'm additionally grateful for the love of her family.

We have continued to update our home over the years. Chris methodically carted off my pool table, packed up my Christmas tree, moved all of my cool pictures to the laundry room and the downstairs and hired a trash service. I think a shredder is a better solution than periodic and often overdue trips to the landfill. My world shrunk to the basement, garage and airplane hangar.

The big deck we had installed on the back enables us to have summer dinners with friends. She has great taste and talent, and has decorated the house over the years. I am proud to entertain friends and family in our home. Chris and I have a true love story that has not ended.

Our 20 years together have been enlivened and enriched by wonderful pets. Hunter, a German shepherd-chow mix, was both beautiful and graceful. She was the protector and loving companion to the family until she died of cancer.

Vinny was a Maltese with a unique personality. We bag-trained him and brought him along, just about everywhere, including Florida where we visited Gina and Rob. He weighed four pounds and was welcomed just about everywhere because he was better behaved than most children.

Nico also was bag trained, and we took him everywhere as well. The Maltese breed is generally affectionate, smart and playful. We had such a great experience with them that we then acquired Tessa Bella, a feisty female with a temper when she doesn't get her way. She hunches down on all fours, peers up at us, then spins in circles and zooms through the house to let us know who the boss is. Kind of reminds me of my wife. Like all true dog lovers, our canines have always been family and losing any of them is heartbreaking.

In 2005, we acquired a condo on a lake in the mountains—our secret retreat to get away from everything. We would live there for extended periods of time. When we purchased It the drapes, carpets and countertops were dated. We updated all of those items including granite tops, artwork and put mountain furniture in it over the years and it now looks great. It already had a lot of updates done to it when we bought it.

We put a mantle on the fireplace from the back bar in our restaurant that survived the fire. All of the owners heard we had done this and had to come see how we did it so they could do the same. Our condo has a big covered patio overlooking the lake and mountains. We feel lucky to have this refuge.

For some time, I wrote stories about retired police officers. Many of them were ill, and I wanted to recount their stories for a retiree newspaper called "After the Badge." My column was called "My Watch." Mike Mullan, the glue who has held the retirees together for years, asked me to write the stories. Some of the tales were long, and the editors pared them down. I protested.

Finally, one former cop went through the roof about his story, which was no longer his story because it had been so dramatically shortened by the editors of "After the Badge." I agreed with him. I provided him with the original story I had submitted, but I don't believe it helped with his outlook on the experience.

The president of the retirement association did nothing—not a retraction, not an offer to print an accurate version of the story. So, I quit writing the stories because they were a classic example that "the juice was not worth the squeeze."

In reflecting back through my life, I have some personal truths to share:

- Fame is fleeting.
- Faith, Family, and Friends are virtually always the most important things in life.

- Your health is very important. I wish I had good health.
- Some friends are imposters posing as friends.
- Being defiant has its price.
- Knowing the difference between "love and in love" is a gift.
- Proving you are right does not mean you won.
- Jealousy and ego can bring out the worse in someone.
- No. 1 rule: Survive the day at all costs and go home to your family.
- Be true and believe in yourself, always.
- For one small moment in time, I was the "best" at something.
- Always follow your gut feelings about women and bad guys.
- They created me.
- Never let anyone have psychological power over you.
- Take no shit off of anyone.
- Never lose your sense of humor.
- When you believe in what you are doing, let no one break your spirit to prevent you from doing it. They are jealous, and they are stepping on their egos.
- If you are good at something, go ahead and flaunt it.
- If you like or love someone, be sure to tell them today.
- Hug and kiss your Mom and Dad every time you see them.
- Mend fences.
- Learn to say you are sorry.

- The 1st and the 15th are not the most important days of the month.
- Sometimes the end justifies the means.
- Believe nothing of what you hear and half of what you see.
- Keep tabs on your enemies as much as you can.
- Focus on what you have, not what you don't have.
- The element of surprise is key.
- Don't try to keep up with what others have.
- Your partner is your most important asset on the department.
- Never turn your back on a bad guy.
- Very few people will have your "six" during your life. Don't depend on the unproven.
- The media is truly a double-edged sword.
- Never give up a fellow officer. We don't eat our own.
- Never go to bed mad.
- Make time to have dinner with your wife and kids. You won't believe what you may learn and can teach.
- Don't burn bridges. You may want to cross back over one in the future.
- Think before you hurt someone or affect their family, livelihood or feelings.
- Women need to stand up for themselves and let no man hit or use her.
- Always kiss and tell your spouse and kids you love them before you leave the house for work. You may not be back.
- To those who criticize you, invite them to walk around the block with you.

- Always be a loyal, good friend. Accept your friends for who they are and enjoy their company. They are a gift.
- He who hesitates is lost or dead.
- Don't answer your door to strangers and never trust one.
- Always carry your gun whether you are a man or woman.
- Take time to enjoy your toys. You earned them.
- Spend time and teach your grandkids what you have learned.
- In a fight, it's better to give than to receive. Win at all costs.
- Passion will make you excel and be great.
- Luck is when preparation meets opportunity.
- Blood makes you relatives. Loyalty makes you family.
- Persistence leads to success.
- Always have someone at the back door when you are kicking the front door.
- Be a good listener in life. Everybody has a story, and their moment of fame they want to share.
- Always have a dog. They are always happy to see and love you. It's therapy and the best companionship.
- In marriage Listen, Love, and Laugh together.
- Sleep on it before you respond when you are really mad at someone.
- Inheritance is a gift, not a right.
- Always ride out of battle on the same horse you rode into battle on.
- Don't break the "Code of The West."
- You have to be a friend to have a friend.

- Money won't buy you happiness, but I have found that it helps a lot.
- Never talk to a federal agent. Remember Martha Stewart.
- Never give a statement incidental to Miranda. They want the missing piece of the puzzle.
- Internal Affairs is not your friend.
- Always have a Plan B.
- I cheated death another day.
- Failure was never an option.
- Timing is a game changer.
- Allegations always leave an air of suspicion behind.

This work has been my way to tell the story of my amazing life, up to this point. I want readers to "take a walk around the block with me." I want people to share what I experienced as a child and growing up, then what I reveled in and endured in 20 years as a Denver Police Officer. I consider my career the fulfillment of a childhood dream and the ultimate adventure of playing "cops and robbers" in the real world, with life-or-death stakes on every bet.

None of my critics bothered to get to know me or my past, and now I can share the story with them—as well as with my many friends. Most of the naysayers never cared about the truth and only believed what suited their motives and prejudices—whether they were based on fact or fiction.

I was a good cop and did not commit the terrible things they alleged. I wonder if anyone's opinion of me will change after reading my book. This is my version, my truth, based on facts. I have chosen to relate stories from a tiny fraction of the hundreds of investigations and arrests in which I participated and initiated.

* * * *

To be a cop today, you are risking being ambushed, targeted and killed for no reason other than wearing a uniform and a badge. In my day, every time we made a stop, contact or kicked in a door we were putting our lives on the line. Today it is different, and cops are reluctant to be proactive because they have little to no backing—inside or outside the substation and Headquarters buildings. They increasingly are suspended, fired or prosecuted if they are involved in a shooting—particularly of a minority individual.

The establishment has surrendered to the media and political correctness. In many areas, crime is accepted or even escalating because criminals know police are not going to confront them as they did in the past. I believe the crime rate is soaring, but it would require astute analysis of the data reported by the FBI and local police departments to get a true picture because of the way crimes are now reported and recorded.

When I was a street cop, our daily log sheets reflected our day's work effort. Class One actions were generated from the police dispatch, directing the uniformed officer on the street to a location. Class Two actions are initiated by officers in the field, for actions such as traffic stops on to clear the occupants for warrants and to create contact cards, and make on-site arrests. My guess is an examination of log sheets nowadays would show a shocking lack of proactive, Class Two police work.

Today's street cop does not want to be suspended or fired and not be able to support his family because he took the initiative. The ugly cycle results in citizens becoming the victim of society's failure to back the police.

It's also worth noting that when the media reports a police shooting and the cop is immediately accused of wrongdoing, then cleared, there is no balance in the coverage. The accusation receives a front-page headline, and the exoneration gets a two-paragraph story on the bottom of page 17.

There tends to be a rush to judgment to appease the families and community action groups. Police departments are quick to suspend an officer and unlikely to defend him, allowing the courts to decide the fate of an officer who had to act in a split second.

Courts are glutted with cases in which the victims' families are in pursuit of "free money." There seems to be plenty of insurance money to spread around, even after an officer is cleared of charges.

These are sad and dangerous times for my fellow officers in Blue.

The system gave me a hundred reasons to quit doing police work my way, but something inside of me would not allow me to be broken like many before me. I felt I owed it to each victim to try to solve the crime and apprehend the "bad guy." The job was a daily challenge that I welcomed and looked forward to, despite the constant undermining of my credibility by foe and supposed friend alike. It proved to be a lonely, dangerous journey.

I elected not to air the dirty laundry of my fellow officers in this book. Police officers are human and succumb to poor choices in life. During my career, I saw officers being rolled up for all sorts of crimes for which they had sworn to keep the public safe, including sale and use of drugs, sexual assault, theft, pimping, and domestic violence.

Some had character flaws long before they became policemen. Others were good cops at one time, honoring their oath to serve and protect, and then falling from their mission. Many of my comrades in arms were great crime fighters and put their lives on the line countless times.

Acknowledgments

This book has been an adventure and a test of perseverance. I thank my wonderful wife, Chris, who had to put up with my many mood swings, struggles with the story line, and the continued in-depth research needed to complete this book. She stuck with me through the whole, difficult process for a year. That's love.

It would not have been possible without my brother Matt, who brought me together with the publisher, Barbara Terry. She believed in my story, and the book became a reality. My brother and I designed the cover, which displays the shirt I was wearing October 3, 1971, when I was shot.

Author Bios

Daril Cinquanta was born in St. Mary's, Pennsylvania in 1948. He grew up in the family restaurant business in Riverside, California and Boulder, Colorado. Growing up in Boulder, he was expelled from two junior high schools and two high schools during his rollercoaster childhood. He lost his driver's license three times before the age of 18. He attended Harbor Junior College taking Police Science courses in pursuing his childhood dream of becoming a Crime Fighter.

Cinquanta became a Denver Police Officer upon entering the Police Academy in 1970. Early in his twenty-year career, he admitted that being a cop was the only thing he was ever good at. He was called a "Super Cop" after amassing thousands of arrests.

Cinquanta's work was legendary in Colorado police circles. Through his investigations, he generated a great deal of positive and negative publicity. He acknowledges that he often bent, and at times, broke departmental rules and regulations. Nonetheless, he followed the law, resulting in an outstanding and extraordinary conviction rate.

Daril Cinquanta was often controversial, and lawyers, some judges, citizen activists—and even his own administration—routinely attacked his credibility and style. Yet, during his career he received the Police Medal of Honor; the Police Distinguished Service Cross, The Service Cross, The Purple Heart, six Police Merit Awards, Optimist Club Policeman of the Year, Citizens Appreciate Police Award of Honor and over 160 official departmental and outside jurisdiction commendations.

After his retirement, he started his own private investigative firm, Professional Investigators, Inc. in Denver, Colorado.

Dennis Bloomquist began writing professionally for his hometown newspaper when he was 16 years of age. The management of the Aurora Sun entrusted him with a key to the plant and allowed him to lay out and paste up sports pages on dark and stormy nights. He has since written and edited for newspapers, magazines, advertising and marketing agencies, computer hardware and software companies, environmental consulting firms, and was news director for a couple of radio stations.

He graduated from the University of Colorado School of Journalism, now defunct. He interned with Senator Timothy work and KOA Radio-Television. He has been a care coordinator for a healthcare company.

Dennis has taught tennis since he was 16, and was named outstanding player his senior year at Aurora Central High School. He was a teaching pro at Denver Country Club and Brookside Tennis Club. In the fall of 2014, he had the pleasure of watching two of his freshman high school students, representing the Lakewood High School Tigers, compete in the state tournament.

The Bloomquists moved from Iowa to Colorado when he was 18 months old, but he enjoyed several summers on the farm in Corning, Iowa with Uncle Wayne and Aunt Paula Strait. He spent most years of his life in the Denver Metro area, with an idyllic interlude in Indian Hills, and is familiar with every intersection and park fountain described in Daril's story.

His most meaningful accomplishment is raising his son, Grant.